Anonymous

Charges and General Information Relating to Patents

Including all the principal countries of the world. Vol. 1

Anonymous

Charges and General Information Relating to Patents
Including all the principal countries of the world. Vol. 1

ISBN/EAN: 9783337428365

Printed in Europe, USA, Canada, Australia, Japan

Cover: Foto ©Suzi / pixelio.de

More available books at **www.hansebooks.com**

SECOND EDITION—APRIL, 1891.

CABLE ADDRESS: "NYMERAB, NEWYORK."

STRICTLY PRIVATE.   FOR PATENT SOLICITORS ONLY.

ALL FORMER CIRCULARS ARE HEREBY WITHDRAWN.

CHARGES

AND

GENERAL INFORMATION

RELATING TO

PATENTS,

INCLUDING ALL THE

PRINCIPAL COUNTRIES

OF THE

WORLD.

RICHARDS & CO.,
INTERNATIONAL PATENT SOLICITORS,
38, BROADWAY, NEW YORK, U.S.A.

TO PATENT SOLICITORS.

WE desire to call your attention to the fact, that we devote ourselves exclusively to the transaction of foreign business for Patent Solicitors. We neither solicit nor receive orders from inventors. We have direct agencies and correspondents in almost every country in the world that grants patent and trade-mark protection, and are prepared to attend to all manner of work in this line.

We respectfully solicit your orders, and promise you promptness, fidelity and despatch in the transaction of any business that you may entrust to us.

RE/SERVICE.—Our agents have been selected with the utmost care, and are, in every instance, the best and most reliable we have been able to find in their respective countries, and we can vouch for the proper and careful treatment of applications that they may prosecute.

RE/CHARGES.—We believe you will find our charges moderate and satisfactory. We are aware that in some instances our charges are somewhat higher than those we have seen quoted by other agents. They are, however, as low as can be given and the best class of work secured.

RE/DOCUMENTS, POWERS OF ATTORNEY, ETC.—We have in print blank powers of attorney for the principal foreign countries, which we furnish to Patent Solicitors without charge. We are always glad to advise and assist our clients in the preparation of any documents for foreign applications.

RICHARDS & CO.

38, BROADWAY, NEW YORK, U. S. A.

GENERAL INFORMATION.

Charges.—The charges given in this book apply only when all the documents required are sent to us completely and correctly prepared as indicated.

Preparation of Applications.—When desired we will attend to the preparation of any application or applications, furnishing all the necessary drawings and documents (one copy of the specification and a tracing or blue print of the drawing being furnished us). Our charges for such services are as follows:

1. COPYING DOCUMENTS, on legal cap, in the English language, 5 cents per 100 words for each copy ; on parchment, 15 cents per 100 words.

2. DRAWINGS.—It is not possible to fix, beforehand, a charge that will meet all cases, but we quote $5.00 per sheet for each country, as an approximate amount for average cases, which will include all requisite copies. Our correspondents are respectfully asked to add the above to their remittances when they request us to prepare any or all of the documents for an application. Should the cost exceed this sum, in case of complicated or difficult drawings, any balance can be settled when the work is completed.

We will also attend to the photo-lithographing of drawings when requested to do so. Our charge for this is usually $8.00 per sheet (U. S. size), which includes the cost of materials, and as many as twenty copies of the drawing. Where a larger number of copies is desired our charge will be a little more, and in accordance with the actual extra cost to us for materials and work. Inasmuch as photo-lithographs are very much cheaper than hand drawings, where a number of copies of the same drawing are to be used, and can be used—if first-class—for any foreign country, Solicitors will see the advantage of their use wherever practicable.

Translations into English.—Where the documents are required to be filed in the English language, we have made no note of translations in the body of this book. When documents are sent to us in any other language than English, however, unless in the language of the country in which they are to be filed, the following amount must be added to our usual charge, for each 100 words contained in the specification, to cover cost of translation here, *viz.*: Translations from French, German, Italian or Spanish, 35 cents ; Scandinavian or Portuguese, 50 cents ; Russian, 85 cents. Will our foreign correspondents please make note of this.

Execution of Documents.—It is important that *full names*, the *full address*, and *the occupation* of each applicant should be clearly set forth in the preamble to the specification. In signing documents the applicants should write out all their names in full, as for instance, *John Henry Augustus Smith*. When the specifications sent are not written in the English language, the signatures of the inventor and witnesses for each specification required, should always be sent on separate sheets of paper in the following form :

" In witness whereof, I have hereunto set my hand at...

this.....................day of...... ....18......"

(Signature of Inventor.)

Witnesses :
(*Signature of two Witnesses.*)

Where the applicant is a *corporation*, all documents should be executed in the following manner:

The...........................Company,
By (Name of Officer who signs).
(Title of Officer.)

Printed Powers of Attorney, Assignments, Etc.—We always have in print, blank forms of Powers of Attorney, and of Assignments, for all the principal foreign countries. We furnish any needed supplies of these to such Patent Solicitors as transact their foreign business through us, *free of charge*, upon application.   Other Solicitors may obtain them by remitting 10 cents for each form ordered, except assignments, for which the charge is $1.00 for each complete set for each country, but this payment will be applied on account of our charge for registering the assignment, if the deed is recorded through our Agency. We issue the printed Powers of Attorney for European and South American applications in books containing 10 forms each, with directions for the proper execution of the same printed in full upon the cover of each book.

Models and Specimens.—Models or specimens are seldom required to be filed in any of the foreign countries.   They are still necessary in the following countries :

Canada.   While an application may be filed without a model, and a filing date obtained, the Patent Office will, at the present time, neither grant nor issue the patent until a model or specimen is received.

Germany.   A model is required where the invention relates to skates or firearms, and two models, one of which must be a sectional model, if the invention relates to spools, spindles, or shuttles.   Samples are required in case the invention relates to chemicals or dyes.

Switzerland.   The filing of models is obligatory when the invention concerns the movements of watches or portable firearms, or, when the object invented is composed in whole or in part of substances or combinations of substances the nature of which is difficult to determine.

Newfoundland.   The law requires the production of a model or specimens, but the Governor in Council has power to dispense with the requirement, and in our practice we have seldom been asked to send one.

Full particulars as to special requirements will be found under each country in the body of the book.

Importation of Patented Articles.—None of the principal foreign countries, except France, Canada, Tunis, Turkey and Peru, make any restrictions as to the importation of patented articles.   In Canada, unless an extension of time is procured, the patented article must be imported by the patentee, or by others with his knowledge or consent, after the expiration of one year after the issue of the patent.   In the other countries, patented articles must not be imported at all except under special permit. Such permit may usually be obtained for the importation of a single model or sample, at a cost of about $10.00.   France and Tunis now belong to the International Union, however, and citizens or subjects of countries belonging to the International Union may now import into these countries without restriction, but others are prohibited from so doing under the penalty of forfeiture of the patent.

Marking of Patented Articles.—It is not compulsory to place any mark upon articles to indicate that they are patented, except in Canada, where the word *"Patented"* and the year of the date of patent must be stamped or engraved on each article, as *" Patented*, 1887," or as the case may be, and in Switzerland, where all patented articles must be marked with the Federal Cross (✛) and the number of the patent.

The German Patent Office has suggested that patented articles be marked *" Deutsches Reiches Patent,"* or with the letters *" D. R. P.,"* adding thereto the official number of the patent.   For France, if the articles are marked at all, or if the patentee mentions his title of patentee, or his patent, in advertisements, prospectuses or signboards, or by means of marks or stamps, the words *" Sans Garantie du Gouvernement"* must be added, under the penalty of a fine of from fifty to one thousand francs.   In the event of a repetition of the offence the fine may be doubled.   The patentee is liable to the same fine if he uses the title or mark after the patent has expired.   The usual practice is to employ the initial letters *S. G. D. G.*, although several persons have, at various times, been condemned for not using the words in full.   The law in Tunis and Turkey on this subject is substantially the same as in France.

Searches.—We undertake searches as to the novelty of an invention in any country. Owing to the defective manner in which the records are kept in many countries, this work is usually more expensive than in America or England.

Opinions.—We undertake to give, through our agents, formal opinions upon points of law, or with regard to any other matters pertaining to patents. The cost will be proportionate to the amount of work necessary to make a complete investigation of the subject.

Copies of Patents.—We can obtain upon short notice, copies of any patent as issued in any country. It should be noted that printed copies of patents can be obtained in but very few countries, and that it is necessary therefore in most cases to make hand copies of both drawings and specifications, thus requiring considerable time and labor. Our charges for printed copies of patents in the principal foreign countries are :

Great Britain, 50 cents for each shilling of the published price.
Germany, 75 cents each.
Switzerland, 75 cents each.

Amendment of Specifications.—Specifications may be amended either before or after the issue of the patent, in many foreign countries, but not in all. We give below a list of the countries in which such amendment is possible, together with a statement of our charges in connection therewith, the amount of same being based in all cases upon the amount of work and time involved.

Before issue of Patent.—When the application has been rejected because the title is too large, or the specification or drawings are insufficient or incorrect:

Austria,	charge	from	$2.50 to $10.00	Russia,	charge from	$5.00 to	$20.00
Canada,	"	"	2.50 " 7.50	South Australia, "	"	2.50 "	10.00
Germany,	"	"	2.50 " 10.00	Straits Settlements,	"	20.00 "	30.00
Great Britain,	"	"	2.00 " 7.50	Sweden,	" "	2.50 "	10.00
Italy,	"	"	2.50 " 10.00	Switzerland,	" "	2.50 "	10.00
Mauritius,	"	"	20.00 " 30.00	Tasmania,	" "	5.00 "	10.00
Norway,	"	"	2.50 " 10.00				

After the issue or grant of patent, by way of disclaimer or memorandum of alteration:

British Guiana,	charge from	$25.00 to $35.00	Natal,	charge from	$15.00 to 30.00
British Honduras,	" "	15.00 " 20.00	Newfoundland,	" "	15.00 " 25.00
Canada,	" "	7.50 " 20.00	New Zealand,	" "	10.00 " 25.00
" (Re-issue)		35.00	Queensland,	" "	15.00 " 25.00
Cape Colony,	from	20.00 to 30.00	South Australia, "	"	15.00 " 25.00
Fiji Islands,	" "	20.00 " 30.00	Straits Settlements,	"	20.00 " 30.00
Great Britain,	" "	35.00 " 40.00	Tasmania, "	"	25.00 " 35.00
India,	" "	15.00 " 25.00	Trinidad,	" "	25.00 " 35.00
Jamaica,	" "	15.00 " 25.00	Victoria,	" "	15.00 " 25.00
Leeward Islands,	" "	25.00 " 40.00			
Mauritius,	" "	20.00 " 35.00			

When the English Application has been Amended :

Hongkong, charge from $25.00 to $35.00 | St. Helena, charge from $25.00 to $35.00

Provisional Patents or Caveats.—*Provisional protection* may be obtained in the following countries and for the following terms:

British Guiana,	12 months	New Zealand,	12 months
British Honduras,	6 "	Orange Free State,	6 "
Fiji Islands,	6 "	Queensland,	12 "
Great Britain,	9 "	South Australia,	12 "
Leeward Islands,	6 "	South African Republic,	6 "
New Zealand,	9 "	Switzerland,	2 years
Natal,	6 "	Tasmania,	6 months
New South Wales,	12 "	Victoria,	12 "

Caveats, may be filed, and are operative for the following terms, in
Argentine Republic, 1 year, and may be renewed from year to year.
Canada, 1 year. Russia, 3 months.
Hawaii, 1 " South Australia, 1 year.

Confirmation of Invalid Patents.—Where the patentee is proved not to be the inventor, although he believed himself to be so, in some countries, the patent may be confirmed, or a new patent may be issued to the patentee, confirming the grant.   This is at present the case in : British Guiana, British Honduras, Cape Colony, Jamaica, Leeward Islands, Natal, South Australia, Tasmania and Victoria.   The cost of obtaining such confirmation would probably be from $75.00 to $100.00.

Compulsory Licenses.—Whenever it is shown that by reason of the failure of a patentee to grant licenses, that the patent is not being worked, or that the reasonable requirements of the public with respect to the invention cannot be supplied ; or that any person is prevented from working or using to the best advantage an invention of which he is possessed, the patentee may, in the following countries, be ordered to grant licenses, on such terms as may be just, according to the circumstances of the case :

Germany,	Norway,
Great Britain,	Orange Free State,
Hong Kong,	Queensland,
India,	St. Helena,
Luxembourg,	South African Republic,
New Zealand,	Switzerland.

The State may buy and use an invention which it deems useful, in the following countries :

Bolivia,	Russia,
Ecuador,	Sweden,
Luxembourg,	Switzerland.
Norway,	

Patents for Communicated Inventions.—This is a strictly English procedure, and the practice is confined to Great Britain and a few of its Colonies—South Australia, Tasmania, and Victoria.

Abyssinia.

There is as yet no patent law in this country, and, so far as we know, no way in which inventions may be effectually protected.

Aden. (British Arabia.)

This British dependency (including the Somali Coast Protectorate and the Kooria Mooria, Perim, and Socotra Islands) is subject to the Government of Bombay, British India, and is covered by the patent law of India. (See India.)

Afghanistan.

There is as yet no patent law in this country, and, so far as we know, no way in which inventions may be effectually protected.

Algeria.

Algeria is a French colony and is covered by the French patent law. A decree of July 5, 1850, (promulgated in Algeria, August 2, 1850 (declares the law to be in force and prescribes the form and manner of making applications in Algeria. (See France.)

Andamans Islands.

See India.

𝔄rgentine 𝔕epublic.

CHARGES.

```
*PATENT, Cost of, 5 year, all taxes paid ..................... $ 50 00
      "        "     10  "      "        ........................ 275 00
      "        "     15  "      "        ........................ 430 00
*PATENT OF ADDITION, upon a 5 year patent, all taxes paid   75 00
      "        "        "      "  10  "      "        "        150 00
      "        "        "      "  15  "      "        "        225 00
*PROVISIONAL PATENT, for 1 year          "          "         120 00
 ASSIGNMENTS, Recording. .............................        50 00
 WORKINGS...............................from $50 to 100 00
```

*The above charge includes translations up to 2,000 words in the specification, beyond that number $1.00 must be added for every 100 words.

LAW AND PRACTICE.

Who may be Patentee.—The actual inventor or his assignee.

Patents, Kind and Term.—Provisional Patents are granted for the term of one year, and may be renewed from year to year. Patents of Invention are granted for five, ten or fifteen years. A fifteen year patent can be obtained only upon inventions which have not up to the date of application in the Argentine Republic been patented elsewhere, and the applicant must furnish with his application a declaration, under oath, to the effect that he has not as yet applied for any patent in any other country, and that he makes his application in the Argentine Republic before applying elsewhere, because he believes it to be to his interest to do so. When a patent has been previously obtained in another country, the duration of the Argentine patent is limited to the duration of the foreign patent, but not to exceed ten years at most. Patents of Addition will not be granted for a longer period than the life of the original patent, when the latter does not exceed ten years, except when half that time has expired, or when the improvement lessens by half, at least, the cost of production, time, risk or danger, or for other similar reasons, in which case the Commissioner of Patents fixes the term for which the patent may be granted. A patent cannot be extended after its issue.

Unpatentable.—Pharmaceutical compositions; financial schemes; such discoveries or inventions as have, previous to the application, received a sufficient publicity in books, pamphlets or periodicals, either in this or foreign countries, to permit of their being worked; those of a mere theoretical nature having no evidence of their practical use in industry; and finally, inventions contrary to morals, or to the laws of the Republic.

Novelty, Effect of Prior Patent or Publication.—To obtain a valid patent the application must be filed before the invention has received sufficient publicity, in books, pamphlets or periodicals, either in the Argentine Republic or abroad, to enable it to be put into practice. The holder of a prior foreign patent, may, subject to the above requirement, apply for and obtain a valid Argentine patent at any time during the existence of his foreign patent.

Taxes.—There are none after the issue of the patent.

Assignments.—To effect the assignment of a patent, the following documents are necessary: 1. The Letters Patent; 2. An assignment in the Spanish language, signed by the assignor before a Notary Public, and legalized by an Argentine Consul. Care must be taken to make no mention in the assignment of any other patent than the Argentine.

When desired, we can obtain the legalization of the applicant's signature here at a cost of $3.00 for each legalization.

Working.—The invention must be worked within two years of the date of the issue of the patent, and the working must not be interrupted thereafter for two years at a time, except by circumstances beyond the patentee's control, or by accident duly certified by the office.

DOCUMENTS REQUIRED.

The same documents are required for Provisional Patents and Patents of Addition.

1.—**Power of Attorney.**—Signed by applicant, and legalized by an Argentine Consul.

When desired, we can obtain the legalization here at a cost of $3.00.

2.—**Drawings in duplicate.**—On drawing paper or tracing cloth of any suitable size. Must be made in black ink and to metric scale. No signatures necessary.

3.—**Specification in duplicate.**—May be written or printed on any suitable paper. No signatures necessary.

4.—**If a prior Patent exists.**—It is necessary to send a certified copy of such patent, legalized by an Argentine Consul. The Patent Office, in every case, where the inventor is not a resident of that Republic, requires the production of either the declaration called for under the following heading, or of a foreign patent of the invention. It does not, however, insist upon such being the patent of the country where the inventor resides, but it may be that of any other country, so long as the specification and drawings agree *exactly* with those of the Argentine application. Where possible, it is always best to use a certified copy of the Spanish Patent.

When desired, we can effect the legalization here at a cost of $3.00.

5.—**If no prior Patent exists.**—A declaration to that effect signed by the applicant before a Notary Public and legalized by an Argentine Consul. This document must also be furnished in all cases where the specification and drawings of the Argentine application do not exactly agree in all important particulars with those of a prior foreign patent. In such case it will not be necessary to furnish a certified copy of the foreign patent.

When desired, we can obtain the legalization here at a cost of $3.00.

FORMS.

POWER OF ATTORNEY.

Poder.

..................abajo firmado............... ....
domiciliado en... ....
....
declaro...........por las presentes otorgar á D...
....
poder especial amplio y bastante para recabar de las oficinas y autoridades nacionales que correspondan la obtencion.... ....
... ...
á cuyo efecto lo faculto .... para dar ante dichas autoridades todos los pasos necesarios al objeto indicado, elevar solicitudes, formular descripciones, protestas, declaraciones, apelaciones y reclamos; abonar todos impuestos, cuotas y pagos determinados por la ley; recibir todos documentos y valores dando el descargo respectivo; llenar cualesquiera otros requisitos y tomar enfin todas las medidas que creyere conducentes al resguardo de....... ....intereses, declarando desde ahora válido y bueno cuanto hiciere dicho Señor en bien ....
....
Dado y firmado............ ....
(*Signature*)..... ....
....
....

DECLARATION.

.... Abajo firmado............... ....
....

vecino de...
....
jur........................y declar...............................solemnemente que la invencion cuya respectiva
patente solicita y gestiona,................. ..apoderado legal,...
residente en...
y cuyo título es....................... ....
....
es de...........................esclusiva invencion y propiedad; que todavia no he....................
solicitado por ella patente alguna en ningun pais, que nadie la conoce aún; y que al presentar.................. ......preferentemente en la República Argentina, para patentarla por vez
primera, lo hago por creerlo así mucho mas conveniente á......................intereses.
    En fé de lo cual firm...................la presente declaracion en........... ....
....á los........ ....
días del mes de..................................de 189........

              (Sign here,).......... ....
              ....

Austria-Hungary.

The patent covers the entire Empire, which includes Bohemia, Bosnia, Cisleithania, Herzego-
vina, and Lichtenstein.

CHARGES.

* PATENT, Total cost of, all taxes paid for first year.............. $35 00
† TAXES.—*Payable annually counting from date of issue of patent.*
    Second, Third, Fourth and Fifth years..................each, 20 00
    Sixth   year... 25 00
    Seventh " 30 00
    Eighth   " 33 00
    Ninth   " 36 00
    Tenth   " 39 00
    Eleventh " 45 00
    Twelfth   " 52 00
    Thirteenth " 58 00
    Fourteenth " 64 00
    Fifteenth   " 70 00
ASSIGNMENTS, preparing and recording...................... 7 50
WORKING, Nominal.. 20 00

    * The above charge includes translations up to 2,000 words in the specification. Beyond
that number, 35 cents must be added for each 100 words.
    † The patent must always be forwarded when ordering the payment of any tax, that the
payment may be endorsed thereon.

LAW AND PRACTICE.

    Who may be Patentee.—Any person, whether the inventor or not; a firm or a
corporation. Where the invention has been patented in any or several foreign countries,
a valid Austrian patent can only be obtained by the owner of said foreign patent or patents, or by his heirs, or legal successors or assignees. In such case one of the foreign
patents, chosen by the applicant, forms the basis of the Austrian patent applied for.

    Patents, Kind and Duration.—Patents of Invention are granted for fifteen years,
subject to the payment of the required taxes, and the legal working of the invention. In
former years it was the custom of the Austrian office to issue the patent for the exact
number of years for which the taxes were paid at the time of issue. This is no longer
the case, the Minister of Commerce having decided (Decisions of July 27, 1882, and July
18, 1888) that Austrian patents are, without exception, granted for the maximum term
of fifteen years, subject to the payment of the legal taxes, etc., and the forms of the patent
documents have now been changed, so as to leave no doubt as to the term of the grant.
In case an Austrian patent is based upon a prior foreign patent, it is limited in term and

validity by the term and validity of such foreign patent, but it is quite independent of all other foreign patents for the same invention, without regard to their date.

Unpatentable.—Preparations of food, beverages and medicines ; discoveries, inventions or improvements which cannot be worked for reasons of public health, morals, or safety, or as being contrary to the general interest of the State ; scientific principles, or strictly scientific theorems, even if the principle or theorem lead to the creation of new industrial products, a new means or a new method of production ; inventions, which while worked in any foreign country are not patented there.

Novelty, Effect of Prior Patent or Publication.—To obtain a valid patent the application must be filed before the invention has been made public in Austria, either by a printed publication, or by the invention having been worked there. The printed copies of patents issued by the German Patent Office will not prevent the obtaining of a valid Austrian patent, provided the application for the latter be filed within three months from the day of issue of such print, but a valid patent cannot be obtained after the expiration of this time. Printed copies of patents of other countries can only affect the validity of an Austrian patent when it is proven that they were introduced into Austria before the filing of the application. A valid Austrian patent can be obtained at any time during the life of a prior foreign patent for the same invention, so long as the invention has not been published, or become publicly known, in Austria.

Taxes.—The legal taxes may be paid at once and in a lump sum, or in annual installments, as preferred by the patentee. In the latter case they must be paid yearly in advance, counting from the date of the issue of the patent. The Letters Patent should always be forwarded for the endorsement of such payment thereon. If for any reason it is impossible to forward the patent with the tax, the latter can be paid for one year without the production of this document. In this case, however, it becomes necessary to produce the patent with the next year's tax, or if it be lost, to apply for and obtain a duplicate of the patent. No extension of time for the payment of taxes can be obtained.

Assignments.—The following documents are necessary : 1. An assignment in German, signed by the *assignor* before a Notary Public and legalized by the Austrian Consul. 2. A power of attorney signed by the *assignee* before a Notary Public, and legalized by an Austrian Consul, authorizing the attorney to apply for and obtain the registration of the assignment and pay the taxes in connection therewith.

We can obtain the legalization of these documents here, when desired, at a cost of $3.00 each.

Working.—The invention must be worked within one year from the day of the issue of the patent, and the working must not be discontinued thereafter for any two consecutive years. No extension of time for working can be obtained. To effect a legal working, the invention, if a machine, must be actually constructed in Austria, and of materials procured there ; if a process, it must be put into operation there. Nominal workings, although very frequently made, are not legally valid, and we cannot recommend them. We will secure estimates of cost for actual workings, on receipt of particulars. According to the official decree of June 1, 1889, they must now be proven and entered upon the Patent Registers in connection with the patent to which they relate.

DOCUMENTS REQUIRED.

1. **One copy of Specification.**—Written or printed on any paper. No signatures required.
2. **Drawings in duplicate.**—May be made on tracing cloth, any size and margin. No signatures required.
3. **Power of Attorney.**—Signed by applicant. The usual German power should be used. (See Germany.) The power must be legalized by an Austrian Consul.

When desired, we can obtain the legalization here at a cost of $3.00, which includes Consular and Agency fees.

Azores Islands.

These islands belong to Portugal and are covered by its patent laws.

Bahama Islands.

CHARGES.

PATENT, cost of, all taxes paid for seven years.................$75 00
EXTENSION of patent at end of seventh year.................. 65 00
    "   "   "   "   " fourteenth year............115 00
PRELIMINARY EXAMINATIONS as to Novelty............... 15 00
ASSIGNMENTS, preparing and recording................. ...... 12 50

LAW AND PRACTICE.

Who may be Patentee.—Practically anyone, whether the inventor or not, as the first importer may obtain a valid patent, as well as the first inventor.

Patents, Kind and Term.—Patents of Invention (or Importation) granted for seven years from the filing of the specification, but the duration may be extended for two additional terms of seven years each, (twenty-one years in all) upon due application and payment of the legal fees.

Unpatentable.—Inventions that are not new within the Islands, as to the public use and exercise thereof at the time the application for patent therefor is filed ; if the applicant for the patent is not the true and first inventor within the Islands (the word inventor being held to include the true and first importer) of the invention described in the specification ; inventions which are at the time the specification is filed well-known elsewhere, and also known to some person or persons in the Islands other than the person filing such specification, and inventions already patented there.

Novelty, Effect of Prior Patent or Publication.—To obtain a valid patent the application must be filed before the invention has been published or otherwise publicly known within the Bahama Islands. The fact that prior patents exist, or that the invention has been published, or is publicly known and used in other countries, will not prevent the obtaining of a perfectly valid patent, so long as the invention is new as to the Bahamas at the time the application is filed.

Taxes.—Strictly speaking there are none after the issue of the patent, the same being issued for seven years and the fees paid at the filing of the application being in full for this term. If, however, it is desired to continue the patent in force for a longer time, it may be extended for a second term of seven years upon payment of a fee of £10 and for a third term of seven years upon payment of a further fee of £20.

Assignments.—These should be prepared in duplicate, and in the English language ; almost any form will answer, and no legalization of the document is now held to be necessary. As this practice may be changed at any time it is preferable to have the documents acknowledged before a Notary Public whenever it is convenient to do so.

Working.—Section XI. of the "Patent Act, 1889" required that the invention should be brought into operation in the Colony within three years from the date of the patent. This section was, however, repealed by Section VI. of 53 Vic., Chap 2, "An Act to amend the, 'Patent Act, 1889,'" assented to March 3, 1890, and there are now no requirements as to the working of the invention within the Colony.

Special.—This is one of the four West Indian Colonies that do not issue a formal document or "Letters Patent" to serve as a title deed. It is hoped that the Colony will soon have proper forms printed, and issue such a document to every patentee. Until this is done, however, the only documents that can be forwarded for the use of the patentee are, 1. The certificate of the Registrar of Records that the specification has been filed, and, 2. A copy of the Official Gazette containing a notice of the filing of the specification. If desired, a certified copy of the patent can be obtained, but only at an expense of from $15 to $35 according to the length of the specification, as the fees demanded by the Attorney-General for such copies are very high.

DOCUMENTS REQUIRED.

1. Four copies of the Specification.—These may be written or printed on any suitable paper, and of any size. No signatures nor legalization required.

2. Four copies of the Drawings.—On bristol board or tracing cloth, of any suitable size. No signatures required.

3. Petition.—Signed by applicant, may be on any suitable paper.

4. Declaration.—Signed by applicant, before a Notary Public, or other person authorized by law to administer an oath, who must affix his official seal.

5. Power of Attorney.—Signed by applicant and two witnesses.

6. Where a prior foreign Patent exists.—A certified copy of such patent must be supplied. Where there are several foreign patents, the certified copy may be a copy of any one of them, but it is best, where possible, to file a copy of the United States or British patent.

FORMS.

PETITION.

To His Excellency the Governor of the Bahama Islands in Council:

The humble petition of (*here insert name, address and occupation of petitioner*), showeth:

That your petitioner is in possession of an invention for (*insert title of invention*), which invention he believes will be of great public utility; that he is the true and first inventor thereof and that the same is not in use by any other person or persons to the best of his knowledge and belief.

Your petitioner, therefore humbly prays that your Excellency will be pleased in the name and on behalf of Her Majesty the Queen, to grant unto him, his executors, administrators and assigns, Her Majesty's Letters Patent for these Islands for the term of seven years, pursuant to the Act of Assembly in that case made and provided.

(*Signature.*)..

DECLARATION.

I (*here insert name, full address and occupation of applicant*), do solemnly and sincerely declare that I am in possession of an invention for (*insert title as in petition*), which invention I believe will be of great public utility; that I am the true and first inventor thereof; and that the same is not in use by any other person or persons to the best of my knowledge and belief; and that the instrument in writing under my hand and seal, hereto annexed, particularly describes and ascertains the nature of the said invention and the manner in which the same is to be performed, and I make this declaration conscientiously believing the same to be true.

(*Signature.*)..

Declared to before me........................
this..............day of................18....
(*Signature and title of person before whom declaration is made.*)

SPECIFICATION.

To all whom it may concern : Be it known that I, *(here insert name, occupation and place of residence)*, am in possession of an invention for *(state title of invention precisely as in petition)*, and I, the said *(here insert name of applicant)*, do hereby declare the nature of the said invention and in what manner the same is to be performed, to be particularly described and ascertained in and by the following statement thereof, that is to say : The invention has for its object *(here insert the full specification and claims.)*

Witnesses :   *(Signature.)*........................

POWER OF ATTORNEY.

In the matter of the Patent Act, 1889, of the Bahama Islands, and in the matter of *(name, occupation and address)*, an Inventor.

I, the above-named *(insert name)*,do hereby retain, constitute and appoint..................................
....
....
as my agent and attorney, to apply for and obtain from the Government of the Bahama Islands an exclusive Privilege or Letters Patent for *(insert title of invention precisely as in petition)*, and I authorize him to sign my name to such papers and writings, and do such acts, including the appointment of a substitute or substitutes, as may be necessary or expedient.

Dated this..............uay of................18....

Signed, sealed and delivered in the presence of

....   *(Signature.)*............................[L. S.]

𝕭𝖆𝖑𝖊𝖆𝖗𝖎𝖈 𝕴𝖘𝖑𝖆𝖓𝖉𝖘.

See Spain.

𝕭𝖆𝖗𝖇𝖆𝖉𝖔𝖊𝖘.

CHARGES.

PATENT, total cost of, all taxes paid for seven years.............$ 75 00
EXTENSION of patent at end of seventh year....................   65 00
"   "   " fourteenth year............. 115 00
ASSIGNMENT, preparing and recording.......................   15 00
WORKING...   30 00

LAW AND PRACTICE.

Who may be Patentee.—"The first and true inventor," which is interpreted to include the first and true importer into Barbadoes.

Patents, Kind and Term.—Patents of Invention (or Importation), which are granted for seven years from the filing of the specification; but the duration may be extended for two additional terms of seven years each (twenty-one years in all), upon due application made, and payment of the legal fees.

Unpatentable.—Inventions that are not new in Barbadoes at the time the application is filed ; inventions of which the applicant for patent is not the true and first inventor within the Colony. (The word inventor is held to mean and include the true and first importer.) Inventions which are at the time the specification is filed, well-known elsewhere, and also known to some person or persons in Barbadoes, other than the person filing the specification ; and inventions already patented there.

Novelty, Effect of Prior Patent or Publication.—To obtain a valid patent the application must be filed before the invention has been published, or otherwise become publicly known in Barbadoes, but the fact that prior patents exist, or that the invention has been published, or is publicly known and used in other countries will not prevent the obtaining of a perfectly valid patent, so long as the invention is new in Barbadoes at the time the application is filed.

Taxes.—Strictly speaking there are none after the issue of the patent, the same being granted for seven years, and the fees paid at the filing of the specification, being in full for this term. If, however, it is desired to continue the patent in force for a longer term, it may be extended for a second term of seven years upon payment of a fee of £10, and for a third term of seven years upon payment of a further fee of £20.

Assignments.—The documents must be prepared in duplicate in the English language. The signature of the assignor must be proven under oath before a Notary, and the document must be legalized by a British Consul.
When desired we can obtain the legalization here at a cost of $2.50.

Working.—The law requires that the invention must be "brought into operation within a period of three years after the filing of the specification." The present practice is not to require the actual construction of the patented article in Barbadoes, it being held sufficient to import, or cause the articles to be imported into the Colony, and there offer and expose them for sale. In the case of a process it should be put into practice there.

Special.—Barbadoes is one of the four West Indian Colonies that issues no formal document or Letters Patent, the only document issued to patentees being the official certificate of the filing of the specification. We also supply a copy of the Official Gazette containing the legal notice of the filing of the specification. A certified copy of the patent can be obtained when desired, but this is expensive, costing from $20 to $40, according to the length of the specification.

DOCUMENTS REQUIRED.

1. **Specification in duplicate.**—Signed by the applicant. The form is the same as for the Bahama Islands, which see.

2. **Drawings in duplicate.**—Any convenient size and material. No signatures required.

3. **Power of Attorney.**—Signed by the applicant and two witnesses. The signature of the inventor must be proven by one of the witnesses under oath before a Notary, and the document must be legalized by a British Consul.

4. **Declaration.**—Signed by applicant.

FORMS.

POWER OF ATTORNEY.

In the matter of the Patent Act of 1883, and in the matter of *(name, occupation and address)*, an inventor.

I, the above-named *(insert name)*, do hereby retain, constitute and appoint.....................
....
....
as my agent and attorney, to apply for and obtain from the Government of Barbadoes an exclusive Privilege or Letters Patent for *(insert title of invention as in specification)*, and I authorize him to sign my name to such papers and writings, and do such acts regarding same, as may be necessary or expedient.

Witnesses.

....

....

                                           (Signature of Applicant.) [L. S.]

State of.....................⎫
                       ⎬ ss.
County of....................⎭

...............................*(Name of witness)* being duly sworn deposes, and says, that the above-named *(name of applicant)* is to him known and known to him to be the individual described in, and who executed, the foregoing instrument, and that he witnessed the execution thereof.

                                        (Signature of Witness.)

Sworn to and subscribed before me this.......................day of....................18......

(Notarial Seal.)

                                        (Signature of Notary.)
                                        (Legalization of British Consul.

DECLARATION.

I, (*here insert name, occupation and place of residence*), do solemnly and sincerely declare that I am in possession of an invention for (*state the title of the invention*), which invention I believe will be of public utility, that I am the inventor of the said invention and the same is not publicly known or used in this colony, to the best of my knowledge and belief; and that, to the best of my knowledge and belief, the instrument in writing under my hand, hereunto annexed, particularly describes and ascertains the nature of the said invention, and in what manner the same is to be carried out.

The.........................day of...............18....

(*Signature of Applicant.*)

Belgium.

CHARGES.

*PATENT, cost of, all taxes paid for one year....................$15 00
*PATENT OF ADDITION, all taxes paid........................ 15 00
TAXES, *payable annually, counting from the date of the application.*
There is one month's grace without fine, or six months' grace with
a fine of $2.00.

Second	Year	$ 6 50	Twelfth	Year	$26 50
Third	"	8 50	Thirteenth	"	28 50
Fourth	"	10 50	Fourteenth	"	30 50
Fifth	"	12 50	Fifteenth	"	32 50
Sixth	"	14 50	Sixteenth	"	34 50
Seventh	"	16 50	Seventeenth	"	36 50
Eighth	"	18 50	Eighteenth	"	38 50
Ninth	"	20 50	Nineteenth	"	40 50
Tenth	"	22 50	Twentieth	"	42 50
Eleventh	"	24 50			

ASSIGNMENTS, preparing and recording........................$15 00
WORKING, nominal.. 20 00

*The above charge includes translations up to 2,000 words in the specification. Beyond this number, 35 cents must be added for each 100 words.

LAW AND PRACTICE.

Who may be Patentee.—Any person, whether the inventor or not, a firm or corporation, may obtain a patent. If the applicant is not the inventor, it is desirable that he should have the inventor's written consent permitting him to make the application.

Patents, Kind and Term.—Patents are of three kinds: Patents of Invention, granted to the applicant who applies for his Belgian patent before the actual grant of letters patent in any other country; Patents of Importation, granted to an inventor or his assigns who, previous to lodging his application in Belgium, has obtained letters patent in some other country; Patents of Addition for improvements on inventions already patented.
Patents of Invention are granted for twenty years, subject to the payment of the prescribed taxes, and proper working of the invention. Patents of Importation are limited to the term of the prior foreign patent having the longest term; not, however, to exceed the maximum duration. Patents of Addition are granted for the unexpired term of the original patent and expire with it.

Unpatentable.—Any discovery or improvement that is not capable of being worked as an article of industry or of commerce.

Novelty, Effect of Prior Patent or Publication.—To obtain valid patents, applications for Patents of Invention should be made before any public use or publication of the invention in Belgium, and before any patent for the same invention is actually issued in another country. It is sufficient under the present practice to file the Belgian application upon the date of issue of the United States patent. Applications for Patents of Importation may be made at any time during the term of the foreign patent, provided the patented article has not been worked, or made use of for commercial purposes in Belgium by other parties, or the complete specifications and accurate drawings of the patented article have not been published in a printed work, prior to the date of the application. (Official or other publications prescribed by law, such as the English blue books and the publications of the U. S. Patent Office, do not affect the validity of Patents of Importation.) Applications for Patents of Addition should be made before public use, or publication of the invention in Belgium.

Taxes.—Taxes are payable upon all Belgian patents (except Patents of Addition), in installments, yearly in advance, counting from the date of the filing of the application. There is one month's grace, without fine, for making the payment, or six months' grace with a fine of 10 francs ($2.00).

Assignments.—The documents should be in the French language, and be executed in duplicate before a Notary Public, and legalized by a Belgian Consul.

We can obtain the legalization here when desired at a cost of $2.00 for each legalization.

Working.—The invention must be worked in Belgium within one year of its first commercial working in *any other* country, and the working must not thereafter be discontinued for any twelve consecutive months. The working must be *bona fide.* If the invention relates to machines, tools, instruments or like articles, they should be manufactured in Belgium in sufficient numbers to give the appearance, at least, of putting the invention into commercial use. If the invention relates to a process, the latter should be carried into practice in some manufactory in Belgium, and for a sufficient length of time to obtain proof that the working has been genuine.

The question of working has been left by the law entirely to the discretion of the government, which alone has the power to decide what shall constitute an efficient working, and to judge in each individual case whether the working made is sufficient or not. The courts decline all competency in this matter, and assume that a patent has been properly worked until it has been annulled by the government. In the case of patents which have been annulled for insufficient working, the government has held that it is not sufficient to import the patented articles into Belgium from abroad and put them on sale there, even if large numbers are sold in the country by this means. It is not even considered sufficient to have a number of the patented articles made in Belgium if the same articles are also imported from abroad and sold in Belgium. The mere importation of patented articles, except in limited quantities to serve as samples or models, while not prohibited by law, seems to be considered as contrary to the spirit of the law. To effect a strictly legal working therefore it would seem that the patentee should not only manufacture the patented article in Belgium, but should manufacture all such articles that may be required to meet the commercial demand for them, and abstain from importing similar articles from abroad for the purposes of trade. The government seldom or never interferes as regards the working of an invention unless called upon to do so by an interested party. If the inventor cannot then establish the fact that his invention has been properly worked his patent will be annulled. It is, of course, impossible for us to fix a stated price for legal workings, as the cost of manufacture of different articles varies so greatly. We will, however, furnish estimates of costs in each individual case upon receiving particulars.

Inasmuch as we are constantly receiving orders for nominal workings we quote a price for them, but it must be understood that we do not recommend them.

DOCUMENTS REQUIRED.

1. **One copy of Specification.**—No signatures required.

2. **Drawings in duplicate.**—On tracing cloth. The sheets should measure 34 centimetres (13⅜ inches), in height, by 21 centimetres (8⅜ inches), in width, with a

frame or margin line all around of 4½ centimetres (1¾ inches), from the edge of the sheet. When this size is not sufficient it may be doubled or trebled either way, but the sheet must be capable of folding exactly within the above dimensions. No signatures necessary.

3. **Power of Attorney.**—Signed by the applicant. The form is the same as for France (which see).

Bermuda Islands.

There is at present no patent law in this British Colony. The government will, however, grant protection for inventions by way of special Legislative Act, provided the invention is likely to prove of practical utility in the country.

The cost of such grants varies considerably, we will, however, undertake to procure them at a charge of $400 each. We must ask for an additional remittance in case the cost exceeds this sum, but think this will cover all charges in most cases.

DOCUMENTS REQUIRED.

The same as for the Bahama Islands, changing the name of the Colony, and omitting the title of the act.

Bolivia.

CHARGES.

```
*PATENT, cost of, all taxes paid......................  ...........$400 00
 ASSIGNMENTS .............................................  50 00
 WORKING, exclusive of freight charges and cost of manufacture.  100 00
```
*The above charge includes translation of the specification up to 2,000 words; $1.25 must b added for every 100 words in the specification in excess of 2,000.

LAW AND PRACTICE.

Who may be Patentee.—The true and first inventor, or the true and first importer of an invention into Bolivia.

Patents, Kind and Term.—Patents of Invention are granted for not less than ten, nor more than fifteen years. Patents of Importation are granted for three years if the establishment of the machinery or industry involves an outlay of 20,000 pesos; for six years if the outlay amounts to 50,000 pesos, and for ten years if it requires 100,000 pesos. Patents date from the day upon which they are issued.

Unpatentable.—Inventions contrary to the law or good customs; inventions merely producing modifications of proportions; articles of pure adornment; secret remedies.

Novelty, Effect of Prior Patent or Publication.—In order to obtain a valid Patent of Invention the application therefor must be filed before the invention has been published or described in the press, either in Bolivia or in any other country. In case of a Patent of Importation the application must be filed before the invention has become known or used in Bolivia. A valid patent may be obtained for an invention already patented in another country, at any time, subject to the above requirements as to novelty.

Taxes.—There are none after the issue of the patent.

Assignments.—These should be prepared in duplicate and in the Spanish language, and must be accompanied by a power of attorney authorizing the recording of the assignment and the payment of the fees in connection therewith. All the documents must be legalized by a Bolivian Consul.

We can obtain the legalization here, when desired, at a cost of $3.50.

Working.—Patents must be worked within a year and a day from the date of issue under penalty of forfeiture. In the absence of any decisions upon this point it is difficult to ascertain just what amount of working is necessary. There is little doubt, however, but that an actual *bona fide* working of the invention in Bolivia is requisite, and this working should be proven before the proper authorities.

DOCUMENTS REQUIRED.

The same as for Chili (which see). The power of attorney must be legalized by a Bolivian Consul.

We can obtain the legalization here, when desired, at a cost of $3.50.

Brazil.

CHARGES.

* PATENT, cost of, all taxes paid for first year.................. $130 00

TAXES, *Payable in advance, counting from date of issue of patent,*

Second	Year..........$22 00	Ninth	Year	..........$63 50
Third	" 28 25	Tenth	"	.... 69 00
Fourth	" 34 00	Eleventh	"	.... 75 50
Fifth	" 40 00	Twelfth	"	.... 82 00
Sixth	" 46 00	Thirteenth	"	.... 87 50
Seventh	" 52 00	Fourteenth	"	.... 93 50
Eighth	" 57 50	Fifteenth	"	.... 99 50

† PATENT OF ADDITION................................... 80 00

ASSIGNMENTS... 50 00

WORKING. The charges are variable.........from $50 00 to 100 00

* This charge includes translations up to 2,000 words: $2.00 must be added for each 100 words in excess of 2,000 contained in the specification. Every reference letter, or figure, is counted as a word. This charge covers not only the translations, but also the cost of publishing the specification in the "Diario Oficial." The specification is published in full, and the cost is 12 cents for every 85 letters.

† To this amount must be added $2.00 for each 100 words in excess of 2,000 contained in the specification. Every reference letter, or figure, is counted as a word. There must also be added an amount equal to the tax about to fall due on the original Patent. There are no subsequent taxes on Patents of Addition.

LAW AND PRACTICE.

Who may be Patentee.—The author of any industrial discovery or invention. Joint inventors may obtain a joint patent. Inventors holding foreign patents may obtain a patent in Brazil confirming their rights there. A patent for an improvement on the subject matter of an existing patent (Patent of Addition) can be obtained during the first year of the original patent, by the inventor or his legal representatives only, but afterwards by other inventors, who may file a petition before the expiration of the first year in order to establish priority.

Patents, Kind and Term.—Patents of Invention granted for fifteen years, subject to the payment of the annual taxes. The patent will expire with a prior foreign patent for the same invention. Patents of Addition are granted for the life of the original patent and expire therewith.

Unpatentable.—Inventions contrary to law and morality, or of a dangerous or noxious character, or which do not afford a practical industrial result.

Novelty, Effect of Prior Patent or Publication.—To obtain a valid patent the application must be made before any publication or public use of the invention in Brazil. If an inventor, having obtained a foreign patent, makes his application in Brazil within seven months of the date of the grant of the foreign patent, his right of priority will not be invalidated by reason of events which may occur in the interval, such as the application by another party for the same invention, or the publication, working, or utilization of the same in Brazil. Inventors can also publicly exhibit their inventions in Brazil prior to their applications for patents, on obtaining the necessary permission for the purpose. It should be noted, however, that where a prior foreign patent exists, the inventor can only obtain a valid patent by filing his application therefor within seven months of the date of such prior patent, and in general, a valid patent can only be obtained when the application has been filed before the invention has become known in Brazil in any way, or been published or patented in a foreign country for seven months.

Taxes.—Taxes are payable in yearly installments, in advance, commencing to count from the date of the issue of the patent. Prolongations of time for making these payments cannot be obtained. The tax payable to the government amounts to £2.7.3 for the first year, £3.10.10 for the second, £4.14.6 for the third, and so on, increasing £1.3.7½ yearly.

Assignments.—In order to record an assignment the following documents must be furnished: 1. The Brazilian Patent. 2. A contract of sale or assignment written in the language of the country in which it is executed, legalized by a Brazilian Consul. 3. If the patent was not obtained through us, a Power of Attorney, legalized by a Brazilian Consul.

When desired we can obtain the legalization here at cost of $3.00 for each document, which includes Consular and Agency fees.

Working.—The law requires the patentee to work the patent within three years from the date of its issue. The working must not be suspended at any time for a period exceeding one year. A legal working is effected only by an actual prosecution of the trade to which a patent relates, and the supplying of the article manufactured thereunder in such proportions or quantities as are reasonable, taking into consideration its uses and consumption. The working should be proven before the end of the third year.

To effect and prove a working we require the following documents: 1. A special power of attorney, the form for which we will supply upon request. This power must be legalized by a Brazilian Consul. 2. A statement showing whether the invention is being worked in Brazil, and if so, in what place or places, and any information and data with respect to the invention that may be useful.

We can obtain the legalization here, when desired, at a cost of $3.00.

DOCUMENTS REQUIRED.

1. One copy of the Specification.—May be on any paper and unsigned. It should bear a title designating the object of the invention, and indicate the full name, occupation, nationality, and residence of the applicant. Weights and measures should be shown in accordance with the metrical system, temperature according to the Centigrade thermometer, and density by specific weight.

2. Drawings in triplicate.—The drawings should be made on white drawing board 33 centimetres (13 inches) in height, by 21, 42, or 63 centimetres (8¼, 16½ or 24¾ inches) wide, with a simple margin line, leaving outside that line a margin of 2 centimetres (⅘ of an inch). The drawings should be made to the metrical scale; each sheet of paper bearing number of order, if there be several. The drawings must be signed by the inventor in the lower right hand corner above the marginal line. The signature is sufficient, and it should not be witnessed nor attested by a Notary or others. When the application is for a Patent of Addition, the drawings should indicate, with the same ink, but with dotted lines or points, the modifications made in the original invention.

3. **Power of Attorney.**—Signed by applicant. This should be acknowledged before a Notary and legalized by a Brazilian Consul.

We can obtain the legalization here, if desired, at a cost of $3.00 for each document, which includes Consular and Agency fees.

4. **For Patents of Addition.**—It is necessary to forward the original patent.

FORM.
POWER OF ATTORNEY.
Procuração.

.....................abaixo assignado..
....
morador ....
do....pela presente procuração os poderes mais amplos a...
morador no Rio de Janeiro, para, por.............e em.......................nome obter do Governo da Republica dos Estados Unidos do Brazil...
para..
....
....
....

de conformidade com a lei de 14 de Outubro de 1882. E para este fim do........poderes ao........ bastante procurador para preencher todas as formalidades prescriptas pela lei e regulamento, que baixou com o Decreto n. 8820 de 30 de Dezembro de 1882, rectificar e assignar todas as declarações, relatorios, documentos e requerimentos, inclusive desenhos e descripções, deposital-os ou em caso de necessidade retiral-os; pagar as taxas e impostos; registrar quando fôr preciso a transferencia ou cessão do privilegio; substabelecer todos ou partes dos presentes poderes finalmente fazer tudo o que fôr á bem dos interesses do outorgante representando-o activa e passivamente perante o Governo Brazileiro ou em juizo.

....18   (*Signature.*)

Burmah.

Burmah is now a province of British India and is covered by its patent law.

British Guiana.

CHARGES.

*PROVISIONAL PROTECTION, for 13 months	$ 90 00
COMPLETING PATENT, all taxes paid up to seventh year	210 00
Total	$300 00
Or, COMPLETE in first instance	$290 00
† TAXES, Before the expiration of the seventh year	115 00
ASSIGNMENTS	40 00

* The application may be made with either a provisional or complete specification. In case of the former, the complete specification must be filed, if the patent is to be completed, before the expiration of the provisional protection.
† The patent must be produced for indorsement when paying the tax.

LAW AND PRACTICE.

Who May be Patentee.—The true and first inventor, which is interpreted to include the true and first importer of the invention within the colony.

Patents, Kind and Duration.—Patents of Invention (or Importation), granted for fourteen years, subject to the payment of the prescribed tax. The Patent will expire with any prior foreign patent for the same invention. A patent may usually be extended for an additional term of seven years upon due application made, and the payment of the prescribed tax.

Unpatentable.—The law provides that a patent may be declared void when it is shown that the grant of such patent is contrary to law, or prejudicial or inconvenient to the public in general, or that the invention is not a new invention as to the public use and exercise thereof, or that the patentee is not the true and first inventor within the colony.

Novelty, Effect of Prior Patent or Publication.—To obtain a valid patent the application therefor must be filed before the invention has been publicly known or used in the Colony. Publication of the invention, or prior patents in other countries cannot affect the validity of a patent subsequently obtained in British Guiana, provided the invention has not been publicly known or used there at the time the application is filed.

Taxes.—A tax of $100 is payable to the government before the expiration of the seventh year of the life of the patent, counting from the day of the filing of the application. There is no provision made for obtaining an extension of the time for making this payment, and if the tax is not paid in time the patent will be lost.

Assignments.—These should be in the English language, and in duplicate, and may be in any suitable form. They should be legalized by a British Consul.

We can obtain the legalization here when required at a cost of $2.50 for each legalization.

Working.—There are no requirements.

DOCUMENTS REQUIRED.

1. **Petition.**—Signed by applicant, and legalized by a British Consul.

2. **Affidavit.**—Signed by applicant. This should be made before a Notary Public and legalized by a British Consul.

3. **Specification in duplicate.**—May be written on any paper. Signed by applicant, and legalized by a British Consul.

4. **Drawings in duplicate.**—May be of any convenient size, and on drawing board or tracing cloth. No signatures necessary.

5. **Power of Attorney.**—Signed by applicant, and legalized by a British Consul.

We can obtain the legalization of the documents here when desired, at a cost of $2.50 for each legalization.

FORMS.

PETITION.

To His Excellency (*leave space for name of the Governor*) Governor and Commander-in-Chief, in and over the colony of British Guiana, Vice-Admiral and Ordinary of the same, &c., &c., &c.

The humble petition of (*name, address, and occupation of the applicant*) respectfully showeth: That your petitioner is in possession of an invention for (*insert the title of the invention*), which invention he believes will be of great public utility; that he is the true and first inventor thereof; and that the same is not in use by any other person or persons in this colony, to the best of his knowledge and belief.

Your petitioner, therefore, humbly prays: That your Excellency will be pleased to grant unto him, his heirs, executors, administrators, and assigns, Letters Patent, in the name of Her Majesty, for the sole use, benefit and advantage of his said invention, within the colony of British Guiana, for the term of fourteen years, pursuant to the ordinance in that case made and provided.

And your petitioner will ever pray, &c. *(Signature of Applicant.)*

AFFIDAVIT.

I *(insert name of applicant)*, of *(insert place of residence and occupation)*, having been duly sworn make oath and say, that I am in possession of an invention for *(insert the title as in petition)*, which invention I believe will be of great public utility; that I am the true and first inventor thereof; and that the same is not in use by any other person or persons in this colony, to the best of my knowledge and belief.

(Signature of Applicant.)

Sworn this...................................day of...........A. D..............before me.
(Official Seal.) *(Title of Office.)*

SPECIFICATION.

To all to whom these presents shall come: I, *(insert name of applicant)*, of *(insert place of residence and occupation)*, send greeting:

Whereas, His Excellency *(leave space for name of the governor)* Governor and Commander-in-Chief in and over the colony of British Guiana, &c., &c., &c., by Letters Patent, bearing date the ....day of...................in the year of our Lord one thousand eight hundred and ....in the..............year of Her Majesty's reign, did, in the name of Her Majesty, pursuant to the ordinance in such case made and provided, give and grant unto me, the said *(name of applicant)*, his especial license, that I, the said *(name of applicant)*, my heirs, executors, administrators, and assigns, or such others as I, the said *(name of applicant)*, my heirs, executors, administrators, and assigns, should at any time agree with, and no others, from time to time, and at all times thereafter, during the term therein expressed, should, and lawfully might make, use, exercise, and vend within the colony of British Guiana, an invention for *(insert title of invention)*, upon the condition (amongst others), that I, the said *(name of applicant)*, by an instrument in writing under my hand, should particularly describe and ascertain the nature of the said invention, and in what manner the same was to be performed, and cause the same to be deposited in the Registrar's office for the counties of Demerara and Essequebo, within six calendar months next and immediately after the date of the said Letters Patent. Now, know ye, that I, the said *(name of applicant)*, do hereby declare the nature of my said invention, and in what manner the same is to be performed, to be particularly described and ascertained in and by the following statement, that is to say: *(describe the invention)*.

In witness whereof, I, the said...have hereto set my hand, this....................................day of...A. D. .... in the presence of the subscribing witnesses.

(Signatures of Witnesses.) *(Signature of Applicant.)*

PROVISIONAL SPECIFICATION.

I, *(insert full name, address, and occupation of applicant)*, do hereby declare the nature of the said invention for *(insert title of invention exactly as in petition)* to be as follows: *(here insert specification.)*

Dated this..................................day of..................................A. D., 18.....

(Signature.)

POWER OF ATTORNEY.

In the matter of the Patent Law Ordinance of 1861, of the Government of British Guiana, and in the matter of *(name, occupation and address)* an inventor.

I, the above-named *(here insert name)* do hereby retain, constitute, and appoint................. .... as my Agent and Attorney, to apply for and obtain from the Government of British Guiana an exclusive privilege or patent for *(state the title of invention as in petition)*, and I authorize him to sign my name to such papers and writings, and to do such acts regarding the same, including the appointment of a substitute or substitutes, as may be necessary or expedient.

Dated this................day of...................18....
Signed, sealed and delivered at............ |
                                            }
In the presence of...................... }
(Two witnesses.)

(Signature of Applicant.) (L. S.)

British Honduras.

CHARGES.

* PROVISIONAL PROTECTION for six months............... $90 00
COMPLETING PATENT, all taxes paid for three years....... 95 00

	$185 00

*or COMPLETE in first instance................. .... $175 00

TAXES. At or before the expiration of the third   year 60 00
"   "   "   " seventh " 110 00
ASSIGNMENTS, preparing and recording..................... 20 00

*The above charge does not include the cost of a possible opposition, for which special arrangements will be made in each case.
The application may be made with either a provisional or a complete specification. In case of the former, provisional protection is afforded for a period of six months. The complete specification must be filed before the expiration of that time.

LAW AND PRACTICE.

Who may be Patentee.—The first and true inventor, which is interpreted to include the first and true importer of the invention within the Colony.

Patents, Kind and Duration.—Patents of Invention (or Importation) granted for fourteen years, subject to the payment of the prescribed taxes. Extensions may sometimes be obtained for seven or fourteen years by making due application. In case of prior foreign patents, the patent will expire with the first expiring foreign patent.

Unpatentable.—The law is silent upon this point.

Novelty, Effect of Prior Patent or Publication.—To obtain a valid patent the application therefor must be filed before the invention has been published or otherwise become publicly known or used in British Honduras. Publication of the invention or the fact that prior patents have been obtained in other countries cannot affect the validity of a patent subsequently obtained in the colony, provided the invention is new there at the time the application is filed.

Taxes.—A tax of $50 is payable to the government before the expiration of the third year of the life of the patent, counting from the day upon which the application is filed, and a further tax of $100 is payable before the expiration of the seventh year. There is no provision made for obtaining an extension of time for making these payments.

Assignments.—These should be in the English language and in duplicate, and may be in any suitable form.

Working.—There are no requirements.

DOCUMENTS REQUIRED.

1. **Petition.**—Signed by applicant.

2. **Declaration.**—Signed by applicant. It may be made before any official competent to take the same, but had better be made before a British Minister or Consul when convenient.

3. **Specification in duplicate.**—No signatures necessary.

4. **Drawings in duplicate.**—On drawing board or tracing cloth, any suitable size. No signatures necessary.

5. **Power of attorney.**—Signed by applicant.

FORMS.

PETITION.

No..................

To..

The humble petition of *(here insert name, occupation and address of petitioner)*, for, &c.
Showeth :

That your petitioner is in possession of an invention for *(title of the invention)*, which invention he believes will be of great public utility; that he is the true and first inventor thereof, and the same is not in use by any other person or persons, to the best of his knowledge and belief.

Your petitioner, therefore, humbly prays that............................will be pleased to grant unto him, his executors, administrators and assigns, Letters Patent for the Colony of British Honduras, for the term of fourteen years, pursuant to the statute in that case made and provided.

And your petitioner will ever pray, &c.

(Signature of Applicant.)

DECLARATION.

No....................

I *(insert name, address and occupation of applicant)*, do solemnly and sincerely declare that I am in possession of an invention for *(title as in petition)*, which invention I believe will be of great public utility; that I am the true and first inventor thereof; and that the same is not in use by any other person or persons, to the best of my knowledge and belief *(where a complete specification is to be filed with the petition and declaration, insert these words*: " *And that the instrument in writing under my hand and seal, hereunto annexed, particularly describes and ascertains the nature of the said invention, and the manner in which the same is to be performed*"), and I make this declaration, conscientiously believing the same to be true.

(Signature of Applicant.)

Declared at.....................this...day of...............................

A. D............before me...

(Signature and title of person taking declaration.)

PROVISIONAL SPECIFICATION.

No....................

I *(name, address and occupation of applicant)*, do hereby declare the nature of the said invention for *(insert title as in petition)* to be as follows *(here insert description)*.

Dated this....................day of........................A. D........

(To be signed by Applicant or his Agent.)

SPECIFICATION.

To all to whom these presents shall come :

I *(name, address and occupation of applicant)*, send greeting :

Whereas, Her most Excellent Majesty, Queen Victoria, by her Letters Patent, bearing date the............ ....day of................. ......A. D...........in the....................year of her reign, did for herself, her heirs and successors, give and grant unto me the said *(name of applicant)*, her special license that I, the said *(name of applicant)*, my executors, administrators and assigns, or such others as I, the said *(name of applicant)*, my executors, administrators and assigns, should at any time agree with, and no others, from time to time, and at all times thereafter during the time therein expressed, should and lawfully might make, use, exercise and vend within the colony of British Honduras, an invention for *(insert title as in Letters Patent)*, upon the condition (amongst others) that I, the said *(name of applicant)*, by an instrument in writing, under my hand and seal, should particularly describe and ascertain the nature of the said invention, and in what manner the same was to be performed, and cause the same to be filed in the office of the Colonial Secretary within six calendar months next and immediately after the date of the said Letters Patent :

Now, know ye, that I, the said *(name of applicant)*, do hereby declare the nature of my said invention, and in what manner the same is to be performed, to be particularly described and ascertained in and by the following statement : that is to say *(describe the invention)*.

In witness whereof, I, the said *(name of applicant)*, have hereunto set my hand and seal this ...., ...day of............................A. D............

(Signature of Applicant.) [L. S.]

POWER OF ATTORNEY.

In the matter of the Patent Law Amendment Act of 1882, and in the matter of (*name, occupation and address*), an Inventor.

I, the above-named (*insert name*), do hereby retain, constitute and appoint.....................
....
as my agent and attorney, to apply for and obtain from the Government of British Honduras, an exclusive privilege or Letters Patent for (*title of invention as per petition*); and I authorize him to sign my name to such papers and writings, and do such acts, including the appointment of a substitute or substitutes, as may be necessary or expedient.

Dated this................day of...................18......

(*Signature of Applicant.*)   [L. S.]

Signed, sealed and delivered at...................}
In the presence of............................}

British North Borneo.

LAW AND PRACTICE.

The Colony of British North Borneo has adopted the Patent Law of the Straits Settlements as its own. As the Act is very short, we give below its full text, together with the Governor's Proclamation announcing the same.

PROCLAMATION.

No. 1, of 1887.

A Proclamation to adopt the Straits Settlements Ordinance No. XII., of 1871, entitled "An Ordinance for Granting Exclusive Privileges to Inventors."

(17th March, 1887.)

By WILLIAM HOOD TREACHER, Esquire, Governor and Commander-in-Chief of the Territory of British North Borneo.

[L. S.]

WILLIAM HOOD TREACHER,

Governor.

WHEREAS, it is expedient to make provision by law for the encouragement of Inventors of new Manufactures by giving certain Exclusive Privileges to such Inventors.

It is hereby enacted by the Government of British North Borneo as follows:

Straits Settlements Inventions Ordinances 1871 adopted.

1. The Ordinance of the Legislative Council of the Straits Settlements Numbered XII., of 1871, and entitled "An Ordinance for Granting Exclusive Privileges to Inventors," and enacted on the 15th day of November, 1871, is hereby adopted as the Law of this Territory, so far as the same shall be applicable to the circumstances of this Territory, and any references to persons, places, or subjects in the said Ordinance shall be taken as referring to corresponding or analogous persons, places, or subjects in this Territory.

Short title.
Date of operation.

2. This Proclamation may be cited as the "Patents Proclamation, 1887," and shall come into operation on the 1st of April, 1887.

Given under my hand, and under the seal of the Territory, at Sandakan, this 17th day of March, 1887.

By the Governor's Command,

L. B. VON DONOP,

Government Secretary.

For further particulars, see "Straits Settlements."

Canada.

The patent covers the entire Dominion, composed of the Provinces of Ontario and Quebec, New Brunswick, Nova Scotia, Prince Edward Island, Manitoba, British Columbia, and the Northwest Territories (also including the western part of Labrador, Keewatin, and Great Prairie Territory).

CHARGES.

```
*PATENT, Cost of, all taxes paid for five years.............. .....$27 50
 CAVEATS, operative for one year.............................. 15 00
†TAXES, at or before the expiration of the fifth year.............. 22 50
    "          "          "          "      tenth "  ................ 22 50
 DISCLAIMERS......... ....................................... 7 50
 RE-ISSUE of Patents........................................... 35 00
 IMPORTATION of patented articles.   Preparing and filing applica-
    tion for extension of time................................... 5 00
 ASSIGNMENTS, preparing and recording....................... 5 00
 WORKING............................................... ......... 20 00
 WORKING, preparing and filing application for extension of time.. 5 00
```

* If it is desired that we shall peruse the specifications to modify them, if necessary, so as to conform with the Canadian practice, $5.00 must be added to the above charge.

†If desired, all taxes may be paid in full at the time of making the application.

LAW AND PRACTICE.

Who may be Patentee.—The actual and true inventor, his assigns or his legal representatives. Joint inventors may obtain a joint patent. The patent may be issued to the inventor alone, or to the inventor and his assignees, or to his assignees alone, but the inventor must sign the papers in all cases, if he be alive. If the inventor be dead his assignee or legal representative may sign, stating in the oath that he believes that the inventor was the true and first inventor.

Patents, Kind and Term.—Patents of Invention, which are granted for fifteen years, subject to the payment of the prescribed fees and proper working of the invention. In case of prior foreign patents, the patent will expire with the first expiring foreign patent. Extensions can only be obtained by special legislative act. Caveats may be filed by any intending applicant for a patent who has not yet perfected his invention, and the same will remain in force for one year. There is no provision for the renewal of Caveats.

Unpatentable.—Inventions which have an illicit object in view, or any mere scientific principle or abstract theorem.

Novelty, Effect of Prior Patent or Publication.—To obtain a valid patent the application should be filed before the invention has been in public use or on sale in Canada, with the consent or allowance of the inventor thereof, for more than one year, and in case a foreign patent exists for the same invention, before the expiration of twelve months from the date of such foreign patent. Section 16 of the law empowers the Commissioner of Patents to object to the grant of a patent for an invention which has been described in a book or other printed publication before the date of the application, or that is otherwise in possession of the public.

Taxes.—If the taxes for the full term of fifteen years are not paid before the issue of the patent, a tax of $20 is payable during and before the expiration of the fifth year of the life of the patent, and a further tax of $20 before the expiration of the tenth year. No prolongation of time for making these payments can be obtained.

Assignments.—These should be in the English language and in duplicate. No special form of document is prescribed.

Working.—The patent will be void at the end two of years, unless within that period the working of the invention shall have been commenced, and, after such commencement the construction or manufacture of the invention must be continuously carried on in Canada, in such manner that any person desiring to use it may obtain it, or cause it to be made for him, at a reasonable price, at some manufactory or establishment for making or constructing it in Canada. This term of two years may usually be extended for from six months to one year upon application, which must be made not more than three months before the expiration of the two year period.

It is considered by good authorities in Canada, that the actual and continuous manufacture of the patented invention is not necessary to constitute a legal working, and it is now the practice to work the patent by concluding arrangements with some agent or manufacturer to be prepared to make the patented articles, and then to advertise that they can be obtained on application to the said agent or manufacturer.

Special. *MARKING PATENTED ARTICLES.*—Patented articles must be marked or stamped with the word "Patented," together with the year of the date of the patent ; as, for instance, "Patented 1887," or as the case may be.

IMPORTATION OF PATENTED ARTICLES.—A patent may be declared void if the patentee or his assigns, after the expiration of twelve months from the grant of the patent, imports the invention or causes the same to be imported into Canada. The term for importing may usually be extended for a further period, by making proper application.

AMENDMENT OF SPECIFICATION.—The specification may be amended at any time by way of disclaimer. Patents may be re-issued and amended wherever they are deemed to be inoperative or defective, when it appears that the error arose from inadvertence, accident or mistake, without any fraudulent or deceptive intention.

MODELS OR SPECIMENS.—Whenever the invention admits of being exhibited by a model, a neat and substantial working model must be furnished. It must be so constructed as to show exactly every part of the invention claimed, and its mode of working. In size it should not exceed twelve inches on the longest side, unless a larger size is allowed by special permission.

Whenever the invention is a composition of matter, specimens of the ingredients and of the composition are required, sufficient in quantity for the purpose of experiment. The specimens should be contained in glass bottles. When the ingredients and composition are of an explosive nature, they are to be furnished only when, and as, specially required.

Both models and bottles must, in all cases, bear the name of the inventor, the title of the invention, and the date of the application. Formerly, unless specially needed, they were not required to be furnished until after the grant of the patent, but under the present practice the patent will neither be granted nor issued until the model or specimen is received by the Patent Office.

DOCUMENTS REQUIRED.

The papers should be written or printed on legal cap, on one side only.

1. **Petition.**—Signed by the applicant.

2. **Power of Attorney.**—Signed by the applicant and one or two witnesses.

3. **Specification in duplicate.**—Signed by the applicant and two witnesses.

4. **Drawings in duplicate.**—On tracing cloth. The sheets must measure exactly eight inches wide by thirteen inches high. As many sheets may be used as are necessary. Beside the drawings on tracing cloth it is necessary to furnish an additional view or views upon a sheet of good white bristol board of exactly the same size as the tracings. This last drawing is used by the Canadian Office to photo-lithograph from, and it is not necessary that it should include all the figures of the drawings; a single figure will be sufficient, provided it shows the entire invention clearly and fully. No reference

letters are required upon the bristol board drawing. The drawings need not be signed by the applicant.

5. Oath.—Sworn, or affirmed to, and signed by the applicant. The oath may be made before any Justice of the Peace in Canada ; but if the applicant is not at the time in Canada, the oath may be made before any Minister Plenipotentiary, *Charge d' Affairs,* Consul, Vice-Consul or Consular Agent, holding commission under the government of the United Kingdom of Great Britain, or any judge of a court of record, or a Notary Public, or the Mayor or other chief magistrate of any city, borough or town corporate in the country in which the applicant happens at the time to be. The oath must in all cases be attested by the proper official seal of the officer before whom the oath is taken.

6. The Model or Specimen.—(See remarks under heading of Special.) It is not absolutely necessary to file the model with the application, as the Canadian Patent Office will receive the papers and give a filing date without it, but the patent will neither be granted nor issued until the model is on file in the Patent Office.

FORMS.

PETITION. (BY A SOLE INVENTOR.)

To the Commissioner of Patents, Ottawa :

The petition of (*full name, address and occupation of applicant*).

Showeth :

That he hath invented new and useful improvements in (*title of invention,*) not known or used by others before his invention thereof, and not being in public use or on sale, for more than one year previous to his application, in Canada, with his consent or allowance as such inventor.

Your petitioner therefore prays that a patent may be granted to him for the said invention, as set forth in the specification in duplicate sent herewith, and for the purposes of the Patent Act, your petitioner elects his domicile in the city of Ottawa, Province of Ontario.

(*Place and date of signing.*)　　　　　　　　　　　　　　　(*Signature of Inventor.*)

PETITION BY JOINT INVENTORS.

To the Commissioner of Patents, Ottawa :

The petition of (*full name, address and occupation of one applicant*) and (*full name, address and occupation of the other applicant*).

Showeth :

That they have jointly invented a new and useful improvement in (*title of invention*), not known or used by others before their invention thereof, and not being in public use, or on sale, for more than one year previous to their application, in Canada, with their consent or allowance as such inventors.

Your petitioners therefore pray that a patent may be granted to them jointly for the said invention as set forth in the specification in duplicate sent herewith, and, for the purposes of the Patent Act, your petitioners elect their domicile in the city of Ottawa, Province of Ontario.

(*Place and date of signing.*)　　　　　　　　　　　　　　　(*Signatures of Applicants.*)

POWER OF ATTORNEY.

To the Commissioner of Patents, Ottawa :

The undersigned (*name, full address and occupation*), hereby appoints............................ his attorney, with full powers of substitution and revocation, to prosecute an application for a patent for new and useful improvements in (*title of invention*), to sign the drawings, to receive the patent, and to transact all business in the Patent Office connected therewith.

Signed at (*date and place of signing*).　　　　　　　　　　　(*Signature.*)

In presence of (*signatures of two witnesses*).

OATH (FOR A SOLE INVENTOR).

....⎱
...........................⎰

I, (*name, full address and occupation of inventor*), make oath and say, that I verily believe that I am the inventor of the new and useful improvements in (*title of invention*), described and claimed in the annexed specification in duplicate, and for which I solicit a patent by my petition, dated (*date of petition*). And I further say that the several allegations contained in the said petition are respectively true and correct.

Sworn before me at (*date and place of signing.*)　　　　　　　(*Signature.*)

(*Signature, title of office, and seal of person administering oath.*)

OATH (FOR JOINT INVENTORS).

.... (
....)

We, (*name, full address and occupation of one inventor*), and (*name, full address and occupation of the other inventor*), do hereby severally make oath and say, and

1st. I, this deponent (*name of first inventor*), for myself, do hereby make oath and say that I verily believe that I and the said (*name of other inventor*) are the inventors of the new and useful improvements in (*title of invention*), described and claimed in the annexed specification, in duplicate, for which we solicit a patent by our petition to the Commissioner of Patents, dated (*date of petition*). And I further say that the several allegations contained in the said petition are respectively true and correct, and

2d. I, this deponent (*name of second inventor*), for myself, do hereby make oath and say that I verily believe that I and the above-named (*name of first inventor*) are the inventors of the new and useful improvements in (*title of invention*), described and claimed in the annexed specification in duplicate, for which we solicit a patent by our petition to the Commissioner of Patents dated (*date of petition*). And I further say that the several allegations contained in the said petitions are respectively true and correct.   (*Signatures of Inventors.*)

Sworn before me, by the said (*name of first inventor*), and (*name of other inventor*), this (*date and place of signing*).

(*Signature, title of office and seat of person administering oath.*)

SPECIFICATION FOR A MACHINE.

To all whom it may concern:

Be it known that I, (*name, full address and occupation*), have invented certain new and useful improvements in (*title of invention*), and I do hereby declare that the following is a full, clear and exact description of the same.

Reference being made to the accompanying drawing in which:

(*Here should follow description of drawing and of the invention.*)

Having thus described my invention, what I claim and desire to secure by patent is:

(*Here insert claims.*)   (*Signature of Inventor.*)

(*Date and place of signing.*)

Signed in the presence of

(*Signatures of two witnesses.*)

SPECIFICATION FOR AN ART OR PROCESS (JOINT INVENTORS.)

To all whom it may concern:

Be it known that we (*name, full address and occupation of one inventor*), and (*name, full address and occupation of the other inventor*), have jointly invented a new and useful improvement in the art or process of (*title of invention*), and we do hereby declare that the following is a full, clear and exact description of the same:

(*Here should follow methodical description of invention and process in detail.*)

What we claim as our invention, and desire to secure by patent is (*insert claims*).

(*Signatures of Inventors.*)

(*Date and place of signing.*)

Signed in the presence of

(*Signatures of two witnesses*)

SPECIFICATION FOR A COMPOSITION OF MATTER.

To all whom it may concern:

Be it known that I, (*name, full address and occupation of applicant*), have invented a certain new and useful composition of matter to be used in (*title of invention*), and I do hereby declare that the following is a full, clear and exact description of the same:

(*Here should follow description of invention, stating proportions of ingredients by weight or measure, how compounded, its uses, etc.*)

What I claim as my invention, and desire to secure by patent, is (*insert claims*).

(*Signature of Applicant.*)

(*Date and place of signing.*)

Signed in the presence of

(*Signatures of two witnesses.*)   **CAVEATS.**

The documents required for caveats are:

1. **Petition.**—Signed by applicant.

2. **Specification.**—Signed by applicant and two witnesses.

3. **Drawing.**—(It is not necessary to furnish a drawing if the invention can be comprehended without.)

4. **Oath.**—Signed and sworn to as in case of application for patent.

5. **Power of Attorney.**—As in case of application for patent.

FORMS.

PETITION IN CASE OF CAVEAT.

To the Commissioner of Patents, Ottawa :

The undersigned (*name, full address and occupation of inventor*), an intending applicant for a patent, who has made certain new and useful improvements in (*title of invention*), and has not perfected his invention, prays that this specification may be filed as a caveat in the Patent Office.
(*Here describe the invention.*)   (*Signature of Inventor.*)

.... {

OATH IN CASE OF CAVEAT.

I, (*name, full address and occupation of inventor*), make oath and say that I am the inventor of the invention described in the foregoing specification, and that the allegations contained therein are respectively true and correct.
                                                                  (*Signature of Inventor.*)

Sworn before me (*date and place of signing*).
      (*Signature, title of office and seal of person administering oath*)

Canary Islands

These islands belong to Spain and are covered by its patents.

Cape Colony. (Cape of Good Hope.)

CHARGES.

```
*PATENT, cost of, all taxes paid for three years.................$110 00
 EXTENSION of Patent.......................................  125 00
 TAXES, Third  year ...........................  ...................   60 00
        Seventh  " .........................................  110 00
 ASSIGNMENTS, preparing and recording.......................   25 00
```

*The Attorney General may call to his aid scientific persons or experts in the examination of applications. The fees of such experts are usually from $25 to $50, which is an additional expense. Such expense, however, is seldom incurred.

LAW AND PRACTICE.

Who may be Patentee.—The true and first inventor, which is interpreted to include the true and first importer of the invention within the Colony.

Patents, Kind and Term.—Patents of Invention (or Importation) granted for fourteen years, but will expire with any first expiring prior foreign patent. The patent can sometimes be extended for an additional term of seven and perhaps fourteen years. The patent is dated as of the day upon which the application is filed.

Unpatentable.—The law is silent on this point.

Novelty, Effect of Prior Patent or Publication.—To obtain a valid patent the application therefor must be filed before any publication or public use of the invention within the Colony. Publication, or the fact that an invention has been patented, in a foreign country, does not prevent the obtaining of a perfectly valid patent so long as the invention is new within the Colony, at the time the application is filed.

Taxes.—A tax of £10 is payable before the end of the third year of the life of the patent, counting from the date of the application, and a further tax of £20, before the expiration of the seventh year.   There are no provisions for extending the time for making payment.

Assignments.—Should be prepared in duplicate.   Any suitable form may be used.

Working.—There are no requirements.

DOCUMENTS REQUIRED.

1. **Specification in duplicate.**—May be signed by the applicant or his attorney. May be written on legal cap.

2. **Drawings in duplicate.**—On drawing board or tracing cloth, any convenient size. No signatures necessary.

3. **Power of Attorney.**—Signed by applicant.

FORMS.

SPECIFICATION.

To all to whom these presents shall come: I, (*Insert name, address and occupation*), send greeting: Whereas I am desirous of obtaining letters patent for securing unto me Her Majesty's special license that I, my executors and assigns, and such others as I or they should at any time agree with, and no others, should and lawfully might, from time to time and at all times during the term of fourteen years (to be computed from the day on which this instrument shall be left at the office of the Colonial Secretary), make, use, exercise, and vend within the colony of the Cape of Good Hope, an invention for (*insert the title of the invention*); and in order to obtain the said letters patent, I must by an instrument in writing under my hand, particularly describe and ascertain the nature of the said invention, and in what manner the same is to be performed, and must also enter into the covenant hereinafter contained: Now know ye that the nature of the said invention and the manner in which the same is to be performed, are particularly described and ascertained in and by the following statement, that is to say (*describe the invention*).   And I do hereby, for myself, my heirs and executors, covenant with Her Majesty, her heirs and successors, that I believe the said invention to be a new invention as to the public use and exercise thereof, and that I do not know or believe that any person other that myself is the true and first inventor of the said invention, and that I will not deposit these presents at the office of the Colonial Secretary with any such knowledge or belief as last aforesaid.

In witness whereof I have hereunto set my hand at....................this...............day of ....18....

(Signature of Applicant.)

POWER OF ATTORNEY.

In the matter of Act No. 17, of 1860, of the Government of the Cape of Good Hope, and in the matter of (*name, occupation and address*), an inventor.

I, the above-named (*name of applicant*) do hereby retain, constitute and appoint............... ....as my Agent and Attorney, to apply for and obtain from the Government of the Cape of Good Hope, Letters Patent for (*state title of invention as in petition*), and I authorize him to sign my name to such papers and writings, and do such acts regarding the same, including the appointment of a substitute or substitutes, as may be necessary or expedient.

Dated this...........................day of.................18........

Signed, sealed and delivered at............ }
in the presence of.................... }

(Signature of Applicant.) [L. S.]

Cape Verde Islands.

These islands belong to Portugal and are covered by its patent.

Ceylon.

CHARGES.

PATENT, total cost of, if an English Patent has been obtained....$110 00
" " " if no " " " 150 00
ASSIGNMENTS, recording................................. 25 00

LAW AND PRACTICE.

Who May be Patentee.—The inventor, his assignee, executor, administrator or heir, or the owner, or first importer of the invention into Ceylon.

Patents, Kind and Term.—Patents of Invention (or Importation) which are granted for fourteen years from the date of the filing of the application. Patents may sometimes be extended for an additional term of fourteen years.

Unpatentable.—No person is entitled to a patent, if the invention at the time of application is not a new invention in Ceylon, or if the applicant is not the inventor or importer thereof into Ceylon, or if the specification filed does not particularly describe the nature of the invention, and in what manner the same is to be carried out. The law also provides that the exclusive privilege will cease if the invention or the mode in which it is exercised is declared by the Governor to be mischievous to the State, or generally prejudicial to the public.

Novelty, Effect of Prior Patent or Publication.—To obtain a valid patent the application must be filed before any public use of the invention in Ceylon. The public use of an invention prior to the application is not deemed a public use within the meaning of the law, if the knowledge thereof has been obtained surreptitiously, or in fraud of the inventor, or shall have been communicated to the public in fraud of the inventor, or in breach of confidence, provided the inventor applies for leave to file a specification within six months after the commencement of such public use, and has not previously acquiesced in such public use. The use of an invention in public by the inventor, or by his servants or agents, or by any other person by his license in writing, is not deemed a public use within the meaning of the law. Publication or prior patenting of an invention in a foreign country will not prevent the obtaining of a valid patent provided the application is filed before any public use of the invention in Ceylon.

Taxes.—There are none after the issue of the patent.

Assignments.—These should be prepared in duplicate. Any suitable form and paper may be used.

Working.—There are no requirements.

DOCUMENTS REQUIRED.

All documents should be written on legal cap, one side only.

1. **Petition.**—Signed by applicant.

2. **Declaration to accompany Petition.**—Signed by applicant.

3. **Specification in duplicate.**—Signed by applicant.

4. **Declaration to accompany Specification.**—Signed by applicant.

5. **Drawings in duplicate.**—May be made on drawing board or tracing cloth, any convenient size. No signatures necessary.

6. **Power of Attorney.**—Signed by applicant.

FORMS.

PETITION.

To the Governor of Ceylon:

The humble petition of *(here insert name, occupation and place of residence)* for leave to file a specification under the Inventions Ordinance, 1859.

Showeth:

That your petitioner is in possession of an invention for *(state the title of invention)*, which invention he believes will be of public utility; that he is the inventor or owner of the said invention *(or, as the case may be, the assignee, or executor, or administrator, or heir of the inventor or owner of the said invention)*, and that the same is not publicly known or used in Ceylon, to the best of his knowledge and belief *(or, as the case may be, that he is the first importer into Ceylon of the said invention and that the same is not publicly known or used in Ceylon.*

If Letters Patent have been obtained for this invention in England, here state the fact, the date thereof and the term during which the same are to continue in force.

The following is a description of the invention *(here describe it)*.

Your petitioner therefore prays for leave to file a specification of the invention, pursuant to the provisions of the Inventions Ordinance, 1859, and your petitioner will ever pray, &c.

The.................day of........................18....

(Signature of Applicant.)

DECLARATION TO ACCOMPANY PETITION.

I, *(here insert name, occupation and place of residence)*, do solemnly and sincerely declare that I am in possession of an invention for *(state the title of the invention precisely as in petition)*: that I believe the said invention will be of public utility; that I am the inventor or owner of the said invention *(or, as the case may be, the assignee, or executor, or administrator, or heir of the inventor or owner of the said invention; or that I am the first importer of the said invention into Ceylon)*, and that the same is not publicly known or used in Ceylon, to the best of my knowledge and belief; and that, to the best of my knowledge and belief, my said invention is truly described in my petition for leave to file a specification thereof.

The.................day of................ ....18....

(Signature of Applicant.)

SPECIFICATION.

To all whom it may concern: Be it known that I *(here insert name, occupation and place of residence)*, am in possession of an invention for *(here state title of invention precisely as in petition)*, and I, the said *(here insert name)*, do hereby declare the nature of the said invention, and in what manner the same is to be performed, to be particularly described and ascertained in and by the following statement thereof, that is to say:

The invention has for its object *(here describe the invention fully, with reference to the drawings, if any)*.

Witness.   */Signature of Applicant.)*

DECLARATION TO ACCOMPANY SPECIFICATION.

I, *(here insert name, occupation and place of residence)*, do solemnly declare that I am in possession of an invention for *(state title of invention precisely as in petition)*, which invention I believe will be of public utility; that I am the inventor or owner of the said invention *(or, as the case may be, the assignee, or executor, or administrator, or heir of the inventor or owner of the said invention; or that I am the first importer of the said invention into Ceylon)*, and that the same is not publicly known or used in Ceylon, to the best of my knowledge and belief; and that, to the best of my knowledge and belief, the instrument in writing under my hand, hereunto annexed, particularly describes and ascertains the nature of the said invention, and in what manner the same is to be performed.

The.....................day of............ ....18....

(Signature of Applicant).

POWER OF ATTORNEY.

In the matter of the Inventions Ordinance of 1859, of the Government of Ceylon, and in the matter of *(name, occupation and address)*, an Inventor.

I, the above-named *(here insert name)*, do hereby retain, constitute and appoint.................
.... as my agent and attorney to apply for and obtain from the Government of Ceylon, Letters Patent for *(state title of invention precisely as in petition)*, and I authorize him to sign my name to such papers and writings, and to do such acts regarding the same, including the appointment of a substitute or substitutes as may be necessary or expedient.

Dated this...... ..... day of...............18....

(Signature of Applicant.)   [L. S.]

Signed, sealed and delivered at..............)

in the presence of.................... .. .. {

Channel Islands.

———

The British Patent no longer covers the Channel Islands. When the last English Act was passed, copies were sent to the Legislative Assembly, so that that body might frame a measure upon the same lines, applicable to the islands. Two such Acts were drawn up; the first was not approved by the English Board of Trade and was returned to be improved. The second was passed, but at the date of our last advices it had not yet received the Royal sanction.

It is, however, possible to obtain protection in the Island of Jersey for inventions already patented in Great Britain, by the registration of a certified copy of such patent upon the Rolls of the Royal Court. We undertake such registrations at a charge of $75.00. We understand that similar protection may be obtained in the island of Guernsey, in the same manner and at the same cost. Further particulars will be given on application.

———

Chili.

———

CHARGES.

*PATENT, total cost of, all taxes paid... ....$250 00
ASSIGNMENTS... 60 00
WORKINGS, Nominal 75 00

*The above charge includes the translation of the specification up to 2,000 words; $1 must be added for every 100 words in the specification in excess of 2,000.

LAW AND PRACTICE.

Who may be Patentee.—The author or inventor of any art, manufacture, machine or instrument, preparation of materials or any improvement thereof.

Patents, Kind and Term—Patents of Invention. The law of September 9, 1840, fixed the maximum term of a patent at ten years, but a law of January 20, 1883, gave power to the President of the Republic to extend the term of a patent to as much as twenty years. The term of a patent is fixed by the government in each case. The practice at present is to allow inventors the maximum term in almost all cases.

Unpatentable.—The law is silent upon this point.

Novelty, Effect of Prior Patent or Publication.—To obtain a valid patent, the invention must be unknown in Chili at the time the application is filed. Prior publication or patents in foreign countries will not prevent the obtaining of a perfectly valid patent in Chili, provided the invention is new there at the time the application is filed. Whenever an application is filed for an invention that is known and practiced in a foreign country, the particulars as to the application are published in the *Official Gazette;* and interested parties can, within thirty days from the date of such publication, oppose the grant of a patent upon showing that the invention or industry has been put into practice in Chili, or that steps have been taken and expense incurred for the introduction of the same, prior to the date of the filing of the application.

Taxes.—There are none after the issue of the patent.

Assignments.—The documents should be in the Spanish language and be executed in duplicate, and legalized by a Chilian Consul. In case the patent has not been taken out through our agency, a Power of Attorney, also legalized by a Chilian Consul, should be furnished.

We can obtain the legalization here, when desired, at a cost of $3.00 for each legalization.

Working.—A term is fixed in each patent for the establishment of the machinery, plant, or manufacture of the patented article in Chili, on the conclusion of which the term of the patent will commence to run. If, at the expiration of this term of establishment the invention has not "come into work" the patent lapses, as it will also do if the working is abandoned for more than one year at a time, or if the products are adulterated, becoming inferior to the samples, specimens or models exhibited. It will be seen therefore that a full and actual manufacture of the patented article in Chili is called for. It is of course impossible for us to establish a fixed price at which we will undertake to make actual workings; we will, however, obtain estimates of cost in individual cases upon receipt of necessary particulars.

We quote a price for nominal workings for the reason that many workings of this kind are ordered. It must be understood, however, that we cannot recommend them or become responsible in any way for their sufficiency.

DOCUMENTS REQUIRED.

1. Power of Attorney.—Signed by inventor. Must be legalized by a Chilian Consul. The form is the same as for the Argentine Republic (which see).

2. Specification in duplicate.—Signed by the inventor. Any suitable form.

3. Drawings in duplicate.—On drawing board or tracing cloth, of any convenient size, leaving ample margin at the sides. No signature necessary.

NOTE.—The Chilian law requires an oath, but as the Attorney is allowed to sign same, it is not necessary to send it. When desired we can obtain the legalization of the documents here at a cost of $3.00 each, which includes Consular and Agency fees.

China (Empire of).

There are no existing National laws in China for the protection of inventions, and the only methods by which foreigners can obtain protection, are as follows:

1. By securing a special grant from the National authorities, conferring on the grantee a monopoly of the manufacture and sale of the invention.

2. By registering copies of the specification and drawings of the invention in the Chinese Foreign Office and at a foreign Consulate, and by due publication of the invention and the inventor's rights of ownership in the principal Chinese official newspapers.

The first method is an expensive one, involving a cost of from $1,000 to $5,000 or more, without any certainty of obtaining the grant.

The last method is not so expensive, and would seem to afford fully as much protection as the former.

Under existing arrangements with our agent in China, we are prepared to receive orders for the registration and publication of inventions at a uniform charge of $225.

DOCUMENTS REQUIRED.

A power of attorney in the English language and duplicate copies of specifications and drawings. Almost any form of documents may be used.

Cochin China.

See France.

Colombia (United States of.)

The Isthmus of Panama, from the southern border line of Costa Rica, and the old State of New Granada, now form part of the United States of Colombia.

CHARGES.

*PATENT, Cost of, for 5 years, all taxes paid $150 00
    "   "   10 "   "   " 200 00
    "   "   15 "   "   " 250 00
    "   "   20 "   "   " 300 00
ASSIGNMENT, preparing and recording....................... 50 00
WORKING, Nominal, about 100 00

*The above charge includes translation of the specification up to 2,000 words. $1.00 must be added for each 100 words in the specification in excess of 2,000.

LAW AND PRACTICE.

Who may be Patentee.—The inventor, importer, or holder of a foreign patent for any invention or improvement of mechanical apparatus, combination of materials, or process, or for the making and sale of any manufacture or industrial product.

Patents, Kind and Term.—Patents of Invention (or Importation) granted for five, ten, fifteen, or twenty years as the applicant may elect.   A patent granted in Colombia for an invention already patented in a foreign country expires with the foreign patent.

Unpatentable.—Inventions endangering public health or security, or that are opposed to morality or to existing rights.   The law also provides that no privileges shall be granted for the importation of natural or manufactured productions from foreign countries.

Novelty, Effect of Prior Patent or Publication.—To obtain a valid patent, the application must be filed before the invention is known in Colombia.   Inventions already patented in a foreign country, may be patented in Colombia at any time during the life of such foreign patent, provided the invention is not publicly known in Colombia at the time the application is filed.

Taxes.—There are none after the issue of the patent.

Assignments.—Should be in the Spanish language, and in duplicate.   They must be legalized by a Colombian Consul.

We can obtain the legalization here when desired, at a cost of $3.00 for each legalization.

Working.—The law provides that "A patent for a new industry shall be void when said industry is not practiced during a whole year, unless unavoidable circumstances should have intervened."   In the absence of decisions covering this point, it is not possible to say just what working is required to satisfy the law, and what circumstances will be held to justify a failure to make the first or any subsequent working. There is not much doubt, however, that the intent of the law is to insure the establishment of a new industry in Colombia with the grant of every patent, and to demand that the manufacture of the patented article be carried on there continuously, or at least that such manufacture shall not be interrupted for a whole year at any one time. We cannot quote a fixed charge for actual workings, but will submit estimates of cost in individual cases upon receiving the necessary particulars. We quote a price for nominal workings, as many of these are demanded, but it must be understood that we do not recommend them nor guarantee their sufficiency in any way.

DOCUMENTS REQUIRED.

1. **Specification in duplicate.**—On any paper and in any form. No signatures necessary.

2. **Drawings in duplicate.**—On drawing board or tracing cloth, any convenient size. No signature necessary.

3. **Power of Attorney.**—Signed by applicant. This should be legalized by a Colombian Consul. The form is the same as for the Argentine Republic (which see).

4. **If a prior foreign patent exists,** a certified copy of the same must be furnished, which must be legalized by a Colombian Consul.

NOTE.—If desired we can obtain the legalization of documents here at a cost of $3.00 for each legalization, which includes both Consular and Agency fees.

Congo Free State.

CHARGES.

```
*PATENT, cost of, all taxes paid.............................$110 00
*PATENT OF ADDITION, all taxes paid....................   60 00
 ASSIGNMENTS.......................................  ..........   20 00
```

*The above charge includes translation of the specification up to 2,000 words, 35 cents must be added for each 100 words contained in the specification in excess of that number.

LAW AND PRACTICE.

Who may be Patentee.—Practically anyone, whether the inventor or not. The assignee of an inventor cannot obtain a strictly valid Patent of Invention, but may obtain a valid Patent of Importation. In case the applicant is not the actual inventor, it will be well for him to first obtain the written consent of the inventor, authorizing him to apply for the patent in his own name, and to have this document legalized by a Belgian Consul.

Patents, Kind and Term.—Patents are of three kinds: Patents of Invention granted for a term of twenty years; Patents of Importation, the term of which is limited by the term of the foreign patent upon which it is based; and Patents of Addition (for improvements upon an original invention) which expire at the same time as the original patent. All patents date from the filing of the application.

Unpatentable.—The law makes no exceptions, but provides that every discovery and every improvement capable of being worked as an object of industry or commerce, is patentable.

Novelty, Effect of Prior Patent or Publication.—The law is silent upon this point, but the practice is the same as for Belgium (which see).

Taxes.—There are none after the issue of the patent.

Assignments.—These should be executed in duplicate in the same form as for Belgian assignments, and be legalized by a Belgian Consul.

We can obtain the legalization here when desired, at a cost of $2.50 for each legalization.

Working.—The law makes no requirements.

DOCUMENTS REQUIRED.

The documents required are precisely the same as for Belgium (which see). The Power of Attorney must be legalized by a Belgian Consul.

We can obtain the legalization here when desired, at a cost of $2.50.

If the application is for a Patent of Addition, information should be supplied setting forth the date and term of the original patent, and the country where it was granted.

Corea.

There is at present no law for the protection of inventions in this country. It is believed, however, that special grants, having the same force as patents, would be allowed should any application be made for them. In case any demand for such protection in this country should arise, we will arrange for the same.

Corsica.

See France.

Costa Rica.

There is as yet no patent law in this country. The government will, however, grant protection for inventions by way of special Legislative Act, provided the invention is likely to prove of practical utility in the country.

The cost of such grants varies considerably. We will undertake to procure them at a charge of $300 each, but we will have to ask for an additional remittance in case the cost exceeds this sum. This amount will be sufficient in most cases.

DOCUMENTS REQUIRED.

The same as for Chili. The power of Attorney should be legalized by a Consul of Costa Rica.

We can obtain the legalization here, when desired, at a cost of $3.00.

Cuba.

***

Article 8 of the Spanish Law, provides that all patents shall be considered as granted, not only for the Peninsula and adjacent islands, but also for the provinces beyond the sea, thus including Cuba, but before the patent can be enforced, or any legal formalities in connection with the patent, such as prosecution for infringement, transfer of rights, etc., take place in Cuba, the patent must be officially registered for the Colonies, at the Colonial Office at Madrid.   This may be done at any time during the life of the patent.   Our charge for this registration, including all fees, is $10.00.

***

Cyprus.

***

A law for the protection of inventions, trade-marks and copyrights was lately introduced in the Legislative Council by the government, but was rejected by reason of the strenuous opposition of the native members, who command a majority in the Council. We are advised that unless the Colonial Office exercises its power of legislating upon the subject by order in Council, there is little prospect of there being any patent law in Cyprus for some time to come.   It is possible that special grants could be obtained, but all such measures would doubtless be strongly opposed by the natives.

***

Danish West Indies.

***

CHARGES.

*PATENT, cost of, all taxes paid........................... ....$75 00
ASSIGNMENTS.. 27 50
WORKING........... .... 50 00

*The above charge includes translation of the specification up to 2,000 words; 50 cents must be added for each 100 words contained in the specification above 2,000.

LAW AND PRACTICE.

There is as yet no special law, but patents are granted upon application by the King of Denmark, upon the same general terms and conditions as the Danish patent. (See Denmark for further particulars.)

DOCUMENTS REQUIRED.

Same as for Denmark, which see.

Denmark.

CHARGES.

```
*PATENT, cost of, all taxes paid...............................$35 00
 ASSIGNMENT, preparing and recording........................ 10 00
 WORKING (not including freight charges)...................... 30 00
```

*The above charge includes translation of the specification up to 2,000 words. Beyond that number, 50 cents must be added for each 100 words.

LAW AND PRACTICE.

No patent laws have been passed in Denmark, but inventions are protected by Royal Letters Patent, granted through the Ministry of the Interior, in accordance with rules prescribed by the traditional practice of that department.

Who may be Patentee.—Any person, whether the inventor or not, a firm or corporation.

Patents, Kind and Term.—Patents of Invention and Importation. The duration of the patent is fixed by the government, and may be three, four or five years. Important inventions are protected for ten, and, in exceptional cases, for fifteen years. Patents are seldom granted to foreigners for more than five years. The patent will expire with the expiration of any prior foreign patent. The patent dates from the date of its issue.

Unpatentable.—All new and useful inventions are patentable.

Novelty, Effect of Prior Patent or Publication.—A valid patent may be obtained at any time, and without regard to prior patents or publication, provided the invention has not been used in Denmark at the time the application is filed.

Taxes.—There are none after the issue of the patent.

Assignments.—The documents should be in duplicate, and should be legalized by a Danish Consul. It is best to have the documents prepared in Denmark.

We can obtain the legalization here, if desired, at a cost of $3.00, which includes Consular and Agency fees.

Working.—The invention must be worked within one year of the issue date of the patent, and the working must be repeated each year. In the case of machinery or apparatus, it is considered sufficient to import one or more of the patented articles into Denmark, and expose and advertise it or them for sale. In case of a process, it should be carried into practice in Denmark. Official proof of each working should be obtained.

DOCUMENTS REQUIRED.

1. **Specification.**—Written or printed on any paper. No signatures necessary.

2. **Drawings in duplicate.**—On any material, tracing cloth preferred, any convenient size. No signatures necessary.

3. **Power of Attorney.**—Signed by applicant. No witnesses or legalization are necessary. The usual French power may be used. (See France.)

Dutch East Indies

AND

Dutch West Indies.

These Colonies have been declared members of the International Convention for the protection of industrial property, but have no patent laws as yet.

Dutch Guiana (Surinam).

There is as yet no patent law in this colony, and we know of no way in which inventions can be protected there.

Ecuador.

CHARGES.

*PATENT, cost of, all taxes paid................................$200 00
ASSIGNMENTS, preparing and recording............. .... 40 00
WORKING, not including freight charges or cost of manufacture. 75 00

*The above charge includes translation of the specification up to 2,000 words. Beyond this number, $1.00 must be added for every 100 words.

LAW AND PRACTICE.

Who may be Patentee.—The first inventor or the first importer of a machine or of a new method or process into Ecuador.

Patents, Kind and Term.—Patents of Invention granted for a term not less than ten years or more than fifteen. Patents of Importation, granted as follows : If the introduction of the invention requires a preliminary outlay of 25,000 pesos, the term of the patent is three years ; if the outlay amounts to 50,000 pesos, the term is six years ; if the expense reaches 100,000 pesos, the term is extended to ten years.

Unpatentable.—Inventions contrary to the laws of the State or the public safety, and the regulations of the police ; secret remedies ; articles which show only a slight modification over those already known and practiced, or which merely relate to objects of adornment.

Novelty, Effect of Prior Patent or Publication.—The law provides that a patent shall become void when it is proven that it was obtained for an invention already described and published in the press, either within or without the Republic. A valid patent may be obtained at any time for an invention already patented in a foreign country, provided that the application is made before the invention is known and practiced in Ecuador or described and published in the press of any country.

Taxes.—There are none after the issue of the patent.

Assignments.—Must be recorded at the risk of forfeiting the patent. The documents should be in duplicate, in the Spanish language, and must be legalized by a Consul of Ecuador.

We can obtain the legalization here, when desired, at a cost of $3.00, which includes Consular and Agency fees.

Working.—The invention must be worked within one year and one day from the grant of the patent. In the case of machinery or apparatus it is considered sufficient to import one or more of the articles into Ecuador, and operate same there. In the case of a process, it must be carried into practice there. Patents of Importation must be worked within the same limits of time, and by the actual establishment of the industry to which the invention relates, in Ecuador.

DOCUMENTS REQUIRED.

1. **Specification.**—Written or printed on any suitable paper. No signatures required.

2. **Drawings in duplicate.**—On drawing board or tracing cloth. No signatures required.

3. **Power of Attorney.**—Signed by applicant and legalized by a Consul of Ecuador. The form is the same as for the Argentine Republic (which see).

We can obtain the legalization here, when desired, at a cost of $3.00, which includes Consular and Agency fees.

Egypt.

Nominally, the Turkish patent covers Egypt, but the protection is doubtful. There is no special patent law in this country, and so far as we can learn there is no way in which inventions may be protected there at present. We are informed that the Egyptian government has a patent law under consideration, and that there is some prospect of its being passed in the near future.

Falkland Islands.

There is as yet no patent law in this country. The government will probably grant protection for inventions by way of special Legislative Act, provided the invention is likely to prove of practical utility in the country.

The cost of such grants varies considerably. We will, however, undertake to procure them at a charge of $150 each, but we will have to ask for an additional remittance in case the cost exceeds this sum. This amount will be sufficient in most cases.

DOCUMENTS REQUIRED.

The same as for the Bahama Islands. The power of attorney should be legalized by a British Consul.

We can obtain the legalization here, when desired, at a cost of $2.50.

Faroe Islands.

CHARGES.

```
*PATENTS, cost of, all taxes paid........................ ....$70 00
 ASSIGNMENTS...... .......................................... 22 50
 WORKING.......................  ............................ 50 00
```

*The above charge includes translation of the specification up to 2,000 words; 50 cents must be added for each 100 words in the specification above 2,000.

LAW AND PRACTICE.

There is as yet no special law, but patents are granted upon application by the King of Denmark (the Faroe Islands being a Danish possession), upon the same general terms and conditions as the Danish patent. (See Denmark for further particulars.)

DOCUMENTS REQUIRED.

The same as for Denmark, which see.

Fiji Islands.

CHARGES.

```
*PROVISIONAL PATENT, for six months............... .......$90 00
 COMPLETING same ......................................... 95 00
                                                          $185 00
*Or, COMPLETE in first instance, all taxes paid................ 175 00
 ASSIGNMENT, preparing and recording...................... 22 50
```

*The above charge does not include cost of possible opposition, for which special arrangement will be made in each case.

LAW AND PRACTICE.

Who may be Patentee.—The first and true inventor, his heirs, executors, administrators or assigns.

Patents, Kind and Term.—Patent of Invention, granted for fourteen years. Provisional Patent, granted for the term of six months. Where Provisional Patents are obtained the complete specification must be filed, if at all, before the expiration of the term of the provisional protection. In case of prior foreign patents, the patent will become void immediately upon the revocation, cancellation, or other determination of the first of such Letters Patent.

Unpatentable.—The law provides that no person shall be entitled to a patent. (a) If the invention is of no utility. (b) If the invention at the time of presenting the petition is not a new invention. (c) If the petitioner is not the true and first inventor thereof. (d) If the petition or specification contain a wilfully false statement.

Novelty, Effect of Prior Patent or Publication.—Publication of the invention, or the fact that prior patents have been obtained therefor in other countries will not prevent the obtaining of a perfectly valid patent, provided the application is filed before any publication, or any public use or knowledge of the invention within the Fiji Islands.

Assignments.—Should be prepared in duplicate and in the English language. They may be in any usual form, and had better be acknowledged before a Notary Public.

Working.—There are no requirements.

DOCUMENTS REQUIRED.

1. **Petition.**—Signed by applicant.

2. **Declaration.**—Signed by applicant.

3. **Specification in duplicate.**—Should be written on legal cap, on one side only. No signatures necessary.

4. **Drawings in duplicate.**—May be on drawing board or tracing cloth, any convenient size. No signatures required.

5. **Power of Attorney.**—Signed by applicant.

FORMS.

The form for the complete specification and power is the same as for the Bahama Islands, the name of the colony being changed, and the title of the Act, which for Fiji is, "The Patents Ordinance, 1879." If a provisional specification is filed, the same form can be used as for British Honduras.

PETITION.

I (insert name, address and occupation of applicant), do hereby humbly petition his Excellency the Governor for Letters Patent in respect of an invention, for (state title of invention).
I have furnished with this petition the necessary specifications or instruments particularly describing the nature of the said invention, and a solemn declaration that I am the true and first inventor thereof, in accordance with law.

(Signature of Applicant.)

DECLARATION.

I (insert name, address and occupation of applicant), do solemnly and sincerely declare that I am in possession of an invention for, (insert title as in petition), which I believe will be of great public utility; that I am the true and first inventor thereof, and that the same is not in use by any other person or persons, to the best of my knowledge and belief, and that the instrument in writing under my hand, hereunto annexed, particularly describes and ascertains the nature of the said invention and the manner in which the same is to be performed.

(Signature of Applicant.)

𝕱inland.

CHARGES.

<pre>
*PATENT, cost of, all taxes paid, usually......................$200 00
 ASSIGNMENTS, preparing andr ecording...................... 30 00
 WORKING, (exclusive of freight charges)........from $50 00 to 100 00
</pre>

*The above charge includes the translation of the specification up to 2,000 words. $1.00 must be added for every 100 words in the specification in excess of 2,000.

The cost of Finnish patents varies largely. A tax of 20 marks is payable to the Government for each year of the duration of the patent, which may be from three to twelve years as fixed by the Government; besides this, the patent and the description must be published three times in the official Finnish and Swedish newspapers, the cost of the publication varying according to the length of the description.

LAW AND PRACTICE.

Who may be Patentee.—The inventor only is entitled to the patent.

Patents, Kind and Term.—Patents of Invention, granted for new inventions and for improvements upon the same. The duration of the patent is fixed by the Government, and may be any term of years, from three to twelve. Where there is a prior foreign patent the Finnish patent will expire with it.

Unpatentable.—Patents are not granted for the preparation of medicines, nor for any invention which is of such a nature that the employment of the same would be contrary to the existing laws, to the public safety, or to good morals. The use of a new principle is not patentable, but the manner, method or means for the employment of such an invention may be made the subject of a patent.

Novelty, Effect of Prior Patent or Publication.—Sec. 3 of the law reads as follows: "If any person has obtained a patent in a foreign country, and has thereby been compelled to publish a description of the manner in which the invention is to be applied, a patent may, nevertheless, be granted to him for a given time in Finland also, but not for a longer period than that within which the patent granted in the foreign country will expire. If no prior patent exists the application should be filed before any publication of the invention and before any introduction of the articles for which the patent is to be obtained into Finland.

Taxes.—There are none after the issue of the patent.

Assignments.—Assignments should be in duplicate, and must be accompanied by a Power of Attorney, in blank, authorizing the execution of all legal formalities, in order to legalize the deed in Finland. All the documents must be legalized by a Russian Consul. It is best to have the papers prepared in Finland.

When desired, we can obtain the legalization here at a cost of $2.50, which includes Consular and Agency fees.

Working.—The invention must be worked within two years of the issue date of the patent, and the working must not be stopped for as long as a whole year at a time thereafter. The Senate *may* limit the time within which the invention must be worked to *one* year, and *may*, on petition, extend it up to four years at the most. In the case of machinery or apparatus, it is considered sufficient to import one of the machines or apparatus and have the same operated there. In case of a process, it must be carried into practice. Proof of the working must be delivered to the Government.

DOCUMENTS REQUIRED.

1. **Specification.**—Written or printed on any suitable paper, any suitable form. No signatures necessary.

2. **Drawings in duplicate.**—On drawing board or tracing cloth, any convenient size. No signatures necessary.

3. **Power of Attorney.**—Signed by applicant, all names in full, and legalized by a Russian Consul. The usual French power may be used. (See France.)

When desired, we can obtain the legalization here at a cost of $2.50, which includes Consular and Agency fees.

4. **When a prior foreign patent exists**, a certified copy of the patent must be furnished. This must be legalized in the same manner as the Power of Attorney.

France.

The patent covers France and all her colonies, which may now be enumerated as follows: Algeria, Cambodia, Cochin-China, French Guiana, Guadaloupe, La Re-Union, Loyalty Islands, Marquesas Islands, Martinique, Micquelon, New Caledonia, St. Pierre, Senegambia, and Tahiti.

CHARGES.

```
*PATENT, cost of, all taxes paid for one year...................$35 00
*PATENT OF ADDITION, all taxes paid........................ 20 00
TAXES, payable annually, counting from date of application, each year.  22 50
ASSIGNMENTS, (Notarial, see "Assignments")................. 5 00
WORKING, Nominal, see "Working")........................ 30 00
```

*The above charge includes translation of the specification up to 2,000 words. Beyond this number, 35 cents must be added for each 100 words.

LAW AND PRACTICE.

Who may be Patentee.—Anyone, whether the inventor or not, a firm, or corporation. In principle, the inventor only can obtain a patent. It has been decided however, that there is nothing to prevent an inventor disposing of his invention to a third party, and with it the right to apply for the patent in his own name. The law only exacts one thing ; that the invention shall not have been practiced or known before the patent is obtained. Where the applicant is not the inventor, it would be well to obtain and keep the written consent of the latter, so that should any question be raised at a future time, the patentee could produce proof that he obtained the French patent in his own name with the consent of the inventor.

Patents, Kind and Term.—Patents of Invention are granted for five, ten or fifteen years, as elected by the applicant subject to the payment of the prescribed taxes and the proper working of the invention. Patents of Importation (for inventions already patented abroad) are granted for a term not exceeding the life of the foreign patent upon which it is based, and expire with the first expiring foreign patent for the same invention. Patents of Addition are granted for the life of the original patent and expire therewith.

Unpatentable.—Medical compositions and medicines of every kind, and plans and combinations of credit or finance.

Novelty, Effect of Prior Patent or Publication.—The fact that a prior foreign patent exists will not prevent, in itself, the obtaining of a perfectly valid French patent, but in all cases, to obtain a valid patent the application must be filed before any publication of the invention in any country, and before the discovery or invention has received sufficient publicity in any way to enable it to be worked or put into practice.

Taxes.—The patent is granted subject to the payment of an annual tax of 100 francs. This must be paid yearly in advance, counting from the date of the filing of the application. No extension of time for the payment of taxes can be obtained.

Assignments.—Under the provisions of the French law, no assignment can be recorded until all the taxes are paid for the full term of the patent. This makes the expense of preparing and recording an assignment of a new patent, including payment of taxes, about $300.00. To avoid this expense it is usual to simply prepare a power of attorney authorizing a Notary to effect the assignment. This is signed by the parties, legalized by a French Consul (leaving a blank for the name of the Notary), and is then retained by the purchaser until he is ready to have the assignment made and recorded.

We can obtain the legalization here, when desired, at a cost of $3.00 for each document, which includes Consular and Agency fees.

Working.—The invention must be worked in France within two years from the date of the issue of the patent, and the working must not entirely cease for any two consecutive years thereafter. The law does not indicate what shall constitute a sufficient working, but requires that an invention must be really worked in a practical manner; a single act of working is not usually sufficient. If a patent contain several modes of procedure, it suffices, to comply with the law, that the inventor should have worked one of them. If the object manufactured differs only slighly from the object for which the inventor takes out the patent, there is no ground for forfeiture. (Court of Cessation, May 23, 1859.) An inventor is allowed to explain the causes of his inaction. The court has wide power of discretion in determining what shall constitute a sufficient working, and every case is decided on its merits. In exceptional cases, it has been decided that the absence of pecuniary resources or sickness can be held to justify the default of working. (Court of Paris, January 11, 1859.) The inventor who has caused his machines to be admitted to public exhibition in France, and who has sold one of them to a third party, has sufficiently worked it thereby to avoid forfeiture. (Court of Paris, May 11, 1836.) It should be noted that this decision was rendered prior to the law of 1844.

That an insufficiency of capital, the natural result of the commercial crisis of 1848 and 1849 was sufficient to relieve the patentee from the forfeiture of his patent by reason of his inaction. (Court of Paris, March 30, 1855.) That the insufficiency of the pecuniary resources of a ptaentee is a legitimate cause of his inaction especially when this insufficiency of his resources has been augmented by political events such as those of 1849; further when the invention is of such a nature that it cannot be used by the public, but only by a restricted number of industries (by railroad companies for example), it is evident that the refusal of these industries to use this invention during two years cannot result in the forfeiture of the patent to their benefit and justify an infringement. (Rej., Nov. 23, 1859.) That the failure to work does not cause the forfeiture of the patent when the patentee justifies sufficiently the cause of his inaction, by the insufficiency of his personal resources, by the nature of the invention (a telegraph apparatus) of which the uses are restricted by reason of the monopoly of the State. (Amiens, May 29, 1884.) That an inventor of a new product escapes forfeiture resulting from the failure to work when it is proven that he has manufactured and sold the said product, whatever may have been the process he employed. (Trib. Civ. Lyons, July 15, 1865.) That when a patentee has publicly made experiments of his apparatus through parties who may have an interest in adopting them, and has put them to the disposal of all, he must be considered as having satisfied all the requirements of the law and is safe from any action for forfeiture. (Court of Paris, August 10, 1876.)

It has been decided that a single act of manufacture cannot be considered as an industrial working of the patent and cannot relieve the patentee from the forfeiture incurred by him if he does not justify himself by other legitimate causes for inaction. (Court o f Paris, March 23, 1870.) That the working prescribed by Act 32 cannot be accomplished by declarations (proces-verbaux) made every two years through an attorney at the request of the inventor, when such working is shown to be inadequate by the defective state of the machines and their almost impracticable setting up. (Donai, July 20, 1859.)

These provisions apply equally to Patents of Addition, but it is clear that if the Patent of Addition be declared void, the original patent may continue to exist. A patentee can avoid forfeiture by either working the patent himself, or by allowing it to be worked by a third party.

It should be noted that the forwarding of the parts of a machine to France, and the assembling of the parts there, even if one or more parts are actually made in France, does not constitute a legal working. It will, however, serve as a commencement, and give time for the beginning of a complete actual working, (the *bona-fide* manufacturer of the patented article in France, in quantities sufficient to supply the legitimate demands of trade,) which must follow within a reasonable time thereafter.

We will furnish estimates for the legal working of inventions upon application.

In cases where a patentee is not willing to incur the expenses of manufacture, we can effect a nominal working on being furnished with a model or sample of the invention. This is not, however, in strict conformity with the law, and though such workings are frequently made they cannot be guaranteed as effectual, and we do not recommend them.

Special.—*IMPORTATION OF PATENTED ARTICLES.*—As France is a member of the International Union, citizens and subjects of States belonging to the Union can now import patented articles into France without risk of forfeiture. None others, however, are allowed to import into France under the penalty of the forfeiture of the patent, except that a permit may sometimes be obtained, for the importation of a single model or sample. The expense of obtaining such a permit is about $10,00.

DOCUMENTS REQUIRED.

The documents required for Patents of Addition are precisely the same.

1. Specification.—Written or printed on any paper, and in any suitable form. No signatures necessary.

2. Drawings in duplicate.—On tracing cloth of any convenient size. No signatures necessary.

3. Power of Attorney.—Signed by applicant, all names in full. No witnesses nor legalization necessary.

FORM.

POWER OF ATTORNEY.

Le soussigné..

constitue.......pour........Mandataire spécial aux effets ci-après:
M...

Auquel il.........donne.......pouvoir de 1 our........et en.........nom........ faire toutes les démarches nécessaires pour obtenir du Gouvernement de..

Un Brevet d'.........................de ... .ans
pour...

En conséquence présenter au Chef du dit Gouvernement ou à toute autre autorité compétente toutes Demandes, Pétitions et Requêtes; se présenter à tous Ministéres, Bureaux, Greffes et Commissions que besoin sera; signer et approuver toutes pièces descriptives; requérir tous procès-verbaux contracter tous engagements, verser ou retirer toutes taxes, en prendre quittance ou en donner décharge. Faire toutes demandes Brevet d'Addition ou de perfectionnement, les échanger ou retirer s'il y a lieu; consentir la radiation de toutes inscriptions; retirer également les titres definitifs ainsi que les pièces y afférentes; Signer et présenter toute demande en autorisation d'introduction de modèle. Signer tous actes ou procès-verbaux de desistement des privilèges d'Étranger. Prendre la parole et répondre pour le constituant à toutes réclamations qui pourront surgir rélativement au Brevet dont il s'agit, pendant toute la durée de celui-ci.—Aux fins sus énoncés Élire domicile, substituer tout ou partie des présents pouvoirs, et dans les différents cas qui pourront se présenter, faire généralement tout ce qui sera utile pour arriver à l'obtention du privilège sus relaté promettant le......constituant.....avoir le tout pour agréable, et le ratifier au besoin.

.... Mil-huit-cent-...

Gambia. (British.)

There is as yet no patent law in this colony.   The government will, however, un-doubtedly grant protection for inventions by way of special Legislative Act, provided the invention is likely to prove of practical utility in the country.

The cost of such grants varies considerably.   We will undertake to procure them at a charge of $200 each, but we will have to ask for an additional remittance in case the cost exceeds this sum.   This amount will be sufficient in most cases.

DOCUMENTS REQUIRED.

The same as for the Gold Coast Colony, which see.

German Empire.

Baden, Bavaria, Prussia, Saxony and Wurtemburg no longer have separate patent laws, but are covered by the German Patent.

CHARGES.

*PATENT cost of, all taxes paid for one year......................$30 00
*PATENT OF ADDITION, all taxes paid........................ 20 00
APPEAL in case of refusal....................................... 15 00
TAXES, *payable annually, counting from the date of application, with three months' grace without fine.*

Second	year	...........$15 00	Ninth	year........$102 50
Third	"	.... 27 50	Tenth	" 115 00
Fourth	"	.... 40 00	Eleventh	" 127 50
Fifth	"	.... 52 50	Twelfth	" 140 00
Sixth	"	.... 65 00	Thirteenth	" 152 50
Seventh	"	.... 77 50	Fourteenth	" 165 00
Eighth	"	.... 90 00	Fifteenth	" 177 50

ASSIGNMENTS, preparing and recording...................... 5 00
WORKING, nominal..... .... 15 00

* The above charge includes translation of the specification up to 2,000 words. 35 cents must be added for each 100 words in the specification in excess of 2,000.

LAW AND PRACTICE.

Who may be Patentee.—The first applicant is entitled to the grant, so that any person, whether the inventor or not, a firm or corporation, may obtain a patent.   In case the applicant is not the inventor, however, it is very desirable that he should obtain and keep the written consent of the latter, as, according to the provisions of the German law, "The claim of the petitioner to the grant of a patent is void if the essential part of his application has, without permission, been taken from the description, drawings, models, implements, methods or arrangements of another person, should such person object thereto."

Patents, Kind and Term.—Patents of Invention granted for fifteen years, subject to the payment of the prescribed taxes and proper working of the invention.   Patents of

Addition, for improvements upon former inventions, granted for the life of the original patent and expiring therewith. All patents are dated as of the day following the filing of the application. The lapse of a prior foreign patent does not affect the term.

Unpatentable.—Inventions the use of which would be incompatible with the laws or the public morals ; inventions relating to articles of food (for nourishment or luxuries), of medicines, and of substances produced by chemical process, so far as the invention does not relate to the method of producing such articles.

Novelty, Effect of Prior Patent or Publication.—To obtain a valid patent, the application must be filed before the invention has been described in any printed publication in any country, or publicly used in Germany. Subject to the above requirements valid German patents may be obtained at any time, whether prior foreign patents exist or not.

Taxes.—Taxes upon patents are payable in annual instalments and in advance, counting from the day following the filing of the application. Three months' grace is allowed for these payments, without fine. No further prolongation of time can be obtained. The tax amounts to 3) marks for the first year; 50 for the second, and increases thereafter 50 marks for each succeeding year.

Assignments.—To record an assignment the following documents are necessary: 1. An assignment in the German language signed by the *assignor* before a Notary Public and legalized by a German Consul. The consideration need not be expressed. 2. A power of attorney signed by the *assignee* before a Notary Public and legalized by a German Consul, authorizing the attorney to apply for and obtain the registration of the assignment and pay the taxes in connection therewith.

We can obtain the legalization here when desired at a cost of $3.00 each.

Working.—The invention must be worked within three years from the *grant* of the patent. The law reads as follows :

§ 11. A patent can be declared void after the expiration of three years.
1. If the patentee fails to work his invention in Germany to an adequate extent, or at least to do everything that is necessary to insure its being worked.

According to a decision of the patent office authorities:

The fact of a patent not having been worked within the first three years, has not the effect, by itself, of rendering the same void; on the contrary, the question arises whether, by this circumstance, the Commonwealth has suffered, or at least, whether there is reason to fear that it will suffer, or whether, more particularly, the development of the domestic industry to which the invention relates may be expected to be prevented, or has been prevented, so as to afford a reason for terminating the existence of a patent.

Among the most important decisions relative to the working of inventions are the following: It is only necessary to manufacture the essential parts of the invention; unimportant deviations from the specification are of no consequence (decisions of the Patent Office of October 12, 1882, Reichsgericht of November 12, 1883). In a case where the invention related to compound armor plates, where the inventor offered a license to the only firm in Germany that made such plates, it was held that in consequence of the small sale of armor-plates the patentee could not be expected to start works of his own in Germany, and the action for annulment was rejected. (Decision of the Patent Office, October 19, 1882.) The term of three years as provided by § 11, runs, not from the day after the application of patent, but from the day of the final grant of the patent. (Decision of the Patent Office July 23, 1885.) In the case of the Eagle Automatic Pencil Case, three patents Nos. 6523, 7168 and 12529 were withdrawn on the following grounds: The plaintiff stated that large quantities of the pencil cases had been imported into Germany, although the same could have well been manufactured there, and that such importation did damage to the home manufacturers. The defendant claimed that the sale of the patented articles was a sufficient working under the law, and that a great part of the raw materials for the production of the articles was obtained from Germany. It was held that the object of § 11 of the law is to compel the patentee to manufacture the patented article in Germany as a compensation for the protection granted, and that the industrial and commercial advantages resulting from the manufacture might benefit the country. The fact that the raw materials were obtained in Germany could not be taken into consideration. (Decisions of Patent Office of February 7, 1884; Reichsgericht of November 30, 1885.) It has also been held that the manufacture must be commensurate with the demand, or at least, every possible means must be taken to assure the same. It will be seen, therefore, that the working should be actual and thorough. In cases where the patentee is not prepared to commence the manufacture in Germany himself, an arrangement should be consummated with some manufacturer in that country to be prepared to make the articles, and the fact should then be advertised; also, that such patented articles may be obtained on application to the manufacturer.

We will furnish estimates for the legal working of inventions upon application. We also quote a price for nominal workings, but it must be understood that we neither recommend them nor guarantee their sufficiency.

Special.—*LICENSES.*—A patent may be declared void after three years from its date, when a patentee refuses to grant licenses to others to use the invention, when the same appears to be demanded in the public interest, and adequate compensation and good security have been offered.

MODELS. Applications relating to the following subjects must be accompanied by a model : *Fire-Arms.*—A working model or real piece, must be furnished. *Spools, Spindles and Shuttles* must be accompanied by two models, one of these being in section. *Skates.*—One model is required. All applications relating to the manufacture of chemicals (explosives excepted) should be accompanied by duplicate samples. *Chemicals.*—Should be accompanied by duplicate samples of the materials, which must be sent in glass bottles of about 1¼ inches in diameter, and 3¼ inches in height, provided with glass stoppers, the seal of the applicant, and an exact description of the contents. *Dyes.* Duplicate specimens showing the colors, on samples of wool, silk or cotton, must be supplied. These must be mounted upon paste-board measuring 13 inches in height, by 8¼ inches in width. These different shades of each color must be prepared ; of colors with which it is possible to color in quantities, a sample must be colored with one per cent. while the other two shades may be weaker or stronger. A description must also be furnished stating the exact concentration of the dye, the mordants (if any), the temperature, etc., also whether the dye used was discolored or retained more or less color.

DOCUMENTS REQUIRED.

The documents required for Patents of Addition are precisely the same.

1. Specification.—Written or printed on any suitable paper and in any suitable form. No signatures necessary.

2. Drawings in duplicate.—One copy must be on good drawing paper or bristol board, and one on tracing cloth. The sheets must measure exactly 33 centimetres (13 inches) in height, by 21, 42 or 63 centimetres (8¼, 16½ or 24¾ inches) in width. A single margin line must be drawn all around 2 centimetres (1¾ inch) from the edge of the sheet, and at the top a clear space of 3 centimetres (1$\frac{3}{16}$ inches) must be left between the figures of the drawing and the margin line.

3. Power of Attorney.—Signed by the applicant or applicants, all names in full. No witnesses nor legalizations are required.

FORM.

POWER OF ATTORNEY.
Vollmacht.

Ich Wir Endesunterzeichnete...

....

ernenne........hiermit zu.............Bevollmächtigten...

....und ertheil.......selben Vollmacht für

....und in...Namen alle nothwendigen Schritte zu

thun um...................................... ....Patent..

....

....zu erlangen.

Demnach bei jedem befugten Amte Eingaben, Gesuche und Bittschriften einzureichen, bei allen hohen Ministerien, Aemtern, Beamten und Commissionen zu erscheinen, alle beschreibenden Actenstücke zu unterzeichnen und gut zu heissen, alle nöthigen Protokolle zu verlangen, von Beschreibungen Einsicht zu nehmen oder nehmen zu lassen, alle Taxen einzuzahlen und zurückzunehmen, dieselben zu quittiren oder die Quittungen in Empfang zu nehmen, alle Gesuche um Verlängerungen oder um Patente auf Zusätze oder Verbesserungen zu machen, dieselben umzuändern oder zurückzuziehen, die Durchstreichung alter Aufschriften zu genehmigen, die schliesslichen Urkunden, sowie die dazu gehörigen Acten in Empfang zu nehmen, gegen Patent verletzungen einzuschreiten, bei allen Reclamationen, welche während der ganzen Dauer eines Patentes stattfinden könnten ....nach Massgabe des Gesetzes zu vertreten. Zu den bezeichneten Zwecken alle Acten gutzuheissen und zu unterzeichnen, Domicil zu wählen, Submandatare für die ganze gegenwärtige Vollmacht o der einen Theil derselben zu bestimmen und in den verschiedenen Fällen, welche sich zeigen sollten, überhaupt Alles zu thun, was gesetzlich nothwendig oder nützlich sein sollte. Versprechend das Ganze als gut und rechtskräftig aufrecht zu halten und es nöthigenfalls zu bestätigen.

..............................am...................... ....18....   (*Signature.*)

Gibraltar.

There is as yet no patent law in this country. The government will, however, grant protection for inventions by way of special Act, provided the invention is likely to prove of practical utility in the country.

The cost of such grants varies considerably. We will, however, undertake to procure them at a charge of $175 each, but we will have to ask for an additional remittance in case the cost exceeds this sum; this amount will be sufficient in most cases.

DOCUMENTS REQUIRED.

The same as for the Bahama Islands. The Power of Attorney should be legalized by a British Consul.

We can obtain the legalization here when desired at a cost of $2.50.

Gold Coast Colony.

There is as yet no patent law in this British Colony. The government will, however, undoubtedly grant protection for inventions by way of special Legislative Act, provided the invention is likely to prove of practical utility in the country.

The cost of such grants varies considerably. We will however undertake to procure them at a charge of $200 each, but we will have to ask for an additional remittance in case the cost exceeds this sum. This amount will be sufficient in most cases.

DOCUMENTS REQUIRED.

The same as for the Bahama Islands. The Power of Attorney should be legalized by a British Consul.

We can obtain the legalization here when desired at a cost of $2.50.

Great Britain.

The Patent covers England, Scotland, Ireland, Wales, and the Isle of Man.

CHARGES.

*PATENT, cost of, all taxes paid for four years:
APPLICATION with complete Specification....................$27 50

*Where Provisional Protection is taken:
PROVISIONAL PROTECTION, cost of, for nine months........$12 50
FILING COMPLETE SPECIFICATION to complete Application 20 00

Total..................................$32 50

* Where Provisional Protection is taken, the complete specification should be filed within nine months of the date of application. An extension of one month's time may be had on payment of a fine of $10.00.

The above charges do not include the cost of procedure in case of possible opposition or interference, for which special arrangements will be made in each case, and apply only where the documents are sent to us completely and correctly prepared, ready for filing. Where it is desired that our London agent should peruse the specification, and modify it, if necessary, to suit the English practice, $5.00 must be added to the charge.

†TAXES. Before the end of fourth year.......... ....$255 00
          "   "   eighth year, or in the case of a pat-
ent applied for prior to Jan., 1884, before the end of seventh year.510 00

Or, in lieu thereof, the above taxes may be paid in annual installments, as follows:

Before the end of	Fourth	year	...........................$52 50
"	Fifth	"	.... 52 50
"	Sixth	"	.... 52 50
"	Seventh	"	.... 52 50
"	Eighth	"	.... 77 50
"	Ninth	"	.... 77 50
"	Tenth	"	...........................105 00
"	Eleventh	"	...........................105 00
"	Twelfth	"	...........................105 00
"	Thirteenth	"	...........................105 00

In case of an old patent dated prior to January, 1884, upon which the tax of £50 has been paid, the remaining taxes may be made in the following annual payments:

Before the end of	Seventh	year	....$52 50
"	Eighth	"	.... 52 50
"	Ninth	"	.... 52 50
"	Tenth	"	.... 77 50
"	Eleventh	"	.... 77 50
"	Twelfth	"	...........................105 00
"	Thirteenth	"	...........................105 00

AMENDMENT, according to work involved, from $2.50 up.
‡ASSIGNMENTS, if consideration is nominal.....................12 50

† If the patentee fails, from any cause, to pay the fees within the required time, the time may be extended for a period not exceeding three months. The fines payable to the government for extension are—one month, £3; two months, £7; three months, £10. Our charges for procuring extension, including the above fines, are:
     Extension for one month, $20.00; for two months, $40.00; for three months, $55.00.

‡ If the consideration is real, it is subject to a stamp duty of ten shillings for the first £100, or part thereof, and sixpence for each £5 above £100.

LAW AND PRACTICE.

Who may be Patentee.—The actual inventor, or the first introducer or importer of the invention into Great Britain. Joint inventors may obtain a joint patent. Other persons, a firm or corporation, may join with the inventor and secure a joint patent ; the legal representatives of an actual inventor may make application for a patent within six months of the inventor's death. Patents may be taken out in the name of a resident agent as *a communication from abroad*, and it is not necessary that the person who, re-siding abroad, communicates an invention to a person residing in England, should be the inventor ; any other person, a firm or corporation, may make the communication and obtain a valid patent. A British patent applied for under the provisions of the International Convention will only be granted to the identical person who made the prior foreign application upon which it is based.

Patents, Kind and Term.—Patents of Invention, granted for fourteen years, counting from the date of the filing of the application (or in the case of applications filed under the provisions of the International Convention, from the date upon which the original foreign application was filed), subject to the payment of the prescribed taxes. The expiration or failure of a prior foreign patent does not affect the British patent. Extensions may sometimes be obtained, but are very expensive, the applications fre-quently requiring an expenditure of from $1,500 to $2,000 without any certainty of suc-cess.

Unpatentable.—It has been held that bare principles are unpatentable, and the Comptroller is authorized to refuse to grant a patent for an invention the use of which would in his opinion be contrary to law or morality.

Novelty, Effect of Prior Patent or Publication.—To obtain a valid patent the application therefor must be made before the invention has been published. or is other-wise publicly known by means of books, or in any other way, in Great Britain. Prior publication or public use of the invention in a foreign country does not affect the valid-ity of a British Patent.

The amount of information given by the prior publication in Great Britian must, in order to invalidate a patent, be equal to that required to be given by a specification, *i.e.*, the invention must be sufficiently disclosed, so that any one skilled in the art to which it appertains, or to which it most nearly relates, may make, construct, compound or use the same.

By the International Convention and section 103 of the Patent Act of 1883 a foreign patentee has an absolute right of priority for his invention for a period of seven months from the date of the filing of his foreign application (not the date of the issue or allowance of the patent), and may obtain a perfectly valid patent notwithstanding any intermediate publication or public use of the invention in Great Britain, by filing his application within this period of time,

Taxes.—A patentee may pay the taxes upon his patent in two installments, viz.: £50 before the expiration of the fourth year of the life of the patent, and £100 before the end of the eighth year, or he may pay the same in annual installments, as follows: £10 before the end of each of the fourth, fifth, sixth and seventh years; £15 before the end of each of the eighth and ninth years, and £20 before the end of each of the tenth, eleventh, twelfth and thirteenth years. If for any reason the patentee fails to make any payment within the required time, the time may usually be extended for not to exceed three months upon payment of the following fees: Extension for one month, £3; two months, £7; three months, £10. The sums here named are the government fees only, for our terms for making the payments see "Charges."

Assignments.—In order to record an assignment, the following documents should be supplied: 1. Assignment in duplicate signed by the inventor and two witnesses. 2. A request to enter the name of the new proprietor upon the Register of Patents (Form L), signed by the assignee.

Working.—There are no requirements.

DOCUMENTS REQUIRED.

These forms are to be used for all ordinary applications: for applications under the provisions of the International Convention see "Documents Required (Convention)", and the forms following.

1. Application with Declaration.—Signed by applicant or applicants; all names in full. No witnesses nor legalization necessary.

2. Specifications in duplicate.—They may be either written, type-written, or printed upon one side only of good white, stiff paper, the sheets of which are exactly eight inches wide by thirteen inches high. A margin of two inches must be left upon the left hand side. Thin paper should not be used. Both copies should always be originals, *i.e.*, not carbon copies, if type-written copies are furnished. It is not necessary that the inventor should sign either copy of the specification, as our English agents can sign the same as attorneys, but if the inventor signs the specification at all, he should sign both copies.

3. Drawings in duplicate.—Both of these are to be upon sheets of good, white bristol board. The sheets must measure exactly eight inches wide by thirteen inches high, or sixteen inches wide by thirteen inches high. The smaller size should always be used if practicable. A single margin line should be drawn, all around, exactly ½ inch from the edge of the sheet. *The reference letters must be ⅛ inch or more in size* to admit of photo-lithographing. All reference letters and numbers should be made in ink upon *one* of the sheets, and upon the other in blue pencil. The latter requirement has not yet been rigidly insisted upon, but this method of lettering is desired. Good lithographs are accepted. No signatures are necessary.

4. Authorization.—Signed by applicant or applicants; all names in full. No witnesses nor legalization necessary.

NOTE.—Drawings are not required with provisional specification, but may be forwarded with the complete specification, when completing the application. When the patent is taken as a communication, the specifications and drawings in duplicate are the only documents required.

FORMS.

APPLICATION WITH DECLARATION.
(For Inventor alone.)
Patents, Designs and Trade Marks Acts, 1883 to 1888.
Form A.
Application for Patent.

I (*full name, address and occupation of applicant*), do hereby declare that I am in possession of an invention the title of which is (*insert title of invention*); that I am the true and first inventor thereof: and that the same is not in use by any other person or persons, to the best of my knowledge and belief; and I humbly pray that a patent may be granted to me for the said invention.

Dated this...................day of............ ......18.... (*Signature of Applicant.*)

FORM OF APPLICATION WITH DECLARATION.
(For an Inventor, and a Person not an Inventor.)
Patents, Designs and Trades Marks Acts, 1883 to 1888.
Form B.
Application for Patent.

We (*insert full names, addresses and occupations of both applicants*), do hereby declare that we are in possession of an invention the title of which is (*insert title of invention*); that said (*insert name of inventor*) is the true and first inventor thereof; and the same is not in use by any other person or persons, to the best of our knowledge and belief; and we humbly pray that a patent may be granted to us for the said invention.

Dated this...................day of............ ....18...... (*Signatures of Applicants.*)

FORM OF AUTHORIZATION.

Application for British Patent.

Authorization.

I, the undersigned applicant for a patent for (*insert title as in declaration*), do hereby appoint
....of...
London, in the County of Middlesex, to act as my agents in respect of such application, and request that all communications relating thereto may be sent to them at the above address.

Dated this.....................day of........................18......
(*Signature of Applicant.*)

FORM OF PROVISIONAL SPECIFICATION.

Patents, Designs, and Trade Marks Acts, 1883 to 1888.
Form B.
Provisional Specification.
(*Insert Title of Invention.*)

I, (*insert full name, address and occupation of applicant*), do hereby declare the nature of this invention to be as follows:
(*Here insert description of invention without claims, and preferably without reference to drawings. At the end of this description insert the date, as follows:*)

Dated this...................day of.................18..... (*Signature of Applicant.*)

FORM FOR COMPLETE SPECIFICATION.

Patents, Designs, and Trade Mards Acts, 1883 to 1888.
Form C.
Complete Specification.
(*Insert Title of Invention.*)

I, (*insert full name, address and occupation of applicant*), do hereby declare the nature of this invention and in what manner the same is to be performed, to be particularly described and ascertained in and by the following statement:
(*Here write description of invention, after which, and before the claims, the following words are to be written:*)

Having now particularly described and ascertained the nature of my said invention, and in what manner the same is to be performed, I declare that what I claim is:
(*Here write the claims, and after the claims, the date, as follows:*)

Dated this...............day of...................18..... (*Signature of Applicant.*)

DOCUMENTS REQUIRED. (CONVENTION.)

These documents and forms are *only* to be used for applications to be filed under the provisions of the International Convention. For all ordinary applications the preceding documents and forms should be used.

1. Application.—Signed by the applicant or applicants; all names in full. No witnesses or legalization necessary.

2. Declaration.—Signed by the applicant or applicants before a British Minister or person exercising the functions of a British Minister or a British Consul, Vice Consul, or other person exercising the functions of a British Consul, or a Notary Public, or before a Judge or Magistrate.

3. A certified copy of the specifications and drawings (or documents corresponding thereto,) filed by the applicant in the Patent Office of the Foreign State or British Possession in respect of the first foreign application, duly certified by the official chief or head of the Patent Office of such Foreign State or British Possession. It is sufficient to send a certified copy of the printed patent if the certificate distinctly states the date the application was filed.

4. Specifications in duplicate. } The forms and requirements for these docu-
5. Drawing in duplicate. } ments are precisely the same as for ordinary
6. Authorization. } application.

FORMS.

Patents, Designs, and Trade Marks Acts, 1883 to 1888.

Form A2.

Application for Patent under International and Colonial Arrangements.

I, (*Here insert name, full address and occupation of applicant*), do hereby declare that I have made foreign applications for protection of my invention of (*here insert title of invention,*) in the following Foreign States and on the following official dates, viz.: (*Here insert the names of each Foreign State followed by the official date of the application in each respectively*), and in the following British Possessions and on the following official dates, viz.: (*Here insert the names of each British Possession, followed by the official date of the application in each respectively.*)

That the said invention was not in use within the United Kingdom of Great Britain and Ireland, and the Isle of Man by any other person or persons before the (*here insert the official date of the earliest foreign application*), to the best of my knowledge, information and belief, and I humbly pray that a patent may be granted to me for the said invention in priority to other applicants, and that such patent shall have the date (*here insert the official date of the earliest foreign application*).

(*Signature.*).... ....
To the Comptroller, 25 Southampton Buildings,
    Patent Office, Chancery Lane, London, W. C.

DECLARATION.

Patents, Designs, and Trade Marks Acts, 1883 to 1888.

Application for Patent under International and Colonial Arrangements.

I, (*Here insert full name, full address and occupation of applicant*)..................................
do solemnly and sincerely declare that the invention of (*here insert the title of invention exactly as in the other papers*) ....
in respect of which the accompanying Application for British Patent is made is identical with the Invention in respect of which the First Foreign Application for Patent, referred to in the accompanying Application, was made.

And I make this solemn declaration conscientiously believing the same to be true.

(*Signature*)..

....

Declared at..
this...day of.................................18................
    Before me
        (*Signature and title of person before whom the declaration is made.*)

Greece.

There is as yet no patent law in this country. The government will, however, grant protection for inventions by way of special Legislative Act, provided the invention is likely to prove of practical utility in the country.

The cost of procuring such grants varies from $250 to $2,500. We will, however, undertake to procure them upon receipt of a remittance of $250 each, but we will have to ask for additional remittances from time to time to meet expenses in case the cost exceeds this sum.

DOCUMENTS REQUIRED.

The same as for France. The power of attorney should be legalized by a Consul of Greece.

We can obtain the legalization here, when desired, at a cost of $5.00.

Grenada (West Indies).

There is as yet no patent law in this country. The government will, however, grant protection for inventions by way of special Legislative Act, provided the invention is likely to prove of practical utility in the country.

The cost of such grants varies considerably. We will, however, undertake to procure them at a charge of $115 each, but we will have to ask for an additional remittance in case the cost exceeds this sum. This amount will undoubtedly be sufficient in most cases.

DOCUMENTS REQUIRED.

The same as for the Bahama Islands. The Power of Attorney should be legalized by a British Consul.

We can obtain the legalization here, when desired, at a cost of $2.50.

Guadeloupe.

See France.

Guatemala.

CHARGES.

*PATENT, cost of, all taxes paid for one year....................$175 00

*The above charge includes translation of the specification up to 2,000 words. Beyond that number, $1.00 must be added for every 100 words.

†TAXES, *payable annually, counting from the grant of the patent.*
AGENCY fee for paying.............................each year, $5 00
ASSIGNMENTS, preparing and recording...................... 30 00
WORKING (not including freight charges or cost of manufacturing) 40 00

†The annual tax is fixed by the government at the time of granting the patent, and varies from $5.00 to $50.00, according to the importance of the invention. The maximum tax is seldom imposed.

LAW AND PRACTICE.

Who may be Patentee.—The true inventor or his duly authorized attorney. Under the present law, to be entitled to a patent, the applicant must be a citizen of Guatemala, a foreigner domiciliated in Guatemala, or a person who has applied for a patent in some country belonging to the International Convention. A bill has been presented in Congress to modify this disposition, and it is expected that it will be passed in the near future.

Patents, Kind and Term.—Patents of Invention granted for from five to fifteen years. Patents for inventions previously patented abroad are granted for the term of the foreign patent upon which they are based, unless the same should exceed fifteen years, in which case the patent is granted for the maximum term.

Unpatentable.—Inventions, the employment of which would infringe prior rights, and those contrary to public health and safety, and to good customs.

Novelty, Effect of Prior Patent or Publication.—To obtain a valid patent, the application should be filed before the invention is publicly known and used in Guatemala. Inventions patented abroad can be patented in Guatemala at any time so long as the invention is new there.

Taxes.—For each patent granted, a tax varying from five to fifty pesos is payable annually in advance, counting from the date of the patent, for each year of the term of the patent. The amount of the tax is fixed by the government when the patent is issued. The maximum tax is seldom imposed. No prolongation of time for making payment can be obtained.

Assignments.—Should be prepared in the Spanish language, and be in duplicate. They should be legalized by a Guatemalan Consul.

We can obtain the legalization here, when desired, at a cost of $3.00 which includes Consular and Agency fees.

Working.—The invention must be worked in Guatemala within one year from the date of the patent, and the working must not be interrupted for more than a year at any one time. In case of machinery or apparatus, it is considered sufficient to import one or more of the machines or apparatus into Guatemala and put them into operation there. In case of a process, it must be carried into practice in the country.

DOCUMENTS REQUIRED.

1. **Specification.**—Written or printed on any paper, and in any suitable form. No signatures necessary.

2. **Drawings in duplicate.**—On tracing cloth, any convenient size. No signatures necessary.

3. **Power of Attorney.**—Signed by applicant or applicants, all names in full, and legalized by a Guatemalan Consul. The form is the same as for the Argentine Republic (which see).

4. **If the Invention is Patented Abroad.**—A certified copy of the patent should be furnished, which must be legalized by a Guatemalan Consul.

We can obtain the legalization here, when desired, at a cost of $3.00 for each document, which includes Consular and Agency fees.

Hawaii. (Sandwich Islands.)

CHARGES.

PATENT, cost of, all taxes paid..$90 00
CAVEAT, all taxes paid...40 00
ASSIGNMENTS, preparing and recording.........................17 50

LAW AND PRACTICE.

Who may be Patentee.—The true inventor.

Patents, Kind and Term.—Patents of Invention granted for ten years from the date of the issue of the patent, but where there are prior foreign patents, it will expire with the first expiring foreign patent. Caveats may be filed by intending applicants, and are operative for one year.

Unpatentable.—The law is silent upon this point.

Novelty, Effect of Prior Patent or Publication.—To obtain a valid patent the application should be made before any public use of the invention in Hawaii or publication in any country. Patents may be obtained at any time, however, for inventions previously patented abroad, unless the thing patented has been introduced into public use in Hawaii for more than one year prior to the application.

Taxes.—There are none after the issue of the patent.

Assignments.—Should be in duplicate, and must be recorded within three months from the date of the execution. The documents may be in any usual form, and should be acknowledged before a Notary Public.

Working.—There are no requirements.

Caveats.—May be filed by intending applicants and are operative for one year.

DOCUMENTS REQUIRED.

The documents required for a Caveat are the same as for a Patent, with the exception of the Petition, the form of which is given below.

1. **Petition.**—Signed by inventor.

2. **Power of Attorney.**—Signed by inventor.

3. **Specification.**—Signed by the inventor and two witnesses. The form is the same as for United States applications.

4. **Drawings in duplicate.**—These must be made on sheets of white drawing board which must measure exactly fifteen inches high and ten inches wide; a single margin line must be drawn all around exactly one inch from the edge, a clear space of one and a quarter inches must be left at the top within the margin line. The drawings need not be signed.

5. **Oath.**—This may be executed before any Minister, *Charge d'Affaires*, Consul or Commercial Agent holding commission under the Hawaiian Government, or before any Notary Public, the oath being attested in all cases by the proper official seal of the office before whom the oath is made.

FORMS.

PETITION.

To the Minister of the Interior :

Your petitioner (*name of applicant*), a citizen (*or subject*) of (*state of what country applicant is a citizen or subject*), residing at (*full address*), prays that letters patent be granted to him for the improvement in (*title of invention*), set forth in the annexed specification.

(*Date.*) (*Signature.*)

POWER OF ATTORNEY.

To the Minister of the Interior :

I, the undersigned, applicant for a patent for (*title of invention*), do hereby nominate and appoint...............of........................my attorney, for me and in my name to make application, for letters patent of the Hawaiian kingdom, to prosecute the said application, to amend the specification, to sign my name for these purposes, to receive the letters patent when granted, and generally to perform all necessary acts in the premises.

(*Date.*) (*Signature.*)

OATH.

....
}
....
} *ss.*

I, (*name of applicant*), the above-named petitioner, residing at (*full address*), being duly sworn, deposes and says that he verily believes himself to be the original, first and sole inventor of the improvement in (*title of invention*), described and claimed in the foregoing specification ; that the same has not been patented to himself or to others with his knowledge or consent, except in the following countries: (*If the invention has been previously patented abroad, insert here the names of all the countries where patented, and the number and date of each patent. If not so patented, omit the words "except in the following countries" and insert in the place thereof the words "in any country"*). That the same has not, to his knowledge, been introduced into public use in the Hawaiian Islands for more than one year prior to his application for a patent; that he does not know or believe that the same was ever before known or used ; and that he is a citizen (*or subject*) of (*state of what country applicant is a citizen or subject*).

Sworn to and subscribed before me
}

this........day of.........A. D. 18
}

(*Signature.*)

(*Official Seal.*) (*Signature of official before whom the oath is taken.*)

PETITION. (CAVEAT.)

To the Minister of the Interior :

The petitioner (*name of applicant*), a citizen (*or subject*) of (*state of what country applicant is a citizen or subject*), residing at (*full address*), represents that he has made certain improvements in (*title of invention*), and that he is now engaged in making experiments for the purpose of perfecting the same, preparatory to applying for letters patent therefor. He therefore prays the protection of his right until he shall have matured his invention ; and that the subjoined description thereof may be filed as a caveat in the confidential archives of the office and preserved in secrecy.

(*Date.*) (*Signature.*)

Hayti.

No special law exists for the protection of inventions, and while special grants can be obtained by Legislative Act, giving an exclusive right to the employment and use of a particular kind of machinery for a special purpose, yet in our opinion such grants would be of little benefit, owing to the chronic revolutionary state of the country and the lax administration of the laws. Further, under the laws in force in the country at the present time, white persons are not allowed to own real estate, and may not engage in any wholesale business in their own names, it being necessary to transact any such business, ostensibly at least, in the name of some native of Hayti.

We have the machinery for securing special grants, however, and will undertake to do so when desired at a charge of $400 each. We cannot, of course, guarantee that any grant will finally be made, and should the cost be in excess of our charge as above, we must ask for an additional remittance.   It is believed that our first charge will not be exceeded in most cases.

DOCUMENTS REQUIRED.

1.   Power of Attorney.—Signed by the applicant and legalized by a Haytian Consul.   The usual French form should be used.

We can obtain the legalization here, when desired, at a cost of $5.00.

2.   Specification in duplicate.—In any form and unsigned.

3.   Drawings in duplicate.—On any suitable material, of any size, and unsigned.

Honduras (Republic of).

There is at yet no patent law in this country.   The government will, however, grant protection for inventions by way of special Legislative Act, provided the invention is likely to prove of practical utility in the country.   The cost of such grants varies considerably.   We will, however, undertake to procure them at a charge of $400 each, but we will have to ask for an additional remittance in case the cost exceeds this sum.   This amount will undoubtedly be sufficient in most cases.

DOCUMENTS REQUIRED.

The same as for Chili.   The Power of Attorney should be legalized by a Consul of Honduras.

We can obtain the legalization here, when desired, at a cost of $3.00.

Hong Kong.

CHARGES.

PATENT, cost of, all taxes paid.................................$115 00
ASSIGNMENTS, preparing and recording..................... 20 00

LAW AND PRACTICE.

Who may be Patentee.—The patentee or the owner, by assignment or otherwise, of any invention for which Letters Patent have already been granted in England.

Patents, Kind and Term.—But one kind of patent is issued, it is granted for the life of the existing English Patent, expiring with it. Extensions may be secured in the event that the English Patent is extended, and for the same term of years.

Unpatentable.—The law is silent on this point.

Novelty, Effect of Prior Patent or Publication.—The invention must not have been publicly used within the Colony before the date of application, but otherwise the patent may be obtained without regard to prior foreign patents.

Taxes.—There are none after the issue of the patent.

Assignments.—The documents should be prepared in duplicate. Any suitable form may be used.

Working.—There are no requirements.

DOCUMENTS REQUIRED.

1. **Petition.**—Signed by applicant.

2. **Declaration.**—Signed by applicant.

3. **Specification in duplicate.**—Signed by applicant. The description of the invention should be identical, as far as practicable, with the complete specification filed in England.

4. **Drawings in duplicate.**—On drawing board or tracing cloth, any suitable size. No signatures required.

5. **Power of Attorney.**—Signed by applicant.

6. **A Blue Book** of the British Patent on which the application is founded.

7. **If the Applicant is the Assignee,** a certified copy of the assignment should be furnished.

FORMS.

PETITION.

To the Governor of Hong Kong:—

The humble petition of *A. B.* (*or, as the case may be, of C. D. as agent for A. B.*) for leave to file a specification under Ordinance No. 14, of 1862.

That your petitioner (*or, as the case may be, that A. B., of whom your petitioner is the agent assignee, executor or administrator*) has obtained Her Majesty's letters patent, dated the............ day of......................18....for (*state the title of the invention as granted*), and that such letters patent are to continue in force for..........................years from the............... .... day of....................18....

That your petitioner believes that the said invention is not now and has not hitherto been publicly used in this colony.

That the following is the description of the said invention : (*Here state the particulars shortly in accordance with the specification on which the letters patent in England were granted.*)

Your petitioner therefore prays for leave to file a specification of the said invention, pursuant to the provisions of Ordinance No. 14, of 1862. And your petitioner will ever pray, &c.

The...............day of....................18....

(*Signature of Applicant.*)

DECLARATION.

I, (*here insert name, occupation and place of residence*), do solemnly and sincerely declare that I am (*or, if made by an agent, that A. B., of..........................is*) in possession absolutely (*or if made in respect of a locally confined interest, then within the colony of Hong Kong or according to fact,*) of an invention for (*state the nature of the invention in terms of the English Patent*), and which invention I believe will, in all probability, be of great public utility within Hong Kong; and that the same is not publicly used within the said colony; and that, to the best of my knowledge and belief, the instrument in writing under my hand hereunto annexed, particularly described and ascertains the nature of the said invention, and in what manner the same is to be performed.

Dated the.....................day of......................18....

(*Signature of Applicant.*)

SPECIFICATION.

To all whom it may concern: Be it known that I *(here insert name, occupation, and place of residence)* am in possession of an invention for *(state the title of the invention as granted)*. and I, the said *(here insert name)*, do hereby declare the nature of the said invention, and in what manner the same is to be performed, to be particularly described and ascertained in and by the following statement thereof, that is to say:—

The invention has for its object *(here describe the invention in accordance with the complete specification on which the English Letters Patent were granted, with reference to drawings, if any).*

(Witness.)   *(Signature of Applicant.)*

POWER OF ATTORNEY.

In the matter of Ordinance No. 14, of 1862, of the Government of Hong Kong, and in the matter of *(name, occupation and address)*, an Inventor.

I, the above-named *(name of applicant)*, do hereby retain, constitute, and appoint.... ....as my Agent and Attorney, to apply for and obtain from the Government of Hong Kong, Letters Patent for *(state title of invention as per petition)*, and I authorize him to sign my name to such papers and writings, and do such acts regarding the same, including the appointment of a substitute or substitutes, as may be necessary or expedient.

Dated this............................day of............................18......

Signed, sealed and delivered at..... ....)

in the presence of..................... .... \

(Signature of Applicant.)   [L. S.]

Iceland.

CHARGES.

```
* PATENTS. Cost of, all taxes paid............        ........ ...$75 00
  ASSIGNMENTS..........................        ........ .. 22 50
  WORKING................................      .... .... ........ 50 00
```

* The above charge includes translation of the specification up to 2,000 words; 50 cents must be added for each 100 words in the specification in excess of 2,000.

LAW AND PRACTICE.

There is as yet no special law in this country providing for the issue of patents, but patents are granted upon application by the King of Denmark, Iceland being a Danish possession, upon the same general terms and conditions as the Danish patent. (See Denmark for further particulars.)

DOCUMENTS REQUIRED.

The same as for Denmark, which see.

India.

The Patent covers the whole of British India, including the newly annexed possessions in Burmah, Aden and the Nicobar and Laccadives Islands.

CHARGES.

PATENT, cost of, all taxes paid for *four* years................ ....$50 00
TAXES.—*Payable yearly, counting from the date of application.*

Before the end of Fourth		Year		....	27 50
"	"	Fifth	"	....	27 50
"	"	Sixth	"	....	27 50
"	"	Seventh	"	....	27 50
"	"	Eighth	"	....	27 50
"	"	Ninth	"	....	55 00
"	"	Tenth	"	....	55 00
"	"	Eleventh	"	....	55 00
"	"	Twelfth	"	....	55 00
"	"	Thirteenth	"	....	55 00

ASSIGNMENTS, preparing and recording....................... 10 00
AMENDMENTS or DISCLAIMERS, including Government fees.. 15 00

If the inventor fail, from any cause, to pay the fees within the required time, the time may be extended for a period not exceeding three months. The fines payable to the government for such extensions are—one month, 10 rupees; two months, 25 rupees; three months, 50 rupees. Our charges for procuring extensions, including the above fines, are:

Extension for one month, $13.00; for two months, $22.00; for three months, $32.00

LAW AND PRACTICE.

Who may be Patentee.—The applicant must be the actual inventor, his assignee, executor or administrator. A mere importer cannot obtain a valid patent.

Patents, Kind and Duration.—Patents of Invention: they are granted for fourteen years from the date upon which the specification is filed, subject to the payment of the prescribed taxes. An exclusive privilege in respect of an invention for which a patent has been obtained in Great Britain will cease on the revocation or expiration of that patent. If a patent has not been obtained in Great Britain, the Indian exclusive privilege will cease on the revocation or expiration of any other prior foreign patent or exclusive privilege. This latter restriction will seemingly oblige many inventors having patents in countries where the grant is only for a short period, or the taxes heavy, to take out and maintain a British Patent, in order to insure the obtaining of the full term of the Indian privilege. Extensions of the duration of privileges are provided for by Sec. 15 of the law. The government fee for such extension is 100 rupees, equal to about $50.00.

Unpatentable.—Patents will not be granted : if the invention is of no utility; if it is not new ; if the applicant is not the inventor ; if the specification does not fulfil the requirements of the Act ; if the application contains a wilful or fraudulent misstatement ; if the application is made after the expiration of a year after the acquisition of a foreign patent for the same invention.

Novelty, Effect of Prior Patent or Publication.—To obtain a valid patent, the application must be filed in the office in Calcutta before the expiration of one year from the date of the acquisition of a Patent or other exclusive privilege in any place beyond the limits of British India and the United Kingdom of Great Britain, and before the invention has been publicly known or used either in India or Great Britain. In case a British Patent has been obtained, the Indian application may be filed at any time within one year from the date of the *actual sealing* of the British Patent, if the said invention was not publicly known or used in India at the time the application was made for the British Patent, notwithstanding any subsequent use or publication before the expiration of the time—a year from date of sealing—allowed for making the application in India. If a public use or knowledge of an invention has been obtained in fraud of an inventor, provided he has not acquiesced in the use, and applies for leave to file a specification within six months of such use, the invention will be deemed new. An inventor himself, or his servant, agent or licensee, may use an invention in public, and the invention be deemed new if the application be lodged within a year from the commencement of such public use.

Taxes.—The law and practice is very similar to that in Great Britain. No taxes are payable after the issue of the patent until the fourth year of its term, when annual taxes commence to fall due. All taxes are payable yearly in advance, counting from the date of application. Should the patentee from any cause fail to pay any tax within

the required time, an extension of time for paying same, but not to exceed three months
at most, can be obtained by making due application therefor, and upon payment of
a fine. (See "Charges" for amount of fine.)

Assignments.—The papers should be prepared in duplicate and must be accompanied by a power of attorney from the assignee, authorizing the registration of such
assignment, and the naming of a place in India where service of any rule, etc., may be
made. Assignments and licenses need not be authenticated by a Notary Public or
Magistrate, but had better bear the signatures and addresses of two witnesses. The
consideration expressed should be nominal.

Working.—There are no requirements.

DOCUMENTS REQUIRED.

NOTE.—The power of the agent in India has been amplified under the new law, and he can now
sign all the papers on behalf of an applicant, provided he be duly authorized in his power of attorney to do so. It is, however, always better to get the applicant himself to sign all the papers
whenever it is possible to do so.
    Where the applicant is the assignee, an assignment must be furnished with the other papers.
    Where the applicant is a Company or Corporation, the petition and all other papers must be
signed by the chief officer or Secretary, and sealed with its seal.
    Where an English Patent has been obtained as a *communication*, the application should never-
theless, be made in the name of the inventor himself. In such cases it is absolutely necessary to
furnish an assignment of the Indian rights from the English agent or other English applicant, to
the applicant for the Indian privilege.
    It is most important that the *Title* of the invention should be described in exactly the same
terms in all the papers. Where an English Patent exists, the title in the paper for Indian applications must correspond precisely therewith.

1. **Petition with Application.**—May be written on any paper. The simple signature of the applicant is sufficient. No witnesses nor legalization necessary.

2. **Five copies of the Specification.**—May be written on any paper. One copy
at least should be signed by the applicant. No witnesses nor legalization necessary.
All alterations or erasures must be initialed by the applicant.

3. **Five copies of the Drawings.**—These may be on any kind of paper, or on tracing cloth. If prepared on thin tracing paper, they should be mounted on thicker paper
or cloth. Copies of drawings taken from the English blue books, or photographs, are
accepted.

4. **Power of Attorney.**—May be written on any paper. Must be signed by the
applicant, whose signature should be attested by two witnesses, who should state
their addresses.

FORMS.

NOTE.—Please note that there are two separate and distinct forms of Petition or Application.
It is important that the correct forms be used in each case.
    Form A. to be used if a Patent has not been obtained in England, but may also be used if an
application for a Patent in England is *pending*.
    Form B *must* be used where a Patent has already *been obtained* in England.

FORM A.   PETITION OR APPLICATION.

To THE GOVERNOR GENERAL IN COUNCIL:

The application of (*here insert name, occupation and address*)
for leave to file a Specification under Part I. of The Inventions and Designs Act, 1888.

1. The applicant is in possession of an invention for (*state the title of the invention*); he is the
inventor thereof (*or, as the case may be, the executor, administrator or assignee of the inventor*);

and, to the best of his information and belief, the invention is new within the meaning of Part I. of The Inventions and Designs Act, 1888, and no circumstance exists which, if the applicant is authorized to file a Specification, and files it in accordance with that Part, will disentitle him to an exclusive privilege thereunder in respect of the invention.

2.   The following is a description of the invention *(here insert a copy of the complete specification.)*

3.   The applicant, therefore, applies for leave to file a specification of the invention pursuant to Part I. of The Inventions and Designs Act, 1888.

(Signature.)

I, the applicant above named, do declare that what is stated in the above application is true to my knowledge, except as to matters stated on information and belief, and as to those matters I believe them to be true.

Dated.............day of...................18....   *(Signature.)*

SPECIFICATION.

To all whom it may concern: Be it known that I *(here insert name, occupation and address)* am in possession of an invention for *(state the title of the invention)*, and I, the said *(here insert the name)*, do hereby declare the nature of the said invention, and in what manner the same is to be performed, to be particularly described and ascertained in and by the following statement thereof, that is to say—
    The invention has for its object *(here describe it fully with reference to the drawings, if any).*

Witnesses :   *(Signature.)*

POWER OF ATTORNEY.

In the matter of Act No........of 18....of the Legislative Council
of India, and in the matter of *(name, occupation and address,)*
an inventor.

I, the above named *(insert name)*, do hereby retain, constitute and appoint.......................
as my agent and attorney, to apply for and obtain from the Government of India an Exclusive Privilege or Letters Patent for *(title of invention as per petition)*, and I authorize him to sign my name to such papers and writings, and do such acts, including the appointment of a substitute or substitutes, as may be necessary or expedient.

Dated this.............day of..................18....

Signed, sealed and delivered at..............
                                                     }
In the presence of........................... }   *(Signature.)* [L. S.]

FORM B.   PETITION OR APPLICATION.

To THE GOVERNOR GENERAL IN COUNCIL:

The application of *(here insert name, occupation and address)* for
leave to file a Specification under Part I. of The Inventions
and Designs Act, 1888.

1.   The applicant *(or, as the case may be, A. B. of whom the applicant is the executor, administrator or assign)* has obtained a Patent in the United Kingdom dated and sealed as on the.....day of........ ....18...., and actually sealed on the..........day of.........18....for *(state the title of the invention).*

2.   To the best of the information and belief of the applicant, the invention is new within the meaning of Part I. of The Inventions and Designs Act, 1888, and no circumstance exists which, if the applicant is authorized to file a specification, and files it in accordance with that part, will disentitle him to an exclusive privilege thereunder in respect of the Invention.

3.   The following is a description of the invention *(here insert a copy of the complete specification).*

4.   The applicant, therefore, applies for leave to file a specification of the invention pursuant to Part I. of The Inventions and Designs Act, 1888.

(Signature.)

I, the applicant above named, do declare that what is stated in the above application is true to my knowledge, except as to matters stated on information and belief, and as to those matters I believe them to be true.

(Signature.)

Dated this.............day of..................18....

International Union.

See end of book.

Italy.

CHARGES.

The patent covers the entire Kingdom of Italy, which includes the Islands of Sicily and Sardinia.

```
* PATENT, Cost of, all taxes paid for one year......................$35 00
     "         "      term tax paid for six years...................... 45 00
     "         "       "      fifteen  "  ................. ..... 63 00
* PATENT OF ADDITION, all taxes paid........................ 25 00
† PROLONGATION of Patent, at end of any term ................. 20 00
```

TAXES, *payable on or before the first day of each successive year of the duration of the patent, the duration being always reckoned from the last day of one of the following months, viz.: March, June, September or December, next following the day on which the application for the patent was made. Three months' grace, without fine is allowed for the payment of annual taxes.*

```
     Second and third years..  ...........................each $12 50
     Fourth, fifth and sixth years............. ............  "    17 50
     Seventh, eighth and ninth years........................  "    22 50
     Tenth, eleventh and twelfth years..................  ......  "    27 50
     Thirteenth, fourteenth and fifteenth years...............  "    32 50

     ASSIGNMENTS (see Assignments)..............................  20 00
     WORKING, exclusive of manufacture or freight charges.........  20 00
```

* The above charge includes translation of the specification up to 2,000 words. Beyond this number, 35 cents must be added for each 100 words.
† Applications for prolongations must be accompanied by a Power of Attorney signed by the applicant and legalized by an Italian Consul, and by the original patent, together with any Patents of Addition which may have been obtained. The application for prolongation must be filed before the expiration of the original patent. To the above charge must be added $2.00 for every year for which the patent is to be prolonged, and also the amount of the next year's tax.

LAW AND PRACTICE.

Who may be Patentee.—The author of a new invention or discovery, or his assign, whether a person, firm or corporation.

Patents, Kind and Term.—Patents of Invention granted for from one to fifteen years as elected by the applicant. Patents of Addition granted for the life of the original patent and expiring therewith. Patents demanded for a less term than fifteen years can be prolonged to this term either in a single prolongation or by successive prolongations of one or more years each. A patent granted for an invention already patented abroad expires with that patent for which the longest term has been granted, but in no case can it exceed the maximum limit of fifteen years. A patent of invention takes effect from the date of its application, and its duration from the last day of that one of the months of March, June, September and December which follows next after the date of application.

Unpatentable.—Inventions or discoveries relating to trades which are contrary to law, morals, or public safety ; inventions or discoveries not relating to the manufacture of material objects ; inventions or discoveries of a mere theoretical nature ; all kinds of medicines.

Novelty, Effect of Prior Patent or Publication.—The application should be filed before the invention has been published, or become publicly known in Italy but in case of an invention previously patented abroad and not yet imported into Italy, although already published by means of such foreign patent, a valid patent may be obtained at any time so long as the application be made before the expiration of the foreign patent, and before the importation or use of the invention in Italy by persons other than the inventor.

Taxes.—Patents are subject to two kinds of taxes : one a proportional or term tax, the other an annual tax. The proportional or term tax consists of as many times 10 lire (about $2.00), as there are years in the term for which the patent is demanded (whether an original patent or a patent of prolongation), and is payable in advance at the time the application is made. The annual taxes are 40 lire for each of the first three years, 65 lire for each of the three following years, 90 lire each for the seventh, eighth, and ninth years, 115 lire each for the tenth, eleventh, and twelfth years, and 140 lire for each of the three last years. All annual taxes are payable in advance, but three months' grace is allowed, without fine.

It is usual to pay the term tax for at least *six* years, as, if a patent is obtained for a shorter term than six years it must be worked within *one* year, whereas a patent granted for six years or longer need not be worked until the second year.

Assignments.—In case the patent is only partially assigned, or is assigned to more than one person in parts or shares, *i. e.*, otherwise than collectively, the registration of the assignment cannot be effected until the whole of the taxes shall have been paid for the remainder of the term of the patent ; that is to say, the term for which the "term tax" was paid.

To effect the recording of an assignment the following documents are necessary. 1. An assignment in duplicate in either the Italian or French languages, signed by the *assignor* and legalized by an Italian Consul. 2. A power of attorney in the same language as the assignment, signed by the *assignee*, and legalized by an Italian Consul, authorizing the recording of the assignment and the payment of the fees in connection therewith.

We can obtain the legalization here, when desired, at a cost of $3.00 for each document, which includes Consular and Agency fees.

Working.—If the invention has been patented for a term less than six years the working must be commenced within *one* year of the date of the patent, and the working must not entirely cease for any one entire year thereafter. If patented for six years or more, the working must be commenced within *two* years of the date of the patent, and the working must not entirely cease for any two years thereafter. The patentee does not forfeit his rights if he can prove that his failure to work his invention is attributable to causes beyond his own control, but the want of pecuniary means is not included in these causes. The courts, in contested cases, seem disposed to construe the law in a sense favorable to the inventor's interests, if he can produce evidence to show that he has reasonably exerted himself to work his invention. It is considered sufficient in case of machinery or apparatus to import one or more of the articles into Italy, and to set up and work it or them there. In case of a process, it must be carried into practice. Proof of working should be obtained and retained by the patentee.

DOCUMENTS REQUIRED.

The documents required for Patents of Addition are precisely the same.

1. Specification.—Written or printed on any paper and in any suitable form. No signatures necessary.

2. **Drawings in triplicate.**—On drawing board or tracing cloth. Three different sizes may be used for the sheets, viz.: 15 centimetres ($5\frac{7}{8}$ inches), in width, by 20 centimetres ($7\frac{7}{8}$ inches) in height; 20 centimetres ($7\frac{7}{8}$ inches) in width, by 30 centimetres ($11\frac{13}{16}$ inches) in height; or 30 centimetres ($11\frac{13}{16}$ inches) in width, by 40 centimetres ($15\frac{3}{4}$ inches) in height. It is important to use the smallest size that the nature of the drawings will permit. No signatures are necessary.

3. **Power of Attorney.**—Signed by the applicant and legalized by an Italian Consul. The usual French power should be used. (See France.)

4. **If Prior Foreign Patent Exists,** a certified copy of the patent should be furnished, which must be legalized by the Italian Consul.

We can obtain the legalization here, when desired, at a cost of $3.00, which includes Consular and Agency fees.

Jamaica.

CHARGES.

PATENT, cost of, all taxes paid	$185 00
PATENT OF ADDITION	185 00
ASSIGNMENTS, preparing and recording	25 00
WORKING, exclusive of freight or cost of manufacture	50 00

LAW AND PRACTICE.

Who may be Patentee.—The true and first inventor or importer, or his authorized agent or assignee.

Patents, Kind and Term.—Patents of Invention (or Importation), granted for fourteen years, and Patents of Addition, which form a part of, and expire with, the original patent. In exceptional cases, the patent may be extended for a further term of seven years. In case of prior foreign patents, the patent expires with the patent having the shortest term.

Unpatentable.—A valid patent cannot be obtained for an invention, the subject of a foreign patent which has already expired.

Novelty, Effect of Prior Patent or Publication.—To obtain a valid patent, the application must be filed before the invention has been introduced into public and common use in Jamaica. Patents may be obtained at any time upon inventions already patented abroad, so long as the foreign patents remain in force and the invention has not been brought into public and common use in Jamaica.

Taxes.—There are none after the issue of the patent.

Assignments.—May be prepared in any usual form, and should be in duplicate.

Working.—The invention must be put into operation within two years of the date of the patent. It is considered sufficient in case of machinery or apparatus to import one or more into Jamaica and put it or them into operation there. In the case of a process it must be brought into practice there.

Special.—Jamaica is one of the few British Colonies that do not issue formal Letters Patent. All Letters Patent are registered and retained in the Office of the Colonial Secretary. The only documents that can be forwarded to inventors, are the official certificate of the filing of the application, and a copy of the *Official Gazette* containing the notice of the same.

DOCUMENTS REQUIRED.

The documents should be written or printed on legal cap, on one side only, *and all should be sent in duplicate.*

1. **Petition.**—Signed by applicant.

2. **Declaration.**—Signed by applicant. The declaration may be taken before a Notary Public or a British Consul.

3. **Drawings in duplicate.**—On drawing board or tracing cloth, of any suitable size. No signatures required.

4. **Specification.**—Signed by applicant and two witnesses.

5. **Power of Attorney.**—Signed by applicant and legalized by a British Consul.

We can obtain the legalization here, when desired, at a cost of $2.50.

FORMS.

PETITION.

To His Excellency, &c., &c., (*here leave blank for the name and title of Governor*).

The humble petition of (*here insert name, occupation and address of petitioner*), for, &c.

Showeth :—

That your petitioner is in possession of an invention for (*insert the title of the invention*), which invention he believes will be of great public utility ; that he is the true and first inventor thereof ; and that the same is not in use by any other person or persons, to the best of his knowledge and belief.

Your petitioner, therefore, humbly prays that your Excellency will be pleased, in the name and on behalf of Her Majesty, the Queen, to grant unto him, his executors, administrators, and assigns, Her Majesty's letters patent for this Island, for the term of fourteen years, pursuant to the statute in that case made and provided. And your petitioner will ever pray, &c.

(*Signature of Applicant.*)

DECLARATION.

I (*insert name, full address and occupation of applicant*), do solemnly and sincerely declare that I am in possession of an invention for (*insert the title as in petition*), which invention I believe will be of great public utility ; that I am the true and first inventor thereof ; and that the same is not in use by any other person or persons to the best of my knowledge and belief ; and that the instrument in writing, under my hand and seal, hereunto annexed, particularly describes and ascertains the nature of the said invention, and the manner in which the same is to be performed ; and I make this declaration, conscientiously believing the same to be true, and by virtue of the provisions of an act made and passed.

Declared at........this........day of........ }

A. D........before me.................. }

(*Signature of Applicant.*)

(*Signature and title of person before whom the declaration is made.*)

SPECIFICATION.

To all to whom these presents shall come : I, (*insert full name, address and occupation of applicant*), send greeting :—

Know ye, that I, the said (*name of applicant*), do hereby declare the nature of my invention, for (*insert title as in petition*), and in what manner the same is to be performed, to be particularly described and ascertained in and by the following statement; that is to say :—

(Here describe the invention.)

In witness whereof, I, the said (*insert name of applicant*), have hereunto set my hand this..... day of..................A. D.....................

We attest :—   (*Signature of Applicant.*)
C. D., of...&c.
E. F., of...&c.

POWER OF ATTORNEY.

In the matter of The Patent Law Amendment Act, 1857, of the Government of Jamaica, and in the matter of (*name, occupation and address*), an Inventor.

I, the above-named (*insert name*), do hereby retain, constitute and appoint.....................
....
...... as my agent and attorney, to apply for and obtain from the Government of Jamaica an exclusive privilege or Letters Patent for (*insert title of invention precisely as in petition*), and I authorize him to sign my name to such papers and writings, and do such acts, including the appointment of a substitute or substitutes, as may be necessary or expedient.

Dated this................day of................18....

Signed, sealed and delivered in the presence of   (*Signature of Applicant.*) [L. S.]

Japan.

New patents, designs and trade-marks laws were passed in Japan on December 18th, 1888, to go into effect on February 1st, 1889.

Under the provisions of these laws *natives* of Japan may secure patents for inventions for five, ten or fifteen years ; patents for designs for three, five, seven or ten years, as they may elect ; and protection for the use of any trade-mark for the term of twenty years, by making due application to the Minister of State for Agriculture and Commerce.

The benefits of these laws do not, however, extend to foreigners, nor can foreigners obtain protection in Japan for inventions, designs or trade-marks, except by securing a special grant, which is a very costly and uncertain undertaking.

We quote the following from the *Japan Mail*, a semi-official journal :

"Foreign patents and foreign trade-marks remain as before without protection in Japan ; nor can they possibly receive protection so long as the provisions of Japanese law— this Patent Law, for example—are not effective in respect of foreigners living in Japan. If the latter cannot be restrained from infringing Japanese patent-rights, neither can they claim protection for their own patents against Japanese infringement."

Upon the passage of the patent law of April 18th, 1884, we instructed our agents to apply to the Japanese Minister of Foreign Affairs for an interpretation of the law as regards the rights of foreigners under it. The Minister's reply, dated at Tokio, August 3d, 1885, was to the effect that the patent regulations were not applicable to foreigners. We have had our agent make similar inquiry with regard to the new laws, and he has been informed that foreigners can derive no benefits from them *at present.*

The cost of a special grant cannot be determined in advance. Upon receipt of particulars we will obtain estimates as to costs through correspondence.

Java.

The Patent Law was repealed in 1870, and there is now no special law upon this subject.

Laccadives Island.

See India.

Lagos.

There is as yet no patent law in this British Colony. The government will, however, undoubtedly grant protection for inventions by way of special Legislative Act, provided the invention is likely to prove of practical utility in the country,

The cost of such grants varies considerably. We will, however, undertake to procure them at a charge of $200 each, but we will have to ask for an additional remittance in case the cost exceeds this sum. This amount will be sufficient in most cases.

DOCUMENTS REQUIRED.

The same as for the Gold Coast Colony, which see.

La Re Union.

See France.

Leeward Islands.

Comprising Antigua, Anguilla, Dominica, Montserrat, Nevis, St. Christopher and Virgin Islands. These several colonies were, for administrative purposes, grouped together in 1871.

CHARGES.

PROVISIONAL PROTECTION, for six months................$150 00
COMPLETING APPLICATION............................... 120 00
$270 00

* COMPLETE in first instance, all taxes paid for three years \$250 00
† TAXES, at or before the expiration of the third year............ 60 00
   "   "   "   "   " seventh " 110 00
   ASSIGNMENTS, preparing and recording......... .... 15 00

*The above charge includes all expenses, except in cases of possible opposition, for which special arrangements will be made in each case.
   The application may be made either with a provisional or a complete specification. In case of the former, provisional protection is afforded for six months' time; the complete specification must be filed before the expiration of the provisional protection.

†In making payment of taxes, the Letters Patent must always be forwarded for the endorsement of the payment thereon.

LAW AND PRACTICE.

Who may be Patentee.—The true and first inventor, which is interpreted to include the true and first importer.

Patents, Kind and Term.—Provisional Patents granted for a term of six months. Patents of Invention (or Importation) granted for fourteen years, counting from the date of the filing of the application, subject to the payment of the prescribed taxes. Extensions may sometimes be obtained. In case of prior foreign patents, the patent will expire with the first expiring foreign patent.

Unpatentable.—The law is silent upon this point.

Novelty, Effect of Prior Patent or Publication.—The invention must not have been known or used in the Colony, at the time the application is filed. Prior publication or patenting in other countries does not prevent the obtaining of a perfectly valid patent, but a valid patent cannot be obtained after the expiration of a foreign patent for the same invention.

Taxes.—A tax of £10 is payable before the end of the third year of the life of the patent, counting from the date of the filing of the application, and another of £20 before the expiration of the seventh year. No prolongation of the time for making payment can be obtained.

Assignments.—These may be prepared in any usual form, and should be in duplicate.

Working.—There are no conditions.

DOCUMENTS REQUIRED.

1. **Petition.**—Signed by applicant.

2. **Declaration.**—Signed by applicant. The declaration may be made before any official competent to take the same, but had better be made before a British Minister or Consul.

3. **Drawings in duplicate.**—On drawing board or tracing cloth, any convenient size. No signatures necessary.

4. **Specification in duplicate.**—Either provisional or complete. Should be written on legal cap, on one side only. May be signed either by the applicant or the agent.

5. **Power of Attorney.**—Signed by the applicant and two witnesses.

   The forms for the documents, except the specification, are the same as for British Honduras (which see), with the exception of the change in the name of the Colony, and the title of the Act, which for the Leeward Islands is "Patent Law Act, 1876." The form for the specification is also the same, with the exception that the first few lines should read:
   To all to whom these presents shall come: I, &c., &c., send greeting:—
   Whereas, His Excellency.........................Governor of the Leeward Islands, by Letters Patent bearing date the...........day of............A. D., in the.............year of Her Majesty's reign, did for Her Majesty, her heirs and successors, give and grant unto me, the said, &c., &c.
   The rest of the form is precisely the same.

Liberia.

CHARGES.

PATENT, cost of, all taxes paid $200 00
ASSIGNMENT, preparing and recording....................... 30 00
WORKING, the charge is variable, usually..................... 75 00

LAW AND PRACTICE.

Who may be Patentee.—The first and true inventor his heirs, executors, admin-strators or assigns.

Patents, Kind and Term.—There is but one form of patent ; this is granted for a term not to exceed twenty years.

Unpatentable.—The law is silent upon this point.

Novelty, Effect of Prior Patent or Publication.—The law requires that where the applicant is a citizen of Liberia, the invention must be one "not known or used by others within the limits of this Republic, and not described in any book or publication in this country" before the applicant's invention or discovery thereof. If the applicant is an alien, the invention must not have been known or used by others within the limits of the Republic at the time the application is filed. The holder of a prior foreign patent may obtain a valid Liberian patent at any time subject to the above requirement of novelty.

Taxes.—There are none after the issue of the patent.

Assignments.—Should be prepared in duplicate. Any usual form will answer.

Working.—Inventions for which aliens obtain patents must be worked ; "put in active operation in the Republic," within three years of the date of the patent.
In the absence of any decision upon this point, it is impossible to state just what amount or form of working is required. It is believed that in the case of machines or apparatus it will be sufficient to import the same into Liberia, and to operate or sell them there.

DOCUMENTS REQUIRED.

1. **Petition.**—Signed by the applicant.

2. **Power of Attorney.**—Signed by the applicant.

3. **Specification in duplicate.**—Signed by the applicant and two witnesses.

4. **Drawings in duplicate.**—Signed by the applicant in the lower right hand corner.

5. **Oath.**—Signed by the applicant before a Notary Public or a Consul of Liberia.

6. **A Certificate,** signed and sealed by the Mayor or Governor of the town in which the applicant resides, or by a Notary Public, to the effect that the applicant is the original and first inventor, or his legal assignee.

NOTE.—Our correspondent informs us that the Liberian Government has not prescribed forms for any of the documents, but says that the documents should be drawn and executed as for United States applications, the name of the country being changed, and the oath setting forth that the invention is not publicly known or used in the Republic of Liberia. The Petition will be addressed "To the Secretary of State." If the applicant is the assignee the documents must so state.

Luxembourg.

CHARGES.

* PATENT, cost of, all taxes paid for one year.....................$25 00
* PATENT OF ADDITION, all taxes paid..... .... 20 00

TAXES, *Payable annually, counting from the date of application, with three month's grace without fine.*

Second year..... ......$ 7 50		Ninth	year.............$21 50
Third " 9 50		Tenth	" 23 50
Fourth " 11 50		Eleventh	" 25 50
Fifth " 13 50		Twelfth	" 27 50
Sixth " 15 50		Thirteenth	" 29 50
Seventh " 17 50		Fourteenth	" 31 50
Eighth " 19 50		Fifteenth	" 33 50

ASSIGNMENTS, preparing and recording...................... 20 00
WORKING, exclusive of freight charges 15 00

*The above charge includes translation of the specification up to 2,000 words. 35 cents must be added for each 100 words in the specification in excess of 2,000.

LAW AND PRACTICE.

Who may be Patentee.—The first applicant; a person, firm or corporation. In case the applicant is not the inventor, however, it is desirable that he should obtain and keep the written consent of the latter, as the patent may be voided should it be proved that the essential features of the invention were taken from the descriptions, designs, models, instruments, tools or processes of another party without his consent.

Patents, Kind and Term.—Patents of Invention granted for fifteen years, subject to the payment of the prescribed taxes, and the proper working of the invention. Patents of Addition granted for the life of, and which expire with, the original patent.

It is useless to take a patent in Luxembourg unless a patent has been, or is to be applied for "in the States with which the Grand Duchy of Luxembourg has a custom house union," (this at present applies to Germany) within three months from the date of the filing of the application in Luxembourg. The Luxembourg patent will also become extinct if the patent applied for in such States be refused, or if having been allowed, it be revoked, annulled or become extinct in any other manner, except by reason of failure to work the invention. The term of the patent commences from the day following the day upon which the application is filed.

Unpatentable.—Inventions which have for their object food or other objects of consumption, pharmaceutical products or substances obtained by chemical means. Any special process for manufacturing these objects is patentable.

Novelty, Effect of Prior Patent or Publication.—An invention is not considered as patentable when at the moment the application is filed it is found to be already so clearly described in any printed matter open to the public, or so openly worked in either the Grand Duchy or any of the States of the German Custom House Union, as to render it possible for execution by other persons expert in the trade to which it refers. The holder of a prior foreign patent may obtain a valid patent in Luxembourg subject to the above requirement as to novelty.

Taxes.—Patents of Invention are granted subject to the payment of annual taxes. The tax amounts to 10 francs for the first year ; 20 francs for the second year, and so on, increasing at the rate of 10 francs each year. Three months' grace, without fine, is allowed for making the payment. No further prolongation of time for making payment can be obtained.

Assignments.—These should be prepared in duplicate, may be in either the French or German language, and must be legalized by a Consul for the Netherlands. It is preferable to have the documents prepared in Luxembourg.

We can obtain the legalization here, when desired, at a cost of $3.00, which includes Consular and Agency fees.

Working.—The patent can be revoked after three years from the date of the patent by a royal Grand Ducal decree, subject to an appeal to the Litigation Committee of the Council of State, if the patentee neglect to put his invention into operation in the Grand Duchy to a suitable extent, or at least to do everything necessary to insure this working. It is considered sufficient to import one or more of the articles into Luxembourg, and to expose them for sale ; or, if this be difficult or impossible, to insert an advertisement in the newspapers offering to supply any demand that may arise.

DOCUMENTS REQUIRED.

The documents required for Patents of Addition are precisely the same.

1. Specification.—Written or printed on any suitable paper. No signatures are required.

2. Drawings in triplicate.—On drawing board or tracing cloth, of any convenient size. No signatures are necessary.

3. Power of Attorney.—Signed by the applicant or applicants, all names in full, and legalized by a Consul for the Netherlands or attested by a Notary Public. The usual French power may be used. (See France.)

We can obtain the legalization here, when desired, at a cost of $3.00, which includes Consular and Agency fees.

Madagascar.

There is no patent law at present, nor do we believe that special grants, having the same force, would be allowed by the government.

Madeira Islands.

These Islands belong to Portugal and are covered by its patent.

Malta.

CHARGES.

PATENT, cost of, all taxes paid for two years....................$75 00
TAXES, (See "Taxes" below.)......................................
ASSIGNMENTS, Preparing and Recording....................... 17 50
WORKING, Nominal... 40 00

LAW AND PRACTICE.

Who may be Patentee.—The true and first inventor or his agent.

Patents, Kind and Term.—Patents of Invention granted for a term not exceeding fourteen years.   In case of inventions patented abroad the patent is granted for the unexpired term of such foreign patent.

Unpatentable.—The law is silent upon this point.

Novelty, Effect of Prior Patent or Publication.—The application must be filed before the invention has been made publicly known in Malta or elsewhere.   An inventor, or his representative to whom a patent has been granted in any other country may obtain a valid patent in Malta for the unexpired term of the original concession so long as the invention has not been made publicly known in any country.

Taxes.—The requirements are quite unusual and peculiar.   A tax of £1 with five per cent. on such portion of the profits as have arisen from the exclusive manufacture (the amount of which is to be declared by an affidavit of the applicant) must be paid every two years during the life of the patent.   As the law is not yet two years old, and we have had no occasion to make any such payments under it, we are unable to state an exact charge for attending to them.   We presume that $10.00 will cover agency fees.

Assignments.—These may be in any suitable form and should be in duplicate.   They should be legalized by a British Consul.
We can obtain the legalization here, when desired, at a cost of $2.50 for each legalization.

Working.—The law reads as follows : " An inventor may be required to assign his right, or to grant the use thereof, for a consideration to be determined by the competent Civil Court, if the invention or modification to which the patent refers shall not have been put into action within twelve months subsequent to the concession, or if its working shall have been suspended for twelve months continuously."   It is believed that it is not the intent of the law to compel the actual manufacture of the invention in Malta, but that it will be sufficient to import and sell the articles there.

DOCUMENTS REQUIRED.

1. Specification in duplicate.—Signed by the inventor.   The form of specification (heading and preamble to claims) may be the same as for British applications.

2. Drawings in duplicate.—May be made upon drawing paper or tracing cloth. and of any suitable size.   No signatures required.

3. Petition.—Signed by the inventor, and legalized by a British Consul.   The application should be addressed to "The Governor of Malta," and may be in the same form as for the Bahama Islands, which see.

4. Power of Attorney.—Signed by the inventor and legalized by a British Consul. It should be in the same form as for the Bahama Islands substituting the words " Ordinance No. XIII. of 1889," for the words "The Patent Act, 1889.
We can obtain the legalization here, when desired, at a cost of $2.50 for each legalization.

Martinique (West Indies).

This Island belongs to France and is covered by its patent.

Mauritius.

CHARGES.

* PATENT, cost of, all taxes paid...................... ....$150 00
ASSIGNMENTS, preparing and recording...................... 25 00

* The above charge is in full, except in case of possible opposition, for which special arrangements will be made in each case.

LAW AND PRACTICE.

Who may be Patentee.—The true inventor, his heirs, executors, administrators, and assigns. Joint inventors must make a joint application. The importer into Mauritius of a new invention is not deemed an inventor unless he is the actual inventor.

Patents, Kind and Term.—Patents of Invention granted for a term of fourteen years. The Governor in Council may extend the patent for a further term not exceeding fourteen years, if he thinks the circumstances warrant such extension. Patents based upon prior British patents cease to have effect if the British patents are revoked or cancelled, and expire with them at the end of their term.

Unpatentable.—Financial schemes and operations of credit, whether commercial or industrial; inventions patented abroad in respect whereof a patent has expired.

Novelty, Effect of Prior Patent or Publication.—To obtain a valid patent, the invention must not, at the time the application is filed, have been publicly used in Mauritius or in any part of the United Kingdom of Great Britain and Ireland, or been made publicly known in Mauritius or the United Kingdom by means of a publication either printed or written, or partly printed and partly written. But, an inventor having obtained a British patent may obtain a patent in Mauritius, provided the application be made within twelve months from the date of the British patent, although the invention be previously known or used in Mauritius, provided that such knowledge or use in Mauritius was not prior to the date of the British patent. The use of an invention in public by the inventor, or by his servants or agents, or by any other person with his license, for a period not exceeding one year prior to the date of the application, is not deemed a public use within the meaning of the ordinance.

Taxes.—There are none after the issue of the patent.

Assignments.—Must be registered and transcribed at the Mortgage Office. The documents may be prepared in any usual form, and should be in duplicate.

Working.—There are no requirements.

DOCUMENTS REQUIRED.

The papers should be written or printed on legal cap, on one side only.

1. **Petition in duplicate.**—Signed by the applicant, all names in full.

2. **Declaration in duplicate.**—Signed by the applicant.

3. **Specification in duplicate.**—Signed by the applicant and a witness.

4. **Drawings in duplicate.**—On drawing board or tracing cloth. No signatures required.

5. **Power of Attorney.**—Signed by the inventor and two witnesses.

PETITION.

To His Excellency, the Honorable Governor of Mauritius:

The humble petition of (*insert full name, address and occupation of applicant*).

Showeth:—

That your petitioner is in possession of an Invention for (*insert title of invention*), which invention he believes will be of great public utility; that he is the true and first inventor thereof, and that the same is not in use by any other person or persons, to the best of his knowledge and belief.

(*If a British Patent has been obtained, here state the fact, giving the number and date in the following form:*) That your Petitioner has obtained Letters Patent of Great Britain for the said invention, said Patent being numbered............of............and dated............)

Your Petitioner, therefore, humbly prays that Your Excellency will be pleased, in the name and on behalf of Her Majesty, the Queen, to grant unto him, his executors, administrators and assigns, Her Majesty's Letters Patent for this Island, for the term of fourteen years, pursuant to statute in that case made and provided. And your Petitioner will ever pray, &c.

The..................day of....................18......

Signature of Applicant.)

DECLARATION.

I, (*full name, address, and occupation of applicant*), do solemnly and sincerely declare that I am in possession of an invention for (*insert title as in petition*), which invention I believe will be of great public utility; that I am the true and first inventor thereof, and that the same is not in use by any other person or persons, to the best of my knowledge and belief; and that the instrument in writing, under my hand hereunto annexed, particularly describes and ascertains the nature of the said invention, and the manner in which the same is to be performed.

The..................day of....................18......

(*Signature of Applicant.*)

SPECIFICATION.

Specification of the invention of (*insert full name, address and occupation of applicant*) for (*insert title as in petition*).

(*Here proceed to describe the invention down to the claims.*)

Having thus described the nature of my invention, and in what manner the same is to be performed, I claim:

(*Insert claims.*)

In witness whereof, I, the said (*insert name of applicant*) have hereunto set my hand and seal this..............day of..............18....

(*Signature of witness.*)   (*Signature of Applicant.*) [L. S.]

POWER OF ATTORNEY.

Use the same form as for India (which see), changing the name of the Colony and the number of the Ordinance, which for Mauritius is " Ordinance No. 16, of 1875."

Mexico.

CHARGES.

*PATENT, cost of, all taxes paid..............................$150 00
PATENT, extension of term of old patents................ ..... 125 00
ASSIGNMENTS 30 00
WORKING, about.......... .... 50 00

*The above charge includes translation of the specification up to 2,000 words; 75 cents must be added for each 100 words in the specification in excess of 2,000.

LAW AND PRACTICE.

Who may be Patentee.—The actual inventor or his lawful representative.

Patents, Kind and Term.—Patents of Invention granted for twenty years, counting from the day of issue, but in case prior foreign patents exist, the Mexican patent will expire with the foreign patent first granted. A patent may be extended for an additional term of five years, in exceptional cases, if the Executive sees fit to do so. The term of existing ten year patents may be prolonged up to a maximum term of twenty years under the new law, upon payment of an additional tax and stamp duty.

Unpatentable.—Inventions or improvements the employment of which is contrary to the prohibitive laws, or to public security ; scientific principles or discoveries, being at the same time merely speculative and not capable of being transformed into a machine, apparatus, instrument, or a mechanical or chemical process or operation, of a practical industrial character.

Novelty, Effect of Prior Patent or Publication.—To obtain a valid patent, the application must be filed before the invention has received sufficient publicity in Mexico or elsewhere to enable it to be worked or executed. This does not, however, include publication of the invention by foreign patent offices, or publicity given in exhibitions. Subject to the above requirement with regard to novelty, a valid Mexican patent can be obtained at any time upon inventions already patented in other countries.

Taxes.—There are none after the issue of the patent.

Assignment.—The document should be prepared in the Spanish language, and must be legalized by a Mexican Consul.

We can obtain the legalization here, when desired, at a cost of $6.00.

Working.—Section 33 of the law requires that a patentee must prove within five years from the date of the patent (the patent dates from its issue) that the patented article is made or used in the Republic or that the necessary steps have been taken to establish such an employment or manufacture. This term cannot be extended and the penalty for non-compliance is the forfeiture of the patent.

DOCUMENTS REQUIRED.

1. **Specification.**—Written or printed on any suitable paper. No signatures required.

2. **Drawings in duplicate.**—On tracing cloth or tracing paper, any convenient size. No signatures required.

3. **Power of Attorney.**—Signed by the applicant or applicants, all names in full, and legalized by a Mexican Consul. The form is the same as for the Argentine Republic (which see).

We can obtain the legalization here, when desired at a cost of $6.00, which includes Consular and Agency fees.

Monaco.

There is no patent law in force, nor do we know of any way in which inventions may be protected there.

Montenegro.

There is no patent law in force, and apparently no disposition on the part of the government to give protection to inventions in any way.

Morocco.

There is no patent law in force as yet, and but little probability that the government would allow special grants affording protection to inventions.

Micquelon.

This Island belongs to France, and is covered by its patent.

Natal.

CHARGES.

```
*PROVISIONAL PROTECTION for six months.................$50 00
 COMPLETING APPLICATION...............................  50 00
                                                       --------
      Total.........................................  $100 00
*COMPLETE PATENT in first instance, all taxes paid for three
      years......................................... ...  90 00
 TAXES, at or before the expiration of three years.................  35 00
     "       "      "           "          seven  "  .................  60 00
 ASSIGNMENTS, preparing and recording......................  40 00
```

*This charge does not include the cost of a possible opposition, for which special arrangements will be made in each case.

The application may be made with either a provisional or a complete specification; in case of the former, the complete specification must be filed within six months of the date of the application.

LAW AND PRACTICE.

Who may be Patentee.—The true and first inventor. The interpretation clause of the Act provides that the word "invention shall bear and have the same meaning as it has in the Act of the Imperial Parliament, the 15th and 16th of Her Majesty, c, 83, entitled, 'An Act for Amending the Law for Granting Patents for Inventions;'" and in the absence of any judicial decision upon the subject in the Colonial Courts, it seems probable the judges would follow the English and the Colonial precedents and construe the " true and first inventor " to include the true and first importer within the Colony.

Patents, Kind and Term.—Patents of Invention granted for fourteen years, subject to the payment of the prescribed taxes. The patent will expire with the first expiring prior foreign patent. The Lieutenant-Governor is empowered to grant an extension of the patent, should the circumstances warrant, for an additional term of not more than fourteen years. The patent dates from the day the application is filed.

Unpatentable.—A valid patent cannot be obtained in Natal for an invention, the subject of a foreign patent which has already expired.

Novelty, Effect of Prior Patent or Publication.—The invention must not have been publicly used in Natal before the application for the patent. Prior patenting or publication in other countries will not prevent the obtaining of a perfectly valid patent providing the invention has not been publicly used in Natal at the time the application is filed.

Taxes.—A tax of £5 must be paid before the expiration of the third year of the life of the patent, counting from the date of the filing of the application, and a further tax of £10, before the expiration of the seventh year. No prolongation of the time for making payment can be obtained.

Assignments.—Should be prepared in duplicate. Any usual form may be employed.

Working.—There are no requirements.

DOCUMENTS REQUIRED.

The documents required and the forms are precisely the same as for Cape Colony (which see), except that the words "Attorney-General" should be substituted for the words "Colonial Secretary" wherever they occur; the name of the colony should be changed; and the title of the Act should read "Act No. 4, of 1870". All the documents including the Specifications (except the drawings) must be signed by the inventor, and the place and date of execution must be given.

Netherlands (Holland).

There is no patent law at present, but it is probable that there will be one soon, as earnest efforts are being made to secure the passage of a liberal law. The Netherlands is a member of the International Convention for the protection of industrial property.

New Caledonia.

See France.

Newfoundland.

The Patent covers Newfoundland and the Eastern coast of Labrador.

CHARGES.

PATENT, cost of, all taxes paid.............................$150 00
RE-ISSUE.................................. .... 150 00
ASSIGNMENT, preparing and recording........................ 15 00
WORKING... 50 00

LAW AND PRACTICE.

Who may be Patentee.—The true inventor, or the owner of a prior foreign patent ; but the assignee cannot make the application in case of an invention made abroad for which no Letters Patent have been obtained.

Patents, Kind and Term.—Patents of Invention granted for fourteen years. In exceptional cases the Governor in Council may insert in the Letters Patent a provision extending the operation thereof for a further term of seven years. In case there are prior foreign patents, the patent will expire with the first expiring foreign patent.

Unpatentable.—A valid patent cannot be obtained in Newfoundland for an invention the subject of a foreign patent which has already expired.

Novelty, Effect of Prior Patent or Publication.—The invention must not, prior to the filing of the application have been known or used, either in the Island or elsewhere, except it has been patented in some other country, in which case it must not have been introduced into public and common use in Newfoundland.

Taxes.—There are none after the issue of the patent.

Assignments.—The documents may be drawn in any suitable form, and should be in duplicate. It is preferable to have them executed before a Notary Public.

Working.—The invention must be brought into operation in Newfoundland within two years of the date of the patent, or the patent will become void. In the absence of any judicial decisions upon this point we cannot say what will constitute a legal working. We are advised, however, that it is believed that the importation and the sale of the patented article in Newfoundland, in quantities sufficient to meet all demands, will be adequate,

Special.—*MODELS OR SPECIMENS.* Section V. of the law provides that in case the invention relate to a machine, that the applicant shall furnish a model ; or, where the invention is a composition of matter, he must furnish specimens of the ingredients and composition of matter sufficient in quantity for the purpose of experiment. The Governor in Council may dispense with the delivery of a model in case of complicated machinery, where the cost may be so great as to prevent any ingenious but poor person from obtaining a patent if the delivery of the model were insisted upon. We should remark here that, while the delivery of a model may be insisted upon with any application, we have found in actual practice that models are not frequently demanded.

DOCUMENTS REQUIRED.

1. **Petition.**—Signed by applicant.

2. **Oath.**—Signed by applicant. The oath may be taken in Great Britain or Ireland, before the Mayor of a city or borough, certified under the corporate seal ; or in any other country before a British Consul or Vice-Consul, and must be certified under his seal of office.

3. Specification in duplicate.—Signed by the applicant and two witnesses. May be written on legal cap, on one side only.

4. Drawings in duplicate.—On any suitable material, tracing cloth preferred, and of any size. No signatures required.

4. Power of Attorney.—Signed by applicant and two witnesses.

6. Model or Specimens.—(See " Special.—Models or Specimens".)

FORMS.

PETITION.

To the Governor of the Province of Newfoundland :

The petition of (*full name, address and occupation of applicant*).
Showeth :

That he hath invented new and useful improvements in (*insert title of invention*), not known or used by others before his invention thereof.

Your petitioner, therefore prays that a patent may be granted to him for the said invention, as set forth in the specification sent herewith, according to the law in such cases made and provided.

(*Signature.*)

(*Place and date of signing.*)

SPECIFICATION.

To all whom it may concern :

Be it known that I (*insert full name, address and occupation of applicant*), have invented a new and useful improvement in (*insert title of invention*), of which the following is a description (*here describe the invention, referring to the drawings, if any.*)

In witness whereof, I have hereunto set my hand in the presence of two attesting witnesses.

(*Signatures of Witnesses.*)   (*Signature of Applicant.*)

............of............

............of............

(*Place and date of signing.*)

OATH.

.... }
.... }

I, (*full name, address and occupation of applicant*), make oath and say, that I verily believe that I am the inventor of the new and useful improvements in (*title of invention*) described and claimed in the annexed specification, and for which I solicit a patent by my petition, dated (*date of petition*); and that, to the best of my knowledge and belief, the said invention has never before been known or used by any person or persons in the Island of Newfoundland, or in any other country.

(*Signature of Applicant.*)

Sworn and subscribed to before me, this................day of..........................18....

[*Official Seal.*]   (*Signature and title of official administering oath.*)

POWER OF ATTORNEY.

I, the undersigned (*name of applicant*), do hereby retain, constitute and appoint...............
as my agent and attorney, to apply for and obtain from the Government of Newfoundland Letters Patent for (*insert title of invention*): and I authorize him to sign my name to such papers and writings, and do such acts regarding the same, including the appointment of a substitute or substitutes, as may be necessary or expedient.

Dated this....................day of..........................18....

Signed, sealed and delivered at................... {
In presence of............................... }   (*Signature of Applicant.*) [L. S.]

𝔑𝔢𝔴 𝔖𝔬𝔲𝔱𝔥 𝔚𝔞𝔩𝔢𝔰.

CHARGES.

PROVISIONAL PROTECTION for twelve months........ .... $30 00
COMPLETING PATENT, all taxes paid....................... 40 00

$70 00
COMPLETE PATENT in first instance, all taxes paid 60 00
ASSIGNMENTS, if consideration is nominal................... 18 50
    "   "   real, and less than $500.................. 15 00
    "   "   more than $500, add $2.50 for each $500 ...

LAW AND PRACTICE.

Who may be Patentee.—An application for a patent or for provisional protection may be made by any person, provided he claims to be either—1. The author or designer of an invention ; 2. the inventor's agent ; 3. the inventor's assignee ; 4. the introducer into the Colony of an invention new to the Colony ; 5. the introducer as to one part of the invention, and the inventor as to the other part ; 6. or the agent or assignee of any person claiming under any of the four preceding sub-sections. Letters Patent and Certificates of provisional protection may also be applied for by trading associations or other corporate bodies; or joint application may be made—1. by individuals ; 2. by two or more corporate bodies ; or, 3. by an association of one or more corporate bodies with one or more individual applicants. The Attorney-General decided in December, 1885, that a patent might be granted to a local agent for a " communicated " invention, and it is presumed that this practice will hold good in future, or until the law is amended.

Patents, Kind and Duration.—Provisional Protection granted for a term of twelve months; Patents of Invention granted for a term of fourteen years counting from the date of the filing of the application.

Unpatentable.—Any invention or improvement in the arts or manufactures may be made the subject matter of a patent, unless such invention or improvement appears to be detrimental to public health, public welfare, morality, or the interest of the State. Scientific principles or theories cannot be patented, but the practical application of them to industrial ends may form the subject of a patent.

Novelty, Effect of Prior Patent or Publication.—The application should be filed before the invention has been published, made, sold or used in New South Wales. Publication of the invention, or the issue of prior patents in other colonies or countries, will not prevent an inventor from obtaining either a patent or provisional protection in New South Wales, unless—1. the invention has been introduced into public use in New South Wales prior to the filing of the application ; or unless 2. such invention has been wholly or in part anticipated in a prior patent or certificate of provisional protection.

Taxes.—There are none after the issue of the patent.

Assignments.—All assignments or licenses are required to be registered in the Patent Office within the following respective periods from the date of execution: 1. within the colony, 14 days ; 2. from any of the other Australian colonies, 30 days ; 3. other places, 90 days. In view of this fact, it sometimes becomes necessary to send out these documents unexecuted, with a power of attorney in blank, authorizing the execution thereof by our agents. In some cases, solicitors prefer to send them out already executed, but not dated, leaving this to be inserted in the colony, but as the Act requires them to be registered within ninety days of their *execution* (and not of their *date*), it seems to be questionable whether this is a correct proceeding. The documents must be in the English language, and in duplicate ; any suitable form.

Working.—There are no requirements.

DOCUMENTS REQUIRED.

1. **Petition.**—Signed by applicant. May be written on any paper. Does not need to be witnessed. Both copies should be originals, that is, not "carbon" copies.

2. **Specification in duplicate.**—Signed by applicant. On any paper. No witnesses needed.

3. **Drawings in duplicate.**—One copy must be made upon stout, white, smooth surfaced drawing paper, and the other copy upon similar paper, parchment or tracing cloth, the sheets of which should be 8 inches wide by 13 inches high ; or 16 inches wide by 13 inches high, having a margin line all around one inch from the edge of the sheet. No signatures required.

4. **In Case of a Communicated Invention an Appointment of Agent.**—Signed by applicant. On any paper.

5. **If the Applicant is an Assignee**, proof of the assignment must be furnished.

FORMS.

PETITION BY A SOLE INVENTOR.

To His Excellency the Governor of the Colony of New South Wales:—
  The humble Petition of (*John Jones, of* 65 *Canal Street, New York City, New York, Machinist,*) Showeth—
  1. That your Petitioner is the author or designer of a certain invention in, or improvement to, the Arts or Manufactures for which he is desirous of obtaining Letters Patent of the Colony of New South Wales.
  2. That communications from the Patents Office relative to this application may be forwarded to your Petitioner's Agent.. ...
  3. That in connection herewith your Petitioner has paid to the Colonial Treasurer the sum of five pounds sterling.
  4. That the title of the invention is (*insert title*).
  5. That to the best of your Petitioner's knowledge and belief, the invention has not been publicly used, or published, or offered for sale within the Colony of New South Wales (*when the invention is the subject of Provisional Protection, add the following :—*"Except under the authority of a Certificate of Provisional Protection dated (*insert date*) for the invention in question.")
  6. That a detailed Specification of the invention, (*if drawings accompanying the specification add the words :—*"illustrated by drawings,") is annexed to this Petition.
  Your Petitioner therefore humbly prays that your Excellency, with the advice of the Executive Council, will be pleased to grant unto him, his executors, administrators, and assigns, Letters Patent for the said invention for the term of fourteen years, in accordance with the provisions of the Act 16 Victoria, No. 24, and of the Patents Law Amendment Act of 1887.
  And your Petitioner will ever pray, &c.

(*Signature.*)
Dated at (*place and date of signing*).

PETITION BY AN INTRODUCER OF AN INVENTION.

The preamble, parts 2, 3, and 4, and the ending are the same as in form above.
Parts 1, 5, and 6 should be changed so as to read :—
  1. That your Petitioner is the author or designer, by virtue of a communication from abroad, of a certain invention in, or improvement to, the Arts or Manufactures, which he desires to introduce into the Colony of New South Wales, and for which he is desirous of obtaining Letters Patent of the said Colony.
  5. That to the best of your Petitioner's knowledge and belief, the invention has not been publicly used or offered for sale within the Colony of New South Wales.
  6. That a detailed specification, illustrated by drawings, is annexed to this Petition.
  Your Petitioner, therefore, humbly prays, etc.

PETITION BY AN APPLICANT WHO IS THE INTRODUCER AS TO ONE PART OF THE INVENTION AND THE INVENTOR AS TO THE OTHER PART.

The preamble, parts 2, 3, 4, and 5, and the ending are the same as in the first form.
Part 7 should be added, and parts 1 and 6 changed so as to read :—
  1. That your Petitioner is the author or designer (partly by virtue of a communication from abroad) of a certain invention in, or improvement to, the Arts or Manufactures, which he desires to introduce into the Colony of New South Wales, and for which he is desirous of obtaining Letters Patent of the said Colony.

6. That a detailed Specification of the invention illustrated by drawings, is annexed to this Petition, and discriminates between the part invented and the part communicated.

7. That the details of the communication from abroad are specified in a document hereto appended.

Your Petitioner, therefore, humbly prays, etc.

PETITION BY AN INVENTOR'S AGENT.

The preamble, ending, and parts 2, 3, 4, 5 and 6 are as in the first form.

Part 1 should be changed so as to read :—

1. That your Petitioner is the Agent of (*here insert the inventor's full name, residence and occupation*), who claims to be the author or designer of a certain invention in, or improvement to, the Arts or Manufactures for which he is desirous of obtaining Letters Patent, in the Colony of New South Wales.

PETITION BY THE INVENTOR'S ASSIGNEE.

The form is the same as for an " Inventor's Agent," except that Part 1 should read :—

1. That your Petitioner is the Assignee of (*here insert the inventor's full name, residence and occupation*), who claims to be the author or designer of, &c.

Where the applicant is the agent of the Assignee, the form will be as follows :—

is the agent of *A. B.*, the assignee of *C. D.*, who claims to be the author, &c.

PETITION FOR AN INVENTOR AND AN ASSIGNEE, JOINTLY.

As in the first form, except that Part 1 should read as follows :—

1. That your Petitioner (*name of inventor*), is the author or designer of a certain invention in, or improvement to, the Arts or Manufactures, that your Petitioner (*name of assignee*), is the assignee of one-half share of and in the same, and that your Petitioners are desirous of obtaining Letters Patent of the Colony of New South Wales, for the said invention.

PETITION FROM A CORPORATE BODY.

As in the first form, except as to the following particulars :—

1. That your Petitioners are the assignees of (*name of inventor*), who claims to be the author or designer of a certain invention in, or improvement to, the Arts or Manufactures, for which they are desirous of obtaining Letters Patent of New South Wales.   *   *   *   *   *   *

Your Petitioners, therefore, humbly pray that Your Excellency, with the advice of the Executive Council, will be pleased to grant unto them, their successors and assigns, &c.

Should be signed in the following form :

		(*Name of Company.*)
Seal of the	By,	(*Name of Officer signing.*)
		(*Title of his Office.*)
Corporation.		

SPECIFICATION.

Specification of

(*insert full name, full address, and occupation of applicant*) for an invention entitled (*insert title of invention.*)

(*Here follows the specification and claims.*)

(*Signature.*)

Dated this (*insert place and date of execution*).

Witness.

APPOINTMENT OF AGENT.   (IN CASE OF COMMUNICATED INVENTION).

Whereas I, (*insert full name, full address, and occupation of applicant*), am the inventor of an invention entitled (*insert title of invention*), for which I am about to apply for Letters Patent in the Colony of New South Wales, I do hereby appoint.. my Agent to represent me in all matters relating to the said application for Letters Patent, and I hereby give him full power to apply for the said patent in his name as my nominee.

Dated this.................day of................one thousand eight hundred and ninety...........

(*Signature.*)

Witness.

ional Protection.

2. That communications from the Patents Office relative to this application may be forwarded to your Petitioner's agent,...

3. That in connection herewith your Petitioner has paid to the Colonial Treasurer the sum of two pounds sterling.

4. That the title of the invention is (*insert the title of the invention*).

5. That, to the best of your Petitioner's knowledge and belief the invention has not been publicly used, or published, or offered for sale, within the Colony of New South Wales.

6. That a detailed specification of the invention, illustrated by drawings, is annexed to this Petition.

Your Petitioner, therefore, humbly prays that your Excellency, with the advice of the Executive Council, will be pleased to grant unto him, his executors, administrators, and assigns, a Certificate of Provisional Protection, in respect of the said invention, and in accordance with the provisions of the "Patents Law Amendment Act of 1887."

And your Petitioner will ever pray, &c. (*Signature.*)

Dated at (*insert place and date of signing*).

NOTE.—Where the Petitioners for Provisional Protection claim to be the agents or assignees of an inventor, or part introducers and part inventors, or where they represent the association of an inventor and his assignee, or of an inventor's assignee and the holder of a sub-assignment, see the corresponding forms of Petition for Letters Patent, and alter the form so as to adapt the language to the relative circumstances of each case.

Omit "illustrated by drawings" where no drawings are furnished.

PROVISIONAL SPECIFICATION.

Provisional Specification of (*insert the full name, address and occupation of applicant*), for an invention entitled (*insert title of invention*).

(*Here follows description of invention, without reference to drawings, and without claims.*)

(*Signature.*)

Dated this...............day of.......................18....

Witness,

NOTE.—When an applicant applies for Provisional Protection or Letters Patent as the assignee of the whole of an invention, he must furnish an assignment, as per following form :—

PROOF OF ASSIGNMENT OF THE ENTIRE INTEREST IN AN UNPATENTED INVENTION.

For the information of the Examiner of Patents, Sydney, New South Wales, I, (*insert name, address and occupation of assignor*), do hereby acknowledge and declare that I am the author or designer of a certain invention entitled (*insert title of invention*), and that I have assigned all right, title, and interest (or an undivided part interest) in and to the said invention, so far as the Colony of New South Wales is concerned (*insert name and address of assignee*), with full power for the said (*name of assignee*) to apply for and obtain Letters Patent for the said invention in the said colony, in his own name (*or in our joint names*).

Dated this (*insert place and date of execution*).

(*Signature.*)

Witness.

When he applies jointly with the inventor as being part assignee of the invention, no assignment is required to be furnished.

New Zealand.

CHARGES.

```
* PROVISIONAL PROTECTION, for nine months................$30  00
† COMPLETING PATENT, all taxes paid for four years...........30  00
                                                            ──────
                                                            $60  00
    † COMPLETE PATENT IN FIRST INSTANCE, all taxes paid for
      four years....................................................  50  00
    ‡ TAXES, upon patents, granted on and after January 1, 1890.
      Before  the  expiration  of  the  fourth  year.................. 35  00
        "            "            "       seventh  "   ....................60  00
    ASSIGNMENTS............. . ..............................17  50
```

    * An extension of time, (not however, to exceed three months) for the filing of the complete
specification can be obtained upon application. The cost of obtaining such an extension, including the government fees of £6, amounts to $40.00.
    † In case the application is opposed or rejected, an additional expense will be incurred, the
amount of which will depend upon the time and work involved.
    ‡ In case the patentee fails from any cause to pay the tax within the required time, an exten-
sion of time, not to exceed three months, can be obtained for making the payment. The cost of
obtaining such an extension, including the government fees of £4, amounts to $30.

LAW AND PRACTICE.

Who may be Patentee.—The true and first inventor; the inventor and assignee or
assignees; the assignee or assignees of the inventor; the nominee or nominees of the
inventor; or the legal representative of a deceased inventor provided he makes the
application within six months of the decease of such inventor. Joint inventors may
obtain a joint patent.   The unauthorized importer of an invention is not entitled to a
patent.

Patents, Kind and Term.—Patents of Invention granted for fourteen years from
the date of the acceptance of the specification.   Provision is made for extending the term
of a patent for seven years, and in exceptional cases for fourteen years.

Unpatentable.—The Registrar may refuse to grant a patent for an invention, the
use of which would in his opinion be contrary to law or morality, or if he knows that
the alleged invention is not new.

Novelty, Effect of Prior Patent or Publication.—The application should be filed
before the invention has been published, or been publicly known or used within
New Zealand. Prior publication or prior patenting in any other country will not prevent the obtaining of a perfectly valid patent provided the invention is new as to New
Zealand at the time the application is filed. The exhibition of an invention at any
colonial, intercolonial or international exhibition will not prejudice the right of an
inventor to apply for and obtain a patent, provided: That in the case of an exhibition
held at any place within the colony: (a) the exhibitor must, before exhibiting the
invention, give the Registrar notice of his intention to do so; and, (b) the application
for patent must be filed within six months from the date of the opening of the exhibition.   In case of an exhibition held at any place outside the colony, the foregoing conditions also apply; but the Governor may exempt the exhibitor from giving the previous
notice to the Registrar. By an order in Council, the provisions of Section 103 of the
British Patents Act, 1883, are applied to New Zealand, and any person who has applied
for protection in England or in any foreign State, a party to the International Convention, is entitled to a patent in priority to any other applicant, provided the application is filed within twelve months from the date of the filing of the English or foreign
application.

Taxes.—A tax of £5 is payable before the expiration of the fourth year of the duration of the patent, counting from the date of the acceptance of the specification; and a

further tax of £10 is payable before the expiration of the seventh year. If a patentee, through inadvertance, accident or mistake, fails to pay a fee within the required time, he may obtain an extension of the time for making such payment, not, however, to exceed three months, upon application and the payment of government fees amounting to £4.

Assignments.—The documents should be in the English language and in duplicate, and must be accompanied by a request to enter name in register, signed by the assignee. No regulations have been made as to the material upon which the assignments and request are to be made, nor have any forms been prescribed. It is suggested that the same forms be used as for British assignments, as these will undoubtedly be accepted.

Working.—There are no requirements as to working, in respect of patents granted on and after January 1, 1890. Patents granted before that date will probably still be required to be worked within two years of their date, although there is some doubt in the minds of some of our correspondents as to the necessity of such working.

DOCUMENTS REQUIRED.

1. Application.—Signed by the applicant and two witnesses.

2. Specification in duplicate.—Signed by the applicant. One of the copies should be certified by the applicant in the following form : " I certify this to be a true copy " and such certification should be signed by the applicant.

3. Drawings in duplicate.—Upon tracing cloth or white drawing paper, the sheets of which should, preferably, not exceed two feet square in size. The drawings must not be folded, and must be signed by the applicant.

4. If the applicant is the assignee or nominee of the inventor, an assignment or authority from the inventor must be furnished, together with a statutory declaration that he is the *bona fide* assignee or nominee of the inventor.

5. If the applicant is the legal representative of a deceased inventor, the application must contain a declaration that the applicant believes such inventor to have been the true and first inventor of the invention, and must be accompanied by an office copy of, or extract from his will, or the letters of administration granted, and such copy or extract must be properly certified.

FORMS.

APPLICATION FOR PATENT.

I, *(insert name, address, and occupation of applicant)*, hereby declare that I am, *(or, that A. B. of —— and I are,* (*as the case may be*) in possession of an invention for *(insert title of invention)*; that I am (*or that A. B. is, as the case may be*) the true and first inventor thereof; and that the same is not in use by any other person or persons to the best of my knowledge and belief; and I humbly pray that a patent may be granted to me (*or us*) for the said invention as described in the specification herewith.

Witness :—

(Signature).

Dated this *(insert place and date of signing).*

COMPLETE SPECIFICATION.

I, *(here insert name, address, and occupation of applicant)*, do hereby declare the nature of my invention for *(insert title of invention)* and in what manner the same is to be performed to be particularly described and ascertained in and by the following statement :—
(Here insert the specification, adding the following just before the claims :) Having now particularly described and ascertained the nature of my said invention, and in what manner the same is to be performed, I declare what I claim is.
(Here insert the claims.)

(Signature of Applicant.)

Dated this *(insert place and date of signing).*

PROVISIONAL SPECIFICATION.

I, (*here insert name, address and occupation of applicant,*) do hereby declare the nature of my invention for (*insert title*) to be as follows:—

(*Here insert description of invention.*)

(*Signature.*)

Dated this (*insert place and date of signing.*)

Nicobars Islands.

See India.

Nicaragua.

There is as yet no patent law in this country. The government will, however, grant protection for inventions by way of special Legislative Act, provided the invention is likely to prove of practical utility in the country.

The cost of such grants varies considerably. We will, however, undertake to procure them at a charge of $300 each, but we will have to ask for an additional remittance in case the cost exceeds this sum. This amount will undoubtedly be sufficient in most cases.

DOCUMENTS REQUIRED.

The same as for Chili. The Power of Attorney must be legalized by a Nicaraguan Consul.

We can obtain the legalization here when desired at a cost of $3.00.

Norway.

CHARGES.

* PATENT, cost of, all taxes paid for one year.....................$35 00
* PATENT OF ADDITION, all taxes paid...................... .... 35 00
TAXES, *payable annually counting from the date of application, with three months' grace ; but, in such case, with the addition of one-fifth of the tax then payable. No taxes are payable on Patents of Addition.*

Second	year	.........$ 6 25	Ninth	year	............$15 00
Third	"	.... 7 50	Tenth	"	.... 16 25
Fourth	"	.... 8 75	Eleventh	"	.... 17 50
Fifth	"	.... 10 00	Twelfth	"	.... 18 75
Sixth	"	.... 11 25	Thirteenth	"	.... 20 00
Seventh	"	... . 12 50	Fourteenth	"	.... 21 25
Eighth	"	.... 13 75	Fifteenth	"	.... 22 50

FIRST APPEAL (in case of refusal).............................. 12 50
† SECOND APPEAL (to Superior Commissioner of Patents)........ 60 00
ASSIGNMENTS, preparing and recording 5 00
WORKING, exclusive of freight charges................. .... 20 00

*The above charge includes translation of the specification up to 2,000 words. Beyond this number, 50 cents must be added for each 100 words. In case the application requires amendment, a small additional charge must be made, the amount of the same being based upon the exact amount of time and work expended.
†Of this amount, $37.50 will be returned if the appeal is successful.

LAW AND PRACTICE.

Who may be Patentee.—The right of obtaining a patent belongs solely to the first inventor, or to him who derives his right from him. In case there are several applicants, and it cannot be clearly shown which was the first inventor, the patent will be granted to the person whose application was filed the earliest. Patents of Addition are granted to the original patentee *only*, during the term of two years from the date of the application for the original patent.

Patents, Kind and Term.—Patents of Invention granted for fifteen years, counting from the date of the application, subject to the payment of the prescribed taxes and the proper working of the invention. Patents of Addition are granted for the unexpired term of the original patent and expire with it.

Unpatentable.—Inventions, the use of which would be contrary to law, morality or public order; inventions, the subject matter of which is a beverage, food or medicine, although in respect of the latter the processes or apparatus specially adapted for their manufacture, may form the subject of a patent.

Novelty, Effect of Prior Patent or Publication.—The application should be made before the invention is so well known in Norway that it can be made use of by other persons. Publications in print or the exhibition of the invention will not prevent the obtaining of a valid patent, provided the application for the patent is made within six months thereafter. In case an application for a patent has been made in a foreign country, the application for the Norwegian patent may be made within seven months from the date of such foreign application.

Taxes.—Taxes are payable upon all patents (except Patents of Addition) in instalments, yearly in advance, counting from the date of the filing of the application. There is three months' grace for the making of these payments, but, in such case a fine must be paid which amounts to one-fifth part of the tax due and payable. The yearly taxes are as follows :—10 kroner for the second year, 15 kroner for the third, and so on, increasing 5 kroner each year. There are no yearly taxes on Patents of Addition.

Assignments.—The documents should be in duplicate, and should be drawn in accordance with the laws of the country where the parties concerned are domiciled ; they must be legalized by a Norwegian Consul, and be duly registered at the Norwegian Patent Office.

When desired, we can obtain the legalization here at a cost of $3.00 for each document, which includes Consular and Agency fees.

Working.—A patent must be worked within three years from the date of its issue, and such working must not be entirely discontinued thereafter for a year at a time. The Commissioners of Patents do not require proof that the patent has been worked. In the case of machinery or apparatus, it is considered sufficient to send one or more of the same to Norway, and have them exposed and advertised for sale. In case of a process, it should be carried into practice in the country. Proof of the working should be obtained each year.

DOCUMENTS REQUIRED.

(The documents required for Patents of Addition are precisely the same.)

1. Specification.—This may be written or printed on any paper. All measures and weights should be indicated by the metric system, and temperature by the Centigrade thermometer. No signatures are necessary.

2. Drawings in duplicate.—These should be made on one or more sheets of strong white drawing paper, or on tracing cloth, which must measure exactly 33 centimetres (13 inches) in height, by 21, 42 or 63 centimetres (8¼, 16½, or 24¾ inches) in width, with a single margin line drawn 2 centimetres (¹³⁄₁₆ inch) from the edge. No signatures are necessary.

3. Power of Attorney.—Signed by applicant, all names in full, and legalized by a Norwegian Consul.

When desired, we can obtain the legalization here at a cost of $3.00, which includes Consular and Agency fees.

Where the applicant is not the inventor, an assignment or similar instrument must be forwarded. This document must be legalized by a Norwegian Consul.

FORM.

POWER OF ATTORNEY.

FULDMAGT.

Undertegnede...
....
der önsker at erhverve patent i kongeriget Norge på...
....
og på senere, forbedringer derved, bemyndiger herved hr.........................i Christiania.
eller den han i sit sted dertil måtte bemyndige, til at være.........fuldmœgtig i denne sag og som
sådan at repræsentere........i alle patentet vedkommende anliggender samt at modtage stevnemål
på........vegne, alt i överensstemmelse med lov om patenter af 16de juni 1885.
      Place and date.............................18....
                                                              (Signature of applicant.)

Orange Free State.

CHARGES.

* † PROVISIONAL PROTECTION for six months..............$165 00
† ‡ COMPLETING APPLICATION, all taxes paid for seven years. 175 00

$340 00

† ‡ COMPLETE PATENT, in first instance, taxes paid for
      seven years.. 325 00
‖ § TAXES, payable on or before the expiration of the third year... 35 00
      "   "   "   " seventh year 65 00
      ASSIGNMENTS................................... 25 00

* Provisional protection may be obtained as a means of establishing priority, but actions against infringers can only be commenced after the complete patent has been obtained. Where provisional protection has been obtained the complete specification must be filed, if at all, before the expiration of six months from the date upon which the application for provisional protection was filed.

† The above charge covers translation of the specification up to 2,000 words. $1.00 must be added for every one hundred words in the specification in excess of 2,000. This charge does not include

the costs of possible opposition, the charge for which will be made the subject of special agreement in each case; nor does it cover reference fees if the Attorney-General calls in the services of experts as he is empowered to do. These expenses will seldom be incurred, however.

‡ The government fee upon the issue of a patent may be any amount from £10 to £50. Our charges, as above, include the payment of a fee of not more than £25, which is the average fee charged. Should the government fix the fee at a larger amount than £25, we shall be obliged to ask for an additional remittance to cover any amount in excess of this sum. It is believed that it will be seldom, if ever, necessary to ask for such additional remittance.

If the patentee fails, for any reason, to make the payment within the required time, an extension of time for making the payment, not to exceed three months, can be obtained upon application, and payment of a fine of £5. Our charge for obtaining the extension and paying the fee is $40.00

§ The patent must be produced for endorsement upon the payment of each tax.

LAW AND PRACTICE.

Who may be Patentee.—The actual inventor. With the inventor may be associated another person, a firm, or corporation. Joint inventors may obtain a joint patent. If an inventor, having obtained provisional protection, dies before obtaining a complete patent, his legal representatives may apply for and obtain the same, provided they do so within three months from the decease of the inventor. When the owner of an invention dies without having applied for a patent, his legal representatives may apply for and obtain a patent, provided they file the application within six months from the decease of the inventor.

Patents, Kind and Term.—Provisional Protection may be obtained for a term of six months. Patents of Invention are granted for a term of fourteen years from the date of the filing of the application. In exceptional cases patents may be prolonged for a further period not to exceed fourteen years. In case a prior foreign patent exists, the patent will expire with the foreign patent if the term of the latter is less than fourteen years, and if there be more than one foreign patent, will expire with that patent having the shortest term.

Unpatentable.—Inventions, the application of which the government may consider contrary to the laws, to the public safety and to good customs; inventions that have already been patented abroad, where such patent has expired.

Novelty, Effect of Prior Patent or Publication.—The application must be filed before the invention has been published or been publicly used in the Orange Free State. Prior publication or prior patenting of the invention in other countries will not prevent the obtaining of a perfectly valid patent, provided the invention is new as to the Orange Free State at the time the application is filed. The exhibition of the invention at an international or industrial exhibition, or the publication of the invention while the exhibition continues, or the use of the invention for making it known at the exhibition, or the use of the invention at some other place while the exhibition lasts, by another person not authorized by the inventor, will not invalidate the right of the inventor or his legal representatives to apply for provisional protection and to obtain a patent for the invention, provided due notice of the intention to make such exhibit is given in writing to the Attorney-General before the exhibit is exposed, and the application for patent is filed within six months after the close of the exhibition.

Taxes.—A tax of £5 is payable on or before the expiration of the third year of the life of the patent, counting from the date of the filing of the application, and £10 before the expiration of the seventh year. In case the applicant, through inadvertence, accident, or mistake, fails to pay a tax within the required time, a prolongation of the time for making payment can be obtained for a time not to exceed three months, upon making application, and paying a fine of £5. For our charges for obtaining such extension, see remarks under "Charges."

Assignments.—The documents should be in duplicate, signed by the assignor, and legalized by a Consul of the Orange Free State, and be accompanied by a Power of Attorney signed by the assignee, and legalized by a Consul of the Orange Free State, authorizing the recording of the assignment and the payment of the fees in connection therewith.

We can obtain the legalization here, when desired, at a cost of $5.00 for each legalization.

Working.—There are no requirements.

Special.—*COMPULSORY LICENSES.* If a person to whom the patentee refuses to grant a license, can prove the following facts to the satisfaction of the government :— (*a*) that the invention is not worked within the Orange Free State ; (*b*) that the invention is not worked in such a manner as to satisfy the reasonable demand of the public ; (*c*) that a party cannot apply and turn to full account an invention to which he has a claim ; the government can then enjoin the patentee to grant licenses under such conditions as it may deem equitable, with due allowance for the nature of the invention and the circumstances of the case.

DOCUMENTS REQUIRED.

1. **Application.**—Signed by applicant, and legalized by a Consul of the Orange Free State.

2. **Specification in duplicate.**—Signed by the applicant and legalized by a Consul of the Orange Free State.

3. **Drawings in duplicate.**—Signed by the applicant and legalized by a Consul of the Orange Free State.

4. **Power of Attorney.**—Signed by the applicant and two witnesses, and legalized by a Consul of the Orange Free State,

We can obtain the legalizations here, when desired, at a cost of $5.00 each.
The applicant is required to advertise the fact that he has made the application in a form prescribed by law, once in the Gouvernements Courant, once in another newspaper printed in Bloemfontein and twice in a newspaper published in or circulating in the place where the applicant uses his invention and lives. Copies of the papers containing these advertisements must be produced before the patent will be granted.

FORMS.

APPLICATION.

....
....
van beroep...
verklaar....hierbij dat...... ....bezit ben van eene uitvinding
voor...
....
dat...........de serste en ware uitvinder......daarvan..........; dat die uitvinding, voor zoover
.........................en geloof, niet toegepast of gebruikt wordt door eenen anderen persoon
of andere personen: en.............vcrrock....met verschuldigden serbied, dat.............voor
gezegde uitvinding een octrooi worde verleend.
....den..dag der maand
.......................van het jaar onzes Heeren.
                      (*Signature.*)..

PROVISIONAL SPECIFICATION.

....
....
van beroep..
verklaar....hierbij, dat.......................wezen.........................uitvinding
......................................van...
....
is als volgt: (*The specification is to be inserted here.*)
Verklaard op heden den.......... 189
                      (*Signature.*)

COMPLETE SPECIFICATION.

....
....
van beroep..
verklaar....hierbij, dat.......................wezen.........................uitvinding

FORM.

POWER OF ATTORNEY.

O abaixo assignado...............................morador..
pela presente procuração poderes a.....................................morador em Lisboa para
por.......................em.....................nome, obtenha do Governo Portuguez uma patente
de Invenção por................annos para..
....

Com este fim póde preencher todas as formalidades prescriptas pelas leis; fazer e assignar todas as declarações e requerimentos, assignar e depositar todos os documentos exigidos, retirar, sendo preciso os depositos passando recibos; pagar as respectivas taxas e impostos e substabelecer todos ou parte dos presentes poderes. Esta procuração terá força para pedir qualquer prorogação de praso ou certificado de addição a que esta patente possa dar logar.

Feita em.........aos............... ....

Portuguese Guiana.

A Portuguese Colony and covered by its laws.

Queensland.

The Patents, Designs and Trade Marks Act of 1884 has been amended by an Act of 1886, bearing the same title.

CHARGES.

* PROVISIONAL PROTECTION for 12 months					....	$25 00
* COMPLETING PATENT, all taxes paid for 4 years......						40 00
				Total Cost	....	$65 00
* COMPLETE, in first instance, taxes paid for 4 years............ ..						60 00
† TAXES, before end of 4 years from date of patent............						32 50
‚‘	‘‘	‘‘	8	‘‘	‘‘	‘‘ ....| 57 50

Or, in lieu of the above the following Annual Taxes :

Before end of 4th year from date of patent...					....	12 50
‘‘	‘‘	5th	‘‘	‘‘	‘‘	12 50
‘‘	‘‘	6th	‘‘	‘‘	‘‘	12 50
‘‘	‘‘	7th	‘‘	‘‘	‘‘	12 50
‘‘	‘‘	8th	‘‘	‘‘	‘‘	15 00
‘‘	‘‘	9th	‘‘	‘‘	‘‘	15 00
‘‘	‘‘	10th	‘	‘	‘‘	17 50
‘‘	‘‘	11th	‘‘	‘‘	‘‘	17 50
‘‘	‘‘	12th	‘‘	‘‘	‘‘	17 50
‘‘	‘‘	13th	‘‘	‘‘	‘‘	17 50
ASSIGNMENT, registering..						15 00

*The above charge does not cover the cost of possible oppositions, appeals, or rejections, in which cases there will be extra expenses based upon the amount of work involved; such expenses are seldom incurred, and will be made the subject of special agreement as to amount, in each individual case.

†In case the patentee fails, from any cause, to make payment of any tax within the prescribed time, an extension of time, not to exceed three months at most, can be obtained for making the payment. The government fees in such cases are: for enlargement of time not exceeding one month, 10 shillings; two months. 15 shillings; three months, £1.0.0, Our charge for obtaining such extensions, including the government fees, are; for one month, $7.50; two months, $8.75; three months, $10.00.

LAW AND PRACTICE.

Who may be Patentee.—The true and first inventor; the inventor and an assignee or assignees, the assignee or assignees of an inventor; the inventor and a capitalist. Patents for communicated inventions can no longer be obtained. Joint inventors may obtain a joint patent. If a person having obtained provisional protection dies, the patent may be granted to his legal representatives. And if a person possessed of an invention dies before filing his application, a patent may be obtained by his legal representatives, provided the application is filed within six months of the decease of such inventor.

Patents, Kind and Term.—Provisional Protection is granted for twelve months from the date of the filing of the application. Patents of Invention are granted for fourteen years, dated from the date of the filing of the application, subject to the payment of the prescribed taxes. The term of a patent may, in exceptional cases, be extended for an additional term of from seven to fourteen years.

Unpatentable.—The law is silent upon this point.

Novelty, Effect of Prior Patent or Publication.—The application should be filed before any publication or public use of the invention in Queensland. Prior publication or patenting of the invention in another country will not prevent the obtaining of a perfectly valid patent, provided the invention is new as to Queensland at the time the application is filed. The exhibition of the invention at an international or industrial exhibition, or the publication of the invention while the exhibition continues, or the use of the invention for the purpose of such exhibition in the place where the exhibition is held, or the use of the invention during the exhibition by any person elsewhere without the consent of the inventor, will not prejudice the right of the inventor or his legal representatives to apply for and obtain a patent, provided due notice of the intention to exhibit is given to the Registrar before the opening of the exhibition, and that the application is filed within six months after such opening.

Taxes.—Patents are granted subject to the payment of the following taxes; £5 before the expiration of the fourth year of the life of the patent, counting from the date of the filing of the specification, and £10 before the expiration of the eighth year; or in lieu of the above, taxes may be paid in annual installments, as follows: £1 before the expiration of each of the fourth, fifth, sixth and seventh years; £1. 10. 0 before the expiration of each of the eighth and ninth years; and £2 before the expiration of each of the remaining four years. If the patentee, through inadvertence, accident or mistake, fails to pay any tax within the required time, an enlargement of time, not, however, to exceed three months, may be obtained for making the payment. See "Charges" for amount of fees in such cases.

Assignments.—An assignment of a patent may be prepared upon any suitable material and of any size, and should be signed by the assignor and two witnesses. When forwarding same for registering the following must also be supplied, viz: (a) a request to enter name in register, and (b) an examined copy of the assignment. All other documents containing, giving effect to, or being evidence of, transmission of patent or effecting its proprietorship (except such documents as are matters of record), must be produced to the Registrar. When a document is a matter of record an official or certified copy must be supplied. The Registrar now refuses to register an assignment unless the patent assigned, or partly assigned, is produced at the same time, so that he may endorse thereon a certificate of the assignment registered. Inasmuch as it is essential that these documents be in the exact form prescribed by the Registrar, and the requirements change from time to time, it will be well to write for and obtain fresh forms whenever it is desired to record an assignment.

3. Power of Attorney.—Signed by applicant or applicants, all names in full, legalized by a Peruvian Consul. The form is the same as for the Argentine Republic (which see).

We can obtain the legalization here, when desired, at a cost of $4.00, which includes Consular and Agency fees.

Philippine Islands.

The same remarks apply as in the case of Porto Rico, which see.

Porto Rico.

Art. 8 of the Spanish Law provides that all patents shall be considered as granted, not only for the Peninsula and adjacent islands, but also for the provinces beyond the sea, thus including Porto Rico ; but before the patent can be enforced, or any legal formalities in connection with a patent, such as prosecution for infringement, transfer of rights, etc., take place in Porto Rico, the patent must be officially registered for the Colonies at the Colonial Office at Madrid. This may be done at any time during the life of the patent. Our charge for this registration is $10.00.

Portugal.

The patent covers Portugal and all her colonies, which include the Azores, Cape Verde and Madeira Islands.

CHARGES.

* PATENT, Cost of, all taxes paid for one year					$ 90	00
" " " "			five years		125	00
" " " "			ten "		175	00
" " " "			fifteen "		225	00
* PATENTS OF ADDITION, all taxes paid					40	00
† PROLONGATION OF PATENTS (*see note below*)					70	00
ASSIGNMENT, preparing and recording					35	00
WORKING, exclusive of freight charges				$50 00 to	75	00

* The above charge includes the translation of the specification up to 2,000 words. Beyond this number, 50 cents must be added for each 100 words.

† Where a patent has been obtained for less than the full term of fifteen years, the protection may be continued during the whole of that term by taking one or more *patents of prolongation* which must be applied for before the expiry of the patent to be prolonged. $7.50 must be added to the above charge for each year of the term for which the patent is to be prolonged.

LAW AND PRACTICE.

Who may be Patentee.—Practically, any one, whether the inventor or not, or a firm or corporation, may apply for a patent ; but if the applicant is not the inventor, it would be well to obtain and keep the written consent of the latter, so that should any question be raised at a future time, the patentee could produce proof that he obtained the Portuguese patent in his own name with the consent of the inventor.

Patents, Kind and Term.—Patents of Invention granted for from one to fifteen years as elected by the applicant. In case of a patent granted for a less term than fifteen years, it may be prolonged to the maximum term, either in a single prolongation or by successive prolongations of one or more years each. Patents of Addition are granted for the unexpired term of the original patent and expire with it. In case a prior foreign patent exists, the Portuguese patent cannot be granted for a longer time than the unexpired term of the foreign patent. The patent dates from the date of issue.

Unpatentable.—Inventions or discoveries relating to unlawful industries or articles; medicines; articles of food ; simple changes in the form of an article already patented ; and ornaments.

Novelty, Effect of Prior Patent or Publication.—An invention can be patented, although it may already be patented or be in public use in another country, but the application should be made before the invention is known to the public, practically or theoretically, through any technical description divulged in home or foreign documents, or by any other means.

Taxes.—There are none after the issue of the patent.

Assignments.—Transfers or sales of Portuguese Patents can, under Article 627, of the Civil Code, only be legally effected by a Notarial deed drawn up in Portugal, and endorsed by the Patent Office upon the original Letters Patent. The usual way is for the assignor to give power to an attorney residing in Portugal to sell, and the assignee to give power to another attorney to accept the sale. Both attorneys then go before a Lisbon Notary who inscribes the proper deed in his books, and gives two official copies thereof, one of which is delivered to the purchaser, and the other is filed at the Patent Office, the patent being handed in at the same time for endorsement.

Our charge for the legalization of the powers here is $3.00 each.

Working.—The invention must be worked within two years, counting from the date of the issue of the patent, and the working must not entirely cease thereafter for any two consecutive years. In the case of machinery or apparatus, it is considered sufficient to import one or more of the patented articles into Portugal, and there expose and advertise it or them for sale. Official proof of this working should be obtained. In case of a process, it should be carried into practice in Portugal and official proof thereof be obtained.

DOCUMENTS REQUIRED.

The documents required for Patents of Addition are precisely the same.

1. **Specification.**—Written or printed on any paper. No signatures necessary.

2. **Drawings in duplicate.**—On any material, tracing cloth preferred, and of any convenient size. No signatures required.

3. **Power of Attorney.**—Signed by the applicant and legalized by a Portuguese Consul.

We can obtain the legalization here, when desired, at a cost of $3.00, which includes Consular and Agency fees.

....van..

....

en de wijze van uitvoering daarvan nauwkeurig en in bijzondetheden worden uiteengezet door de volgeende beschrijving: (*Here insert the specification.*)

Verklaard op heden den..18....

POWER OF ATTORNEY.

BIJZONDERE LASTGEVING.

Ondergeteekende...

....

verklaar.....................bij deze te magtigen...

....

....

om namens...............en ten...............behoeve...

....

....

....

....

ten voorschreven einde in regten te verschijnen, zoowel eischende als verwerende in hooger beroep te komen, regterlijke magtigingen te vragen, Agenten en Procureurs te benoemen, benoodigde Acten en stukken te doen maken, te beteekenen en te doen teekenen, en in het algemeen datgene te doen wat vereischt wordt; alles met de magt van plaatsbekleeding, belofte van goedkeuring, schadeloosstelling, eene billijke belooning in verband als naar regten.

Geteekend te....................op den...

dag van...........................Achttien Honderd...

Als Getuigen

....   (*Signature.*)..............

....

Paraguay.

There is as yet no patent law in this country. The government will, however, grant protection for inventions by way of special Legislative Act, provided the invention is likely to prove of practical utility in the country. It should be noted that the proceedings to obtain such grants are slow and uncertain.

The cost varies considerably. We will, however, undertake to procure grants at a charge of $400 each, but we will have to ask for an additional remittance in case the cost exceeds this sum. This amount will be sufficient in most cases.

DOCUMENTS REQUIRED.

The same as for Chili. The power of attorney should be legalized by a Paraguayan Consul.

We can obtain the legalization, when desired, at a cost of $3.00.

Persia.

There is no patent law in this country and the only manner in which inventions can be protected is by way of a special grant, a costly and uncertain procedure and of doubtful value.

Peru.

CHARGES.

* PATENT, cost of, all taxes paid for one year....................$300 00
TAXES, *payable annually, counting from the date of application.*
    Each year... 115 00
ASSIGNMENTS, preparing and recording............. .... 50 00
WORKING, exclusive of cost of manufacture.................... 75 00

* The above charge includes translation of the specification up to 2,000 words. $1.25 must be added for each 100 words in the specification in excess of 2,000.

LAW AND PRACTICE.

Who may be Patentee.—The true and first inventor.

Patents, Kind and Term.—Patents of Invention granted for a term of ten years, counting from the date of the issue of the patent.   Extensions can only be obtained by special legislative act.

Unpatentable.—Pharmaceutical preparations, and remedies of every description ; financial schemes ; all operations to improve known industries the use of which is free both in and out of the Republic.

Novelty, Effect of Prior Patent or Publication.—Article 14 of the law provides as follows :   "Any discovery, invention, or application, either in Peru or any foreign country, that may exist, anterior to the date of application, and which shall have had sufficient publicity to have been put into use, will not be considered as new." It follows, therefore, that the application should be filed before the publication, or the public use or knowledge of the invention in any country.

Taxes.—A tax of $100 must be paid, yearly in advance, for each year of the life of the patent.   No prolongation of the time for making the payment can be obtained.

Assignments.—Should be prepared in duplicate in the Spanish language, and should be executed before a Notary Public, and be legalized by a Peruvian Consul. The consideration expressed should be nominal

We can obtain the legalization here, when desired, at a cost of $4.00 for each document, which includes Consular and Agency fees.

Working.—The invention must be worked in Peru within two years (the usual time), or within such other term as may be expressed in the patent, unless the cause of the delay can be legally justified.   The working must be actual and commercial, the manufacture being carried on in the country.

Special.—*IMPORTATION OF PATENTED ARTICLES.*—Article 15, Section 3 of the law, prohibits the importation of patented articles under pain of the forfeiture of the patent, with the exception of models of machinery, whose introduction shall be authorized after formal inspection by the Government.

DOCUMENTS REQUIRED.

1. **Specification.**—Written or printed on any suitable paper.   No signatures required.

2. **Drawings in duplicate.**—On drawing or tracing cloth, any suitable size.   No signatures required.

CHARGES.

* † PATENT of Invention for 3 years, all taxes paid						$ 90 00
"	"	5	"	"	"		120 00
"	"	10	"	"	"		300 00
"	of Importation for 1		"	"	"		70 00
"	"	2	"	"	"		100 00
"	"	3	"	"	"		135 00
"	"	4	"	"	"		170 00
"	"	5	"	"	"		210 00
"	"	6	"	"	"		245 00
* CAVEAT, all taxes paid							25 00
ASSIGNMENTS, preparing and recording							30 00
WORKING						from $40 00 to	50 00

*The above charge includes translation of the specification up to 2,000 words; 85 cents must be added for each 100 words in the specification in excess of 2,000.

†In case a patent is refused, the following amounts will be returned: On applications for patents of invention for three years, $30.00; five years, $60.00; ten years, $200.00. On applications for patents of improvement for one year, $20.00; two years, $40.00; three years, $75.00; four years, $100.00; five years, $140.00; six years, $175.00.

LAW AND PRACTICE.

Who may be Patentee.—Any person, a firm or corporation. The patentee may be the actual inventor or his assignee. Joint inventors are entitled to a joint patent. The proprietor of an invention, though not the inventor, or formal assignee, may generally obtain a valid patent of invention. The mere importer of an invention may obtain a valid patent of importation, but not a strictly valid patent of invention; yet patents thus obtained can be contested by the inventor only.

Patents, Kind and Term.—Patents of Invention are granted for either three, five or ten years, as elected by the applicant. A Patent of Importation is granted for one, two, three, four, five or six years, subject to the expiration of any prior foreign patent. A patent cannot be extended after its issue, but where an inventor has applied for a short term patent, and desires to enlarge its duration, the change in the term can usually be effected at any time within about six months after the filing of the application, by paying the difference in the cost, and an agency fee of $5.00 in addition. The term of a patent commences from the date of issue, but protection is afforded from the date the application is filed. A Caveat may be filed by an inventor who intends to make application for a patent, but in case a Caveat is filed the application must be lodged before the expiration of three months from the day upon which the Caveat was filed.

Unpatentable.—(a) Fundamental or elementary principles, without their application or combination produces some new results in the arts, presenting a special and new apparatus. (b) Trifling or unimportant discoveries, inventions or improvements indicative only of inventive genius, without offering any real advantages or utility. (c) Discoveries, inventions or improvements that may become dangerous to society or detrimental to the government revenues. (d) Medicines, although patents may be granted for cosmetics if reported to be harmless by the medical board. (e) Discoveries, inventions, or improvements relating to munitions of war, as, for instance, guns, projectiles, and other materials required for artillery, armor plates, torpedoes, gunpowder magazines, revolving turrets, etc., use of which can only be made by the government.

Articles which, although used by armies, may also be used by private persons, such as hand fire-arms, metallic cartridges, bullets, and other appurtenances of such arms, are capable of being patented; the grant still remaining subject to the rights of the Army and Navy Departments to use the inventions or improvements freely and without compensation. Although the government does not grant patents for improvements in munitions of war, the Army and Navy Departments are empowered to acquire, by purchase or gift, the benefit of any inventions relating to these improvements.

Novelty, Effect of Prior Patent or Publication.—The application should be made before the invention has been publicly worked in Russia. Prior patents, or publication of the invention in any other country will not prevent the obtaining of a perfectly valid patent, provided the application is filed before the public use and exercise of the invention within the Empire of Russia.

Taxes.—There are none after the issue of the patent.

Assignments.—The documents should be prepared in duplicate, and may be in any form, and in the language of the country in which the assignment is made. After execution, the assignment must be legalized by a Russian Consul, who must state that the transfer has been made according to the laws of the country in which it is executed. The assignment must be accompanied by a power of attorney, legalized by a Russian Consul, authorizing the execution of all legal formalities, in order to legalize the deed in Russia. There is no prescribed form for this power. The consideration expressed should be nominal.

When desired, we can procure the legalization of these documents here at cost of $3.00 each, which includes Consular and Agency fees.

Working.—The patentee is obliged to put the invention into practice or execution within the Empire, during the first quarter of the term for which the patent is granted, and within six months thereafter to present to the Department of the Ministry, from which the patent was issued, a certificate from the local authorities to the effect that the invention has been put into practical use. In case of machinery or apparatus, it is considered sufficient to import one or more of the same and put it or them into operation. In the case of a process, it should be carried into practice in Russia. One working is sufficient to keep the patent in force during its entire term.

DOCUMENTS REQUIRED.

1. **Specification in duplicate.**—These may be written or printed in any form and on any paper. It is not necessary that the applicant should sign the specifications.

2. **Drawings in duplicate.**—These may be made on sheets of drawing board or tracing cloth of any convenient size. Drawings of agricultural implements must be made to a scale, and the scale indicated on the drawings. The drawings are not to be signed.

3. **Power of Attorney.**—Signed by the applicant ; all names in full. No legalization is required, nor does the signature need to be witnessed. The form is the same as for France (which see).

NOTE.—When the application is made by an assignee, an assignment, legalized by a Russian Consul, should be provided. There is no special form prescribed ; it will be sufficient to state in it that the inventor gives permission to the assignee to take out the Russian patent in his own (the assignee's) name. When desired, we can obtain the legalization here at a cost of $3.00, which includes Consular and Agency fees.

DOCUMENTS REQUIRED FOR CAVEAT.

A caveat consists of a single document containing the name, address and occupation of the inventor, and an abridged specification of the invention, accompanied by drawings on tracing cloth, where the nature of the invention admits of them. The inventor should sign the document. No power of attorney is necessary.

NOTE.—The application for patent must be filed *before the expiration of three months* from the day of lodging the caveat.

St. Helena.

CHARGES.

LETTERS OF REGISTRATION, cost of, all taxes paid..........$100 00
ASSIGNMENTS, preparing and recording...................... 25 00

APPLICATION BY ASSIGNEE ALONE.

(A 2.)

"Patents, Designs, and Trade Marks Act, 1884."

(Patent.)

Application for a Patent.

(By the Assignee of the Inventor alone.)

I, *(here insert name, address and occupation of assignee,)* hereby apply that a Patent may be granted to me, for an invention for *(insert title of invention)* and I do hereby solemnly and sincerely declare that I am the Assignee of the said Invention from *(insert name, address and occupation of inventor)* by virtue of a deed of assignment made by the said *(insert name of inventor,)* dated the............day of............one thousand eight hundred and ninety   ; and I further solemnly and sincerely declare that I am in possession of the said invention and the said *(insert name of inventor)* is the first and true inventor thereof; and that the same is not in use by any other person or persons in the Colony of Queensland to the best of my knowledge and belief, and I make this solemn declaration conscientiously believing the same to be true and under and by virtue of *(here recite Statute under which declaration is made).*

(Signature.)

Declared at............in..........this..........day of..........189....

Before me *(signature of person taking declaration).*

STATEMENT OF ADDRESS AND APPOINTMENT OF AGENT.

—

Queensland.

Under the Patents, Designs, and Trade Mark Rules.

(Patents.)

SIR.

I beg to inform you that I do hereby nominate, constitute, and appoint.........to apply for and obtain Letters Patent in the Colony of Queensland, in my favor, for my invention, entitled *(insert title of invention),* and for that purpose to sign my name, and as my act and deed to seal and deliver all documents (except the application) that my said Agent may think necessary or desirable, and I further empower my said Agent to alter and amend such documents, whether originally signed by me or otherwise, in any manner which may be necessary, and I authorize and request you to send all notices, requisitions, and communications in connection with my said application to him at his address as above given.

In witness whereof I have hereunto ⎫
  affixed my signature this   ⎬   *(Signature.)*
  day of   A.D. 189 ⎭

        Witness—

To the Registrar of Patents,
  Patents Office, Brisbane, Queensland.

ASSIGNMENT TO GO WITH APPLICATION WHEN APPLICANT IS THE ASSIGNEE.

—

Assignment.

This Deed made the   day of   189   between *(insert name, address, and occupation of assignor)* (hereinafter called the assignor) of the one part, and *(insert name, address, and occupation of assignee)* (hereinafter called the assignee) of the other part........................ Whereas the said assignor is the inventor of an invention entitled *(insert title of invention).* Now this deed witnesseth that in consideration of the premises and of the sum of *(insert consideration)* sterling in hand well and truly received by the said assignor from the said assignee at or before the signing and sealing of these presents, the receipt whereof the said assignor doth hereby acknowledge, he the said assignor doth hereby sell and assign, transfer and set over unto the said assignee, his executors, administrators, and assigns, all his right, title, and interest of and in the said invention so far as the Colony of Queensland is concerned, with full power to the said assignee to apply for and obtain Letters Patents therefor in his own name in Queensland aforesaid. In witness whereof the said assignor has hereto set his hand and seal the day and year first above written.

Signed, sealed, and delivered ⎫
  by the said   ⎬   *(Signature)*
  in the presence of   ⎭

COMPLETE SPECIFICATION.

—

(C.)

"Patents, Designs, and Trade Marks Act, 1884."

(Patents.)

Complete Specification.

(To be furnished in duplicate.)

(*Title of Invention.*)

    I, (*name, address, and occupation*), do hereby declare that the nature of my invention for (*title of invention*), and the manner in which the same is to be used, are particularly described and ascertained in and by the following statement :—

(*Insert Specification.*)

    Having now particularly described and explained the nature of my said invention, and in what manner the same is to be performed I declare that what I claim is :—

(*Insert Claims.*)

1—
2—
3—

Dated this...........day of }
....................A. D. 189   }   (*Signature*)..........................

PROVISIONAL SPECIFICATION.

—

(B.)

"Patents, Designs, and Trade Marks Act, 1884."

(Patents.)

Provisional Specification.

(To be furnished in Duplicate.)

(*Title of Invention.*)

    I (*name, address, and occupation*) do hereby declare the nature of my invention for (*title of invention,*) to be as follows :—(*insert specification.*)

Dated this   day of   18

[*Signature.*]

    N.B.—The provisional specification must be without claims, or it will be treated as a complete specification, and a fee of £3 will have to be paid, in addition to the fee of £2 payable on filing a provisional specification.

Roumania.

    There is as yet no patent law in this country, and while it is possible that special Legislative grants, having the same force as a patent, may be obtained, we are not aware that any have been granted up to the present time. We are informed that the government has a projected patent law under consideration, and that some legislation upon the subject will be made soon.

Russia.

    The patent covers the entire Russian Empire, including Russia, Poland, Siberia and the Caucasus.

Working.—There are no requirements.

Special.—*COMPULSORY LICENSES.*—If, on the petition of any person interested, it is proved to the Governor in Council that by reason of the default of a patentee to grant licenses on reasonable terms—(*a*) the patent is not being worked in the colony ; or (*b*) the reasonable requirements of the public with respect to the invention cannot be supplied ; or (*c*) any person is prevented from working or using to the best advantage an invention of which he is possessed ; the Governor in Council may order the patentee to grant licenses on such terms as may be deemed just, having regard to the nature of the invention and the circumstances of the case.

DOCUMENTS REQUIRED.

Note.—The Queensland Patent Office is exceedingly strict in its practice, and much delay and trouble is caused by the slightest deviation from the prescribed forms.

All documents must be written or printed in legible characters in the English language, upon strong, wide-ruled paper (on one side only) of a size of thirteen inches in height by eight inches wide, leaving a margin of two inches on the left hand side.

Erasures are not allowed under any circumstances, in ANY *document. Corrections must be effected by ruling a red line through the incorrect word or words and writing the correction above in red ink. Each alteration must be initialed by the person signing the document. Failure in observing any of these conditions insures the rejection of the documents.*

1. **Statement of Address.**—Signed by Applicant or Applicants.

2. **Application with Declaration.**—The declaration forming part of the application must be a statutory declaration. When not made by all the applicants, the applicant making the declaration may sign the application on behalf of all the applicants. When the application extends over more than one sheet, each and every one *must* be signed by the applicant and by the person before whom the declaration is made.

Statutory declarations may be under any Act which substitutes declarations in lieu of oaths, and which renders the person making a false declaration liable to punishment for perjury in the territory in which the declaration is made. The declaration may be made as follows :—

1. In any place in the British Dominions, before any Court, Judge, or Justice of the Peace, or any person authorized to administer oaths there in any Court.

2. In any place out of British Dominions, before a British Minister, or person exercising the functions of a British Minister, or a British Consul, Vice-Consul, or other person exercising the functions of a British Consul, or a Notary Public, or before a Judge or Magistrate.

3. **Provisional or Complete Specification in duplicate.**—Both copies signed by applicant or applicants.

Note.—Under the principal act of 1884 a complete specification is required to be left within nine months and to be accepted within twelve months from the date of the provisional specification. The Registrar has now power to grant extended time, not exceeding three months, on the payment of the prescribed fees, which are as follows :—For a period not exceeding one month $10 ; not exceeding two months, $12.50 ; not exceeding three months, $15.00. The complete specification must then be accepted within eighteen months, and the Letters Patent be sealed within twenty-one months from the date of application.

4. **Drawings in duplicate.**—Neither copy should be signed. They must be made on half sheets or sheets of Imperial drawing paper, or smooth, white bristol board, of a size of 13 inches high by 20 wide, or 13 inches high by 28 wide, with a single margin line all around half-inch from the edge.

FORMS.

APPLICATION BY THE INVENTOR ALONE.

—

(A.)

"Patents, Designs, and Trade Marks Act, 1884."

(Patents.)

Application for a Patent.

(By an Original Inventor, or two or more Inventors, where all the Applicants sign the Declaration.)

I (*here insert name, occupation and address of applicant*), hereby apply that a Patent may be granted to me for an Invention for (*insert title of invention*).

And I, the said (*insert name of applicant,*) do solemnly and sincerely declare that I am in possession of the said Invention, and that I am the true and first inventor thereof, and that the same is not in use within the colony of Queensland by any other person or persons, to the best of my knowledge and belief. And I make this solemn declaration, conscientiously believing the same to be true, and under and by virtue of (*here recite Statute under which declaration is made*).

                         (*Signature.*)   ....
    Declared at................in..............this.................day of..............18....
    Before me (*signature of person taking declaration*).

    NOTE.—If declared by more than one person, and at different times or places, insert after the word " Declared" the words "by the above-named." A separate jurat for each declarant is required.

APPLICATION BY AN INVENTOR AND ANOTHER PERSON.

—

(A1.)

" Patents, Designs, and Trade Marks Act, 1884."

(Patents.)

Application for a Patent.

(When one of the Applicants is not the Original Inventor.)

We (*insert names, residences, and occupation of applicants*) hereby apply that a Patent may be granted to us for an invention for (*state title of invention*).

(*If all the applicants do not join in the declaration, the one who makes the declaration must sign here for himself and the other applicant or applicants.*)

(Witness.
                         (*Signatures.*)   ....
    And I (*or we*), the said (*insert name of party or parties making the declaration*), do solemnly and sincerely declare that we the said (*insert name of one*) and (*insert name of other party*) are in possession of the said Invention, and that I the said (*insert name of declarant*) am [or the said (*insert name of inventor*) is] the true and first inventor thereof, and the same is not in use within the colony of Queensland by any other person or persons to the best of my (*or our*) knowledge and belief. And I (*or we*) make this solemn declaration conscientiously believing the same to be true, and under and by virtue of (*here recite Statute under which declaration is made.*)

                         (*Signature.*)
    Declared at..............in.............this.................day of.............18......
    Before me (*signature of person taking Declaration.*)

    NOTE.—The Registrar of Patents explains that the above form is intended to meet cases under Section 5 of the Amended Act, in which an inventor, being a poor man, may apply to a rich one for pecuniary assistance, with the understanding that they should jointly share the patent, without the trouble and expense of having a deed of assignment drawn up.

APPLICATION BY AN ASSIGNOR WITH THE INVENTOR.

—

(A3.)

"Patents, Designs, and Trade Marks Act, 1884."

(Patents.)

Application for Patent.

(By the Assignee of the Inventor, jointly with the Inventor.)

We (*insert names, addresses and occupations of applicants*) hereby apply that a Patent may be granted to us for an Invention for (*insert title of invention.*)
                         (*Signature of assignee for himself and the inventor.*)
Witness—
    And I the said (*insert name of assignee*) do solemnly and sincerely declare that I am the assignee of an undivided share in the said Invention from the said (*insert name of inventor*) by virtue of a deed of assignment made by the said (*insert name of inventor*), dated the...........................
.................................day of.....................one thousand eight hundred and ninety.......... ....And I further solemnly and sincerely declare that we the said (*insert name of assignee*) and (*insert name of inventor*) are in possession of the said Invention; and that the said (*insert name of inventor*) is the true and first inventor thereof, and that the same is not in use by any other person or persons in the Colony of Queensland to the best of my knowledge and belief. And I make this solemn declaration conscientiously believing the same to be true and under and by virtue of (*here recite Statute under which declaration is made.*)
                         (*Signature.*)
    Declared at...................in................this.................day of.............189....
    Before me (*signature of person making Declaration*)........

LAW AND PRACTICE.

Who may be Patentee.—The grantee of a British patent, his executors, administrators or assigns. The application may be made at any time during the existence of the British patent.

Patents, Kind and Term.—The patent is granted for the unexpired residue of the term of the British patent upon which it based, including any extensions, and expires with it.

Unpatentable.—Any invention the subject of Letters Patent in Great Britain may be patented in St. Helena.

Novelty, Effect of Prior Patent or Publication.—A patent may be obtained at any time during the life of a British patent for the same invention, without regard to prior patenting, or publication of the invention in other countries.

Taxes.—There are none after the issue of the patent.

Assignments.—Should follow the usual British form. The documents should be in duplicate.

Working.—There are no requirements,

DOCUMENTS REQUIRED.

1. **Certified copy** of British patent and specification.
2. **Petition.**—Signed by applicant.
3. **Declaration.**—Signed by applicant.
4. **Power of Attorney.**—Signed by applicant.

The forms for the Petition, Declaration and Power of Attorney are the same as for Hong Kong (which see), with the exception of the name of the Colony and the title of the Act, which for St. Helena is "Ordinance No. 3 of 1872."

St. Lucia (West Indies.)

There is as yet no patent law in this country. The government will, however, grant protection for inventions by way of special Legislative Act, provided the invention is likely to prove of practical utility in the country.

The cost of such grants varies considerably. We will, however, undertake to procure them at a charge of $175 each, but we will have to ask for an additional remittance in case the cost exceeds this sum. This amount will undoubtedly be sufficient in most cases.

DOCUMENTS REQUIRED.

The same as for the Bahama Islands. The Power of Attorney must be legalized by a British Consul.

We can obtain the legalization here at a cost of $2.50 when desired.

St. Pierre.

See France.

St. Vincent (West Indies.)

There is as yet, no patent law in this country. The government will, however, grant protection for inventions by way of special Legislative Act, provided the invention is likely to prove of practical utility in the country.

The cost of such grants varies considerably. We will, however, undertake to procure them at a charge of $150 each, but we will have to ask for an additional remittance in case the cost exceeds this sum. This amount will undoubtedly be sufficient in most cases.

DOCUMENTS REQUIRED.

The same as for the Bahama Islands. The Power of Attorney should be legalized by a British Consul.

We can obtain the legalization here when desired at a cost of $2.50.

Samoa.

There is as yet no patent law. It is probable that the government would give protection for inventions by way of special grants. As yet we have had no demand for such grants, and have not arranged as to prices, etc. We have a reliable agent in Samoa, however, and will undertake any business for these Islands that may be presented, obtaining and giving all desired information through correspondence.

Sandwich Islands.

See Hawaii.

San Domingo.

There is as yet no patent law in this country. The government will, however, grant protection for inventions by way of special Legislative Act, upon application to the Executive through the Corresponding Secretary of State, provided the invention is likely to prove of practical utility in the country. The Dominican Government is disposed to be liberal in its grants; the term of some of which has been fixed as high as fifty years.

The cost of such grants varies considerably. We will, however, undertake to procure them at a charge of $400 each, but we will have to ask for an additional remittance in case the cost exceeds this sum. This amount will undoubtedly be sufficient in most cases.

DOCUMENTS REQUIRED.

The same as for Chili. The Power of Attorney should be legalized by a Dominican Consul.

We can obtain the legalization here when desired at a cost of $5.00.

San Salvador.

There is as yet no patent law in this country. The government will, however, grant protection for inventions by way of special Legislative Act, provided the invention, is likely to prove of practical utility in the country.

The cost of such grants varies considerably. We will however undertake to procure them at a charge of $300 each, but we will have to ask for an additional remittance in case the cost exceeds this sum. This amount will undoubtedly be sufficient in most cases.

DOCUMENTS REQUIRED.

The same as for Chili. The Power of Attorney should be legalized by a Consul of San Salvador.

We can obtain the legalization here, when desired, at a cost of $3.00.

Sardinia.

See Italy.

Senegal.

See France.

Servia.

Servia is a member of the International Union for the protection of industrial property, but up to the present time has passed no patent law. A proposed law was submitted to the legislature a few years ago, but it failed to pass. We are informed that the government is giving the matter renewed consideration and it is expected that a law will be passed in the near future.

Siam.

There is as yet no special law upon the subject of patents in this country, and we know of no way in which inventions can be protected there at the present time.

Sierra Leone.

There is as yet no patent law in this British Colony. The government will, however, undoubtedly grant protection for inventions by way of special Legislative Act, provided the invention is likely to prove of practical utility in the country.

The cost of such grants varies considerably. We will undertake to procure them at a charge of $200 each, but we will have to ask for an additional remittance in case the cost exceeds this sum. This amount will be sufficient in most cases.

DOCUMENTS REQUIRED.

The same as for the Gold Coast Colony, which see.

Sicily.

See Italy.

South African Republic. (Transvaal.)

CHARGES.

```
* † PROVISIONAL PROTECTION for six months...............$100 00
  * COMPLETING PATENT, all taxes paid  for three years........ 110 00
                                                            ----------
                                                             $210 00
* † Or, COMPLETE PATENT in first instance, taxes paid  for three
      years......... ...................................... 200 00
   ‡ TAXES, payable on or before the expiration of three years ..... 35 00
      "          "          "              "    seven  "  ...... 65 00
   ASSIGNMENTS....................................... 25 00
```

*The above charge covers translation of the specification up to 2,000 words. $1.00 must be added for every 100 words in specification in excess of 2,000. The charge does not cover the cost of possible oppositions, or the cost of referees' fees, if the application is referred to experts, as the Attorney-General is empowered to do. Such additional expenses will seldom be incurred, and the charges will be made the subject of special agreement for each individual case.

†The application may be filed with either a provisional or complete specification. Where provisional protection is obtained the complete specification must be filed, if at all, before the expiration of the term of such provisional protection. Provisional protection may sometimes be useful as a means to establish priority, but suits against infringers cannot be commenced until the complete patent is obtained. The filing of the application is required to be advertised, in prescribed form, once in the *Government Gazette*, and in one other paper printed in Pretoria, and twice in a newspaper printed in or near the place where the applicant uses his invention, or where he lives, and the applicant must produce the newspapers containing the advertisements when proceeding to obtain the patent.

‡If by any reason the patentee fails to pay a tax within the required time, a prolongation of the time, not exceeding three months, may be obtained for making the payment, upon payment of a fine of £5. Our charge for obtaining such extension, including the fine, is $40.

LAW AND PRACTICE.

Who may be Patentee.—The actual inventor. Corporations and firms have the same right, but the inventor must be one of the members, and as such be pointed out in the application. Joint inventors may obtain a joint patent. When an inventor, having obtained provisional protection dies before completing his application, his legal representatives may obtain the patent, provided they proceed to do so within three months after his decease. Whenever anyone in possession of an invention dies before having filed his application, his legal representatives may obtain the patent, provided they make their application within six months after the decease of the inventor.

Patents, Kind and Term.—Provisional Protection may be obtained for a term of six months. Patents of Invention are granted for fourteen years, counting from the date of the filing of the application in the Office of the Attorney-General, subject to the payment of the prescribed taxes. In case of a prior foreign patent, the patent will expire with the foreign patent if its term is the shorter, and if there be more than one prior foreign patent, it will lapse with the expiration of the first one of them.

Unpatentable.—Inventions, he application of which is contrary to law, good morals or order, and inventions for which foreign patents have been granted that have already expired.

Novelty, Effect of Prior Patent or Publication.—The application must be filed before any publication or public use of the invention in the South African Republic. Prior publication or patenting of the invention in any other country will not prevent the obtaining of a perfectly valid patent provided the invention is new in the South African Republic at the time the application is filed. The showing of an invention in an international or industrial exhibition, or the working or making known of an invention at such an exhibition, or at some other locality by anyone not authorized to do so by the inventor, does not prejudice the rights of the inventor or his legal representatives to obtain a patent, provided that due notice of the intention to exhibit is given to the Attorney-General, and the application is filed within six months after the opening of the exhibition.

Taxes.—A tax of £5 must be paid on or before the expiration of the third year of the life of the patent, counting from the date of the filing of the application, and £10 before the expiration of the seventh year. If the patentee, through inadvertence, accident or mistake, fail to pay a fee within the prescribed time, an extension of time, not to exceed three months at most, can be obtained for making the payment, upon payment of a fine of £5. See " Charges " for our terms for obtaining an extension.

Assignments.—Should be prepared in duplicate, and be legalized by a Consul of the South African Republic.

We can obtain the legalization here, when desired, at a cost of $5.00 for each legalization.

Working.—There are no requirements.

Special.—*COMPULSORY LICENSES.* When it is proved to the satisfaction of the Government that in consequence of the refusal of a patentee to grant licenses on reasonable terms ; (a) that the patent-right is not being made use of in the State ; (b) that the ordinary demand for the patented article cannot be supplied ; (c) that anyone is prevented from making use of and deriving the full benefit of an invention in his possession; then, the Government may order the patentee to grant licenses upon such terms as may appear reasonable, and the conditions of the case may require.

DOCUMENTS REQUIRED.

1. **Application.**—Signed by the inventor, and legalized by a Consul of the South African Republic.

2. **Specification.**—Signed by the inventor.

3. **Drawings in duplicate.**—Upon bristol board or tracing cloth. No signatures.

4. **Power of Attorney.**—Signed by the inventor and two witnesses, and legalized by a Consul of the South African Republic.

We can obtain the legalization here, when desired, at a cost of $5.00 for each legalization.

5. **Before the patent is issued,** but after the filing of the application, the application must be advertised, and copies of the papers containing such advertisement be supplied. (See note under charges.)

FORMS.

APPLICATION.

....
....
van beroep...: ....

verklaar hierbij dat.........................bezit ben van eene uitvinding voor...................
....
dat.......................de eerste en ware uitvinder daarvan.............................; dat die
uitvinding, voor zoover...............................engeloof, niet toegepast of gebruikt wordt door
eenen aneren persoon of andere personen; en.....................verzoek met verschuldigden
eerbied, dat.................voor gezegde uitvinding een octrooi worde verleend,
....den.........................dag der maand
.....................................van het jaar onzes Heeren.
                             (Signature.) ....

POWER OF ATTORNEY.

Bijzondere Lastgeving.

Ondergeteekende...
....
verklaar.......................bij deze te magtigen...
....
om namens.......................en ten.......................behoeve.........................
....
....

ten voorschreven einde in regten te verschijnen, zoowel eischende als verwerende, in hooger
beroep te komen, regterlijke magtigingen te vragen, Agenten en Procureurs te benoemen, benoodigde Acten en stukken te doen maken, te beteekenen en te doen teekenen, en in het algemeen
datgene te doen wat vereischt wordt; alles met de magt van plaatsbekleeding, belofte van goedkeuring, schadeloosstelling, eene billijke belooning in verband als naar regten.
Geteekend te...op den.................................
dag van.......................................Achttien Honderd.................................
                       (Signature) ....
        Als Getuigen:
....
....

South Australia.

CHARGES.

* PROVISIONAL PROTECTION for twelve months............. $22 50
* COMPLETING PATENT, all taxes paid for three years......... 47 50
                                                              _____
                                                              $70 00
* Or, COMPLETE PATENT in first instance, taxes paid for three
    years.. 60 00
† TAXES, before the expiration of the third year................ 22 50
    "   "   "   seventh " 22 50
‡ ASSIGNMENTS... 15 00

*The above charge does not include cost of a possible opposition, or referee's fees, if the appli-
cation is referred to an Examiner for report. Such additional charges are seldom incurred, and
will be made the subject of a special agreement in each individual case.

†The receipts for the taxes must be endorsed upon the patent, and this document should be
forwarded when the order is given for the payment of a tax. If this is impracticable, however,
the Office will receive the tax without the production of the patent, giving an interim receipt,
and will endorse the patent when it is presented.

‡Assignments must be registered within six months of their date. Under the "Stamp Act,
1886," assignments of patents must pay an *ad valorem* duty of 5 shillings ($1.25) per £100 ($500), or
fractional part of £100, of consideration money. Our charge includes the duty for the first £100
only. Where the consideration amounts to more than this sum, the proper duty must be added
to our charge.

LAW AND PRACTICE.

Who may be Patentee.—The true and first inventor, or his assignee, legatee, or
executor. It is believed that the words, "true and first inventor" include, as in the

other Colonies and Great Britain, the true and first importer, but the local authorities are in doubt upon this point. Patents may be obtained for communicated inventions as in England. Joint inventors may obtain a joint patent.

Patents, Kind and Term.—Provisional Protection is granted for a term of twelve months. Patents of Invention are granted for fourteen years, counting from the date of the filing of the application, subject to the payment of the prescribed taxes. An extension of the term for an additional term of seven years may be obtained in exceptional cases. In case of prior foreign patents, the patent will expire with the first expiring foreign patent. Caveats may be filed by intending applicants for patents and remain in force for one year.

Unpatentable.—Inventions which have been patented abroad, when such patent has already expired before the patent is granted in South Australia.

Novelty, Effect of Prior Patent or Publication.—The application must be filed before the invention has been publicly used or offered for sale in South Australia. Prior publication or patenting in other countries will not prevent the obtaining of a perfectly valid patent so long as the invention is new as to South Australia at the time the application is filed. The mere fact of an inventor having exhibited or tested his invention either publicly or privately is not in itself any ground for refusing him a patent, and will not justify any other person in using the invention, provided that such exhibiting has been made within six months of the date of the application for patent.

Taxes.—A tax of £2.10.0 is due before the expiration of the third year of the life of the patent, counting from the date of the filing of the application, and a further tax of £2.10.0 before the expiration of the seventh year. No prolongation of the time for making payment can be obtained.

Assignments.—These should be in duplicate, and both copies must be endorsed as follows: "Certified correct for the purposes of the South Australian Patent Act, 1877." This certificate must be signed by the principal party to the deed—say the assignee. If not so endorsed, an extra charge of $5 is incurred to pay a local solicitor or agent to give such a certificate. Assignments must be registered within six months after their date. Under the "Stamp Act, 1886," assignments of patents must pay an *ad valorem* duty of 5 shillings per £100, or fractional part of £100, of consideration money. If the consideration is nominal, the duty is £1 ($5.00). It will, therefore, be best to state the consideration at from £5 to £100, as in such case the consideration will only amount to 5 shillings.

Working.—The law provides that a patent *may* be revoked after three years from its date, if the patented invention has not been "used to a reasonable extent for the public benefit." As a matter of fact this provision has never been put into operation, and it is almost certain that the Law Officers would never allow any proceedings to be taken under this section without first calling upon the patentee, either to work the invention himself, or to allow it to be worked by others.

DOCUMENTS REQUIRED.

1. **Petition.**—Signed by applicant. This should be written on legal cap briefwise, and does not require to be witnessed.

2. **Declaration.**—Signed by applicant. Should be written on legal cap briefwise, and may be made before any competent person, such as a Justice of the Peace, Notary Public, &c., but need not be statutory. If the applicant be the assignee there must be *two* declarations and a short assignment as shown in the forms. (See note under "Declarations" in article on Queensland.)

3. **Specification in duplicate.**—Should be written on legal cap briefwise, and must be signed by the inventor himself, or under Power of Attorney from him, and must be attested by two witnesses, who must specify where and when it was signed.

4. Drawings in duplicate.—May be on any material, and must be executed by the inventor (or his attorney) and attested by two witnesses, exactly the same as the specifications.

5. Appointment of Agent or Power of Attorney.—Signed by applicant. Should be written on legal cap briefwise.

6. If the Applicant is the Assignee, a certified copy of the assignment or a short assignment as per form below.

FORMS.

PETITION.

In the matter of "The Patent Act, 1877."

To the Commissioner of Patents for the Province of South Australia:

The Petition of (*name of Petitioner in full*), of (*address and occupation of Petitioner*).

Showeth:

1. That your Petitioner is the true and first inventor of a certain invention for (*here insert the name or title of invention*).

2. That the said invention has not been publicly used or offered for sale within the said Province prior to the date of this present Petition.

3. That your Petitioner's address, to which notices in respect to this Petition may be sent, is at ....in the City of Adelaide.

Your petitioner therefore humbly prays that Letters Patent for the sole making, using, exercising and vending of the said invention within the said Province, for the term of fourteen years, may be granted to your Petitioner, pursuant to "The Patent Act, 1877." And your Petitioner will ever pray, &c.

Dated this...........day of...........18....   (*Signature of Applicant.*).................

(NOTE.—If the Petitioner claims as assignee, legatee, executor, or administrator of the original inventor, alter the form by setting out the name of the inventor, that he was the true and first inventor, and by showing how the Petitioner derives right to apply for a patent.)

DECLARATION.

Declaration.

I, (*name of inventor in full*), of (*address and occupation of inventor*), do hereby solemnly and sincerely declare as follows:—

1. I verily believe I am the true and first inventor of the invention mentioned in the Petition and Specification hereunto annexed, and marked respectively "*A*" and "*B*."

(*If the inventor is also the applicant, add*)

2. The several allegations contained in the said Petition hereunto annexed, and marked "*A*" are true.

(*Signature*)   ....

Declared at..the...........day of ....18....
before me (*signature and title of person taking declaration*).

SECOND DECLARATION (*If Petitioner is not the Inventor*).

Declaration.

I (*name of Petitioner in full*), of (*address and occupation of Petitioner*), do hereby solemnly and sincerely declare as follows:—

1. That I am the assignee of.............................of............................ who is, I verily believe, the true and first inventor of the invention mentioned in the Petition and Specification hereunto annexed, and marked respectively "*A*" and "*B*."

2. I verily believe that the several allegations contained in the Petition hereunto annexed and marked "*A*" (or above written) are true.

(*If the Inventor be dead, add*)

3. I verily believe that (*name of inventor*), formerly of (*his last known address and addition*) was the true and first inventor of the invention mentioned in the said Petition.

Declared at.............................the...........day of......... ....18....

Before me.............................

(*Signature.*)   ....

FORM OF SPECIFICATION.

Specification of (*John Brown, mechanic, of 69 Broadway, New York City, in the State of New York, United States of America*), for an invention of ("*Improvements in Car Couplers.*")

(*Here describe invention.*)

In witness whereof, I, the said (*John Brown*) have hereto set my hand and seal.

(*John Brown.*) [L. S.]

Signed and sealed by the said (*John Brown*) at (*New York*) on the.............................day of......................18...., in our presence.

(*William Smith, New York, Patent Solicitor.*)
(*James Cooke, his clerk.*)

ASSIGNMENT.

NOTE.—WHEN THE PETITIONER IS THE ASSIGNEE, a certified copy of the assignment must be sent or a short document somewhat as follows :—

Assignment.

In consideration of the sum of five pounds to me paid before the execution hereof, I do hereby assign unto................................of..................................all my invention entitled ....so far as the Province of South Australia is concerned, with full power to apply for and obtain Letters Patent therefor in his own name in such colony.

Dated this.......day of............one thousand eight hundred and ninety.....................

Witness :   (*Signature.*)

APPOINTMENT OF AGENT.

(Under Clause 3 of Act No. 201, of 1881.)

I (*A. B.*), of............................ do hereby retain, constitute, and appoint...................
............Agent, with full power of substitution and revocation, to apply for and obtain from the proper authorities Letters Patent in the Province of South Australia for my invention entitled..and for this purpose for me and in my name to sign all papers and writings relative to obtaining such Letters Patent, to alter and amend the same, and generally to do such acts regarding the same as may be necessary or expedient.

Signed at.............................this...........................day of.....................18

Witness :   (*Signature.*)

POWER OF ATTORNEY.

NOTE.—A Power of Attorney is necessary whenever the agent is required to sign the Petition or a Declaration. The appointment of agent is sufficient to enable the agent to sign the specification and drawings. Inasmuch as the authorities hold that Powers of Attorney are liable to a duty of £1, under the "Stamp Act of 1886," the appointment of agent should always be used instead of a Power of Attorney when it is possible to do so. When a Power of Attorney is sent the amount of the duty payable thereon—$5.00, must be added to our usual charge.

Power of Attorney.

Know all men by these presents :—

That I, (*insert full name and occupation of applicant*), of (*insert full address of applicant*), do hereby retain, constitute and appoint...
of.......................................Licensed Patent Agent, my true and lawful attorney, for me and in my name to sign, and as my act and deed to seal and deliver all necessary documents relative to obtaining Letters Patent in the Province of South Australia, for an Invention entitled (*insert title of invention,*) and to alter and amend such documents, and at pleasure to appoint a substitute or substitutes under him for all and any of the purposes aforesaid : I hereby ratifying and affirming, and engaging to ratify and confirm, all that my said attorney or his substitute shall lawfully do by virtue hereof.

In witness whereof I, the said (*insert full name of applicant*) have hereunto set my hand and seal this........day of..................................18....

Signed, sealed and delivered by the said (*full name of applicant*) in presence of (*Signatures of two witnesses.*)   }   (*Signature.*) [L. S.]

DOCUMENTS REQUIRED. (PROVISIONAL PROTECTION.)

1. **Petition.**—Signed by applicant.

2. **Specification.**—One copy. Signed by applicant and two witnesses.

3. **Appointment of Agent.**—Signed by applicant. The form is the same as for Letters Patent.

FORMS.

PETITION.

(In the matter of the " Patents Amendment Act, 1887.")

To the Commissioner of Patents for the Province of South Australia :

The Petition of

SHOWETH—

1. That your Petitioner....entitled to obtain a patent for a certain invention or an improvement in an invention for..
2. That your Petitioner's address, to which notices in respect of this Petition may be sent is at.. ....

Your Petitioner therefore humbly prays that a Certificate of Provisional Protection for the using and publishing of the said invention within the said Province, for the term of twelve months, may be granted to your Petitioner pursuant to "*The Patents Amendment Act*, 1887,"

And your Petitioner will ever pray, &c.

Dated this.............day of...................18....   (*Signature.*)

FORM OF SPECIFICATION:

Specification
of
Thomas Brown, of No. 89 Cannon street, London, in England, for an invention of
"Improvements in dynamo-electric machines."

(*Here describe invention, without reference to drawings, and omitting claims.*)

In witness whereof, I, the said Thomas Brown have hereto set my hand and seal.

(*Signature.*)   [L. S.]

Signed and sealed by the said Thomas Brown,
at London, in England, on the
day................18...., in our presence.

William Smith, London, Patent Agent.
James Robinson, his Clerk.

DOCUMENTS REQUIRED. (CAVEATS.)

Only one document is required. It may be written on one side only of any suitable paper.

FORM OF CAVEAT.

In the matter of " The Patent Act, 1877."

Let no patent be granted until after the expiration of one year from the filing of this Caveat to any person for the invention described in the Schedule hereto, and claimed by me, the undersigned, as my own, without notice to me at the address hereunder written, to which any notice required to be sent to me under clause 47 of " The Patent Act, 1877," may be addressed.

SCHEDULE.

(*Here describe the invention, referring to any drawings that may accompany the Caveat. No claims should be added.*)

Dated this........day of................18   (*Signature of Caveator.*)

Care of.. ......
....

Spain.

The patent covers Spain and all her colonies, which include Cuba, Porto Rico, the Philippine, Balearic and Canary Islands, but in order to obtain protection in the Colonies, it is necessary to have the patent registered for the Colonies in the Colonial Office at Madrid.

CHARGES.

* PATENT, cost of, all taxes paid for one year....................$35 00
PATENT OF ADDITION, all taxes paid........................ 25 00
TAXES, *payable annually, counting from the date of the issue of the patent. There is no grace.*

Second	year.........$ 8 50	Twelfth	year..... .....$28 50
Third	" 10 50	Thirteenth	" 30 50
Fourth	" 12 50	Fourteenth	" 32 50
Fifth	" 14 50	Fifteenth	" 34 50
Sixth	" 16 50	Sixteenth	" 36 50
Seventh	" 18 50	Seventeenth	" 38 50
Eighth	" 20 50	Eighteenth	" 40 50
Ninth	" 22 50	Nineteenth	" 42 50
Tenth	" 24 50	Twentieth	" 44 50
Eleventh	" 26 50		

ASSIGNMENT, preparing and recording........................ 25 00
WORKING, exclusive of cost of manufacture.................. 30 00

*The above charge includes translation of the specification up to 2,000 words; 35 cents must be added for each 100 words in the specification in excess of 2,000.

LAW AND PRACTICE.

Who may be Patentee.—Any person, whether the inventor or not, a firm or corporation.

Patents, Kind and Term.—There are three kinds of Patents: Patents of Invention; Patents of Importation; and Patents of Addition applied for by the inventor, before the invention has become publicly known in Spain or elsewhere, the term will be twenty years. If, at the time of the application in Spain, the invention—although not known in that country—has been already patented abroad, the inventor may obtain a patent for ten years, provided his application be made in Spain within two years of the date of the prior foreign patent; should more than two years have elapsed, the term will be for five years only. If the applicant is the importer, the term is limited to five years. In all cases the duration of the patent is subject to the payment of the prescribed taxes and proper working of the invention. Patents of Addition are granted for the unexpired term of the original patent and expire with it.

Unpatentable.—(1) The result or product of machines, apparatus, instruments, processes, or operations, the working of which will not tend to establish a new industry in the country. (2) The use of natural products. (3) Scientific principles or discoveries, so far as they are of a mere speculative nature, and are not likely to be applicable to machinery, apparatus, instruments, processes, or mechanical or chemical operations of a practical industrial nature. (4) Pharmaceutical or medical preparations of all sorts. (5) Schemes or combinations of credit or finance.

Novelty, Effect of Prior Patent or Publication.—The application should be filed before the invention has been established or executed in the same way or form within the Spanish Dominions. Prior publication, or patenting of the invention in another country will not prevent the obtaining of a perfectly valid patent, but the term of the patent will be shortened thereby. (See remarks under heading "Patents, Kind and Term.")

Taxes.—All patents (except Patents of Addition) are granted subject to the payment of annual taxes, which must be paid yearly in advance, counting from the date of the issue of the patent. The taxes amount to 10 pesetas for the first year, 20 pesetas for the second year, 30 pesetas for the third year, and so on, increasing 10 pesetas each year. There is no grace for the payment of taxes, and no prolongation of the time for making payment can be obtained.   There are no taxes upon a Patent of Addition after its issue.

Assignments.—The law requires that all assignments must be made before a Notary Public ; the signatures must then be legalized by a Spanish Consul, and the instrument recorded in the Spanish Patent Office.

We can obtain the legalization here, when desired, at a cost of $2.50, which includes Consular and Agency fees.

Working.—The invention must be worked in Spain within two years of the date of the issue of the patent, and the working must not entirely cease thereafter for the space of one year and a day at any one time.   The patented article should be actually manufactured in Spain or in a Spanish colony.   The mere importation and running of a machine is not sufficient.   Inventions covered by Patents of Addition must be worked also.   The owners of patents are required to prove the working before the Director of the Conservatory of Arts.
In ordering the working of Spanish patents ample time (from three to six months) should be given us, prior to the date at which the time expires, so that we may have time to arrange with a manufacturer at Madrid or elsewhere, and that we may submit an estimate of the entire cost, with particulars as to what the manufacturer will require to be furnished.

Special.—*COLONIES.*—The Spanish patent covers all the colonies; but before any legal formalities in connection with a patent, such as prosecution for infringement, transfer of rights, etc., can take place in the colonies, the patent must be officially registered at the Colonial Department in Madrid.   This can be done at any time during the life of the patent.   The charge for this registration, including all fees, is $10.00.

DOCUMENTS REQUIRED.

1. **Specification.**—Written or printed on any paper.   No signatures required.

2. **Drawings in duplicate.**—On tracing cloth, any convenient size.   No signatures required.

3. **Power of Attorney.**—Signed by the applicant or applicants; all names in full. No witnesses nor legalization necessary.

FORM.

POWER OF ATTORNEY.

Poder.

.................................que suscribe...
....
domiciliado en...
constituye.........por el presente documento su apoderado general, con facultad de substituir.
á..
....al cual da....poder
general, sin limitacion alguna, para que á su...nombre...y en su representacion, haga toda clase de
diligencias y firme cuantas solicitudes y documentos sean necesarios presentar en España á S. M. el
Rey, ó á sus Ministros, Autoridades y Funcionarios de todas clases SOLICITANDO..............
....
....

En su virtud......poderdante....reconoce......desde hoy, como si personalmente lo hiciese....
cuanto haga en su....nombre....su referido apoderado en la gestion del asunto para que está
autorizado por este documento y cuanto mas sea necesario hacer en cualquier tiempo en bien y
en defensa de sus intereses.

Firmado en...á... ....
de..............de..................................... (*Signature.*)

Straits Settlements.

The patent covers Malacca, Penang, Singapore, and the Province Wellesley.

CHARGES.

* PATENT, cost of, all taxes paid............................$125 00
EXTENSION OF PATENT. The charge is variable, usually
    about... 100 00
ASSIGNMENTS, preparing and recording..................... 30 00

*In case the application is referred to experts to report on the novelty and utility of the invention, their fees, ranging from $50 to $100, are an additional charge. This expense is seldom incurred where a prior British patent has been obtained.

LAW AND PRACTICE.

Who may be Patentee.—The actual inventor, his heirs, executors, administrators and assigns; the first importer, or the holder of a British patent, or patent granted in any British Possession.

Patents, Kind and Term.—Patents of Invention (or Importation), granted for the term of fourteen years from the date of the filing of the specification. Provision is made for the extension of the term of a patent for such further term, not to exceed fourteen years, as the Governor in Council may see fit to direct. In case a prior patent for the same invention has been obtained in Great Britain, or in any British Possession, the patent will be granted for the unexpired term of such prior patent, and will expire therewith.

Unpatentable.—Section 4, of the law provides that no person shall be entitled to any exclusive privilege under the ordinance; if the invention is of no utility, or, if the invention, at the time of presenting the petition for leave to file the specification, was not a new invention within the meaning of the ordinance; or, if the petitioner is not the inventor thereof; or, if the specification filed, or the amended specification (if any), does not particularly describe and ascertain the nature of the invention, and in what manner the same is to be carried out, with the particulars required by section 11 of this ordinance; or, if the original or any subsequent petition relating to the invention, or the original or any amended specification, contain a willful or fraudulent misstatement.

Novelty, Effect of Prior Patent or Publication.—The application must be filed before the invention has been publicly used in Great Britain, in the Colony, or in any other British Possession. Public use of the invention in fraud of the inventor, or if the knowledge thereof shall have been obtained surreptitiously, or in fraud of the inventor, or shall have been communicated to the public in fraud of the inventor, or in breach of confidence, will not be deemed a public use of the invention within the meaning of the ordinance, provided that the inventor shall, within six months after the commencement of such public use, apply for leave to file his specification, and shall not previously have acquiesced in such public use. It is also provided that the use of an invention in public by the inventor thereof, or by his servants or agents, or by any other person by his license in writing, shall not be deemed a public use thereof, within the meaning of the ordinance.

Taxes.—There are none after the issue of the patent.

Assignments.—Should be prepared in duplicate. Any suitable form may be used.

Working.—There are no requirements.

DOCUMENTS REQUIRED.

1. Petition.—Signed by applicant.

2. Declaration to Accompany Petition.—Signed by applicant.

3. Specification in duplicate.—Signed by applicant.

4. Declaration to Accompany Specification.—Signed by applicant.

5. Drawings in duplicate.—On drawing board or tracing cloth, any suitable size. No signatures.

6. Power of Attorney.—Signed by applicant.

7. Blue Book of British Patent, if any exist.

FORMS.

PETITION.

To His Excellency tne Governor of the Colony of the Straits Settlements in Council:—

The Petition of *(here insert name, occupation and place of residence)*, for leave to file a specification under the Inventions Ordinance, 1871.

Showeth:

That your petitioner is in possession of an invention for *(state the title of the invention)*, which invention he believes will be of public utility; that he is the inventor or owner of the said invention *(or, as the case may be, the assignee, or the executor, or administrator, or heir of the inventor, or owner of the said invention)*; and that the same is not publicly known or used in the Colony, to the best of his knowledge and belief *(or, as the case may be, that he is the first importer into the Colony of the said invention, and that the same is not publicly known or used in the Colony)*.

N. B.—If Letters Patent have been obtained for the invention in England, or in any British Possession, here state the fact, the date thereof, and the term during which the same are to continue in force.

The following is a description of the invention *(here describe it)*.

Your petitioner therefore prays for leave to file a specification of the said invention, pursuant to the provisions of the Inventions Ordinance, 1871, and your petitioner will ever pray, &c.

The.....................day of..............18....

        (Signature of Applicant.)

DECLARATION TO ACCOMPANY PETITION.

I, *(here insert name, occupation and place of residence)* do solemnly and sincerely declare that I am in possession of an invention for *(state the title of the invention as in the petition)*; that I believe the said invention will be of public utility; that I am the inventor *(or owner)* of the said invention *(or, as the case may be, the assignee, or executor, or administrator, or heir of the inventor or owner of the said invention, or, that I am the first importer of the said invention into this Colony)*, and that the same is not publicly known or used in the colony, to the best of my knowledge and belief; and that, to the best of my knowledge and belief, my said invention is truly described in my petition for leave to file a specification thereof.

The..............day of................18....

        (Signature of Applicant.)

SPECIFICATION.

To all whom it may concern: Be it known that I *(here insert name, occupation and place of residence)*, am in possession of an invention for *(title of invention)*; and I, the said *(here insert the name)*, do hereby declare the nature of the said invention, and in what manner the same is to be performed, to be particularly described and ascertained in and by the following statement thereof, that is to say:

The invention has for its object *(here describe invention fully with reference to the drawings, if any)*.

      (Witness.)   *(Signature of Applicant.)*

DECLARATION TO ACCOMPANY SPECIFICATION.

I, *(here insert name, occupation and place of residence)*, do solemnly and sincerely declare that I am in possession of an invention for *(state the title of the invention)*, which invention I believe will be of public utility; that I am the inventor or owner of the said invention *(or, as the case may be, the assignee or executor, or administrator, or heir of the inventor or owner of the said invention, or that I am the first importer of the said invention into this colony)*, and that the same is not publicly known or used in this colony, to the best of my knowledge and belief; and that, to the best of my belief, the instrument in writing, under my hand, hereunto annexed, particularly describes and ascertains the nature of the said invention, and in what manner the same is to be carried out.

The..............day of...................18....

        (Signature of Applicant.)

POWER OF ATTORNEY.

In the matter of the Inventions Ordinance, 1871, of the Government of the Straits Settlements, and in the matter of *(name, occupation and address)*, an Inventor.

I, the above-named *(here insert name)*, do hereby retain, constitute and appoint................. ....as my agent and attorney, to apply for and obtain from the Government of the Straits Settlements an exclusive privilege for *(state the title of the invention as per petition)*, and I authorize him to sign my name to such papers and writings, and do such acts regarding the same, including the appointment of a substitute or substitutes, as may be necessary or expedient.

Dated this................day of............. ....18....

(Signature of Applicant.)   [L. s.]

Signed, sealed and delivered at................ }

in the presence of .... }

Sweden.

CHARGES.

```
* PATENT, cost of, all taxes paid for one year...................... $45 00
* PATENT OF ADDITION, all taxes paid......................       45 00
   TAXES, payable annually, counting from the date of application,
      with three months' grace; but in such case, with the addition of
      one-fifth of the tax then payable.  No taxes on patents of addition.
      Second, third, fourth and fifth years........ :..........each,   10 00
      Sixth, seventh, eighth, ninth and tenth years...........  "      18 00
      Eleventh, twelfth, thirteenth, fourteenth and fifteenth....  "   25 00
   ASSIGNMENTS, preparing and recording .....................     12 50
   WORKING (exclusive of freight charges)... ....................    30 00
```

*The above charge includes translation of the specification up to 2,000 words. Beyond that number, 50 cents must be added for each 100 words.

LAW AND PRACTICE.

Who may be Patentee.—An actual inventor or his duly accredited representative. When several persons apply for a patent on the same invention, the preference will be given to the person whose application was filed the earliest.

Patents, Kind and Term.—Patents of Invention granted for fifteen years, subject to the payment of the prescribed taxes, and proper working of the invention. Patents of Addition granted for the unexpired term of the original patent upon which it is based, and expiring therewith.

Unpatentable..—Inventions, the working of which would be contrary to law or morals. With regard to inventions relating to provisions or medicines, patents will not be granted for the commodity itself, but only for special methods for its manufacture.

Novelty, Effect of Prior Patent or Publication.—An invention is not considered as new, if it has, prior to filing the application for a patent with the patent authorities, been described in any published journal, or is so openly worked that any person conversant with the subject may, guided by the information thus gained, work the invention, or if the object of the invention does not essentially differ from products or methods of manufacture which have before become known in such a way. The publication of the invention by foreign patent authorities, or the exhibition of the invention in an international exhibition will not prevent the grant of the patent, provided the application is filed within six months from the day of such publication, or the day the exhibition was opened.   In case an application for patent has been previously filed in a foreign country, the application for the Swedish patent may be made within seven months from the day such foreign application was filed, even if the invention has received publication in the intervening time.

Taxes.—All patents, (except Patents of Addition), are granted subject to the payment of annual taxes, payable yearly in advance counting from the date of the filing of the application.   Three months' grace is allowed within which the payment may be made, but in such case a fine amounting to one-fifth of the tax then due must be paid in addition to such tax.   The taxes are as follows :—25 crowns each for the second, third, fourth and fifth years ; 50 crowns for each of the following five years ; and 75 crowns for each of the remaining five years.   There are no taxes upon Patents of Addition after their issue.

Assignments.—To record an assignment we require : (1) a deed of assignment signed by the assignor, and legalized by a Swedish Consul ; (2) an acceptance of the assignment, signed by the assignee.   Both of the above may be prepared in one document, which should be made and executed in duplicate.

When desired, we can obtain the legalization here at a cost of $3.00 for each legalization, which includes Consular and Agency fees.

Working.—The invention should be worked within three years from the date of the grant of the patent, and the working should not be discontinued thereafter for as long as a year at a time.   The time for working may sometimes be extended to four years, and, in exceptional cases, it rests with the patent authorities to prescribe conditions, by complying with which the patentee is considered to have fulfilled the conditions of working. It is considered sufficient to import one or more of the patented articles into Sweden, in case of machinery or apparatus, and to expose and advertise the same for sale.   In case of a process, it should be carried into practice in Sweden.

DOCUMENTS REQUIRED.

The documents for Patents of Addition are precisely the same.

1. Specification.—Written or printed on any paper.   No signatures necessary. Measures and weights should be given according to the metrical system; the degrees of heat, according to the Celsius' (Centigrade) thermometer; the density should be indicated as specific weight, and in the case of chemical processes the new atomic weights and the molecular formulas are to be used.

2. Drawings in duplicate.—One copy is to be made on smooth, white, thick drawing board, and the other copy on tracing cloth.   Any number of sheets may be used.   The sheets must measure exactly 33 centimetres (13 inches) in height, by 21, 42 or 63 centmetres (8¼ 16½ or 24¾ inches) wide.   A single marginal line must be drawn exactly two centimetres (¼ inch) from the edge of the sheet.   No signatures are necessary.

3. Power of Attorney.—Signed by the applicant; all names in full.   No witnesses nor legalization required.

Note.—If the applicant is not the inventor, an assignment or similar instrument must be forwarded, showing that the applicant is authorized to make the application in his own name.   This document must be legalized by a Swedish Consul.   When desired, we can obtain the legalization here at a cost of $3.00, which includes Consular and Agency fees.

FORM.

POWER OF ATTORNEY.

Fullmakt.

för ....
eller den han i sitt ställe förordnar, att för...
söka och uttaga patent i Konungariket *Sverige* på.................................
..........................af..........................uppfunn...............
....
samt att under hela patenttiden i allt, hvad patentfrågan angår, å.................
vägnar tala och svara; förklaranda...........................nöjd..................
med hvad ombudet dervid lagligen gör och låter.
.........................den.........................18....

(*Signature.*)

Switzerland.

CHARGES.

* PROVISIONAL PATENT, for two years, all taxes paid for one
  year... $27 50
† CHANGING PROVISIONAL to DEFINITIVE PATENT...... 12 50

                                             $40 00

* † DEFINITIVE PATENT in first instance..................... 35 00
* PATENT OF ADDITION, all taxes paid..................... 27 50
TAXES, *payable annually in advance, counting from the date of the filing of the application, with three months' grace without fine.*

Second Year	$ 9 50	Ninth	Year	23 50
Third "	11 50	Tenth "		25 50
Fourth "	13 50	Eleventh "		27 50
Fifth "	15 50	Twelfth "		29 50
Sixth "	17 50	Thirteenth "		31 50
Seventh "	19 50	Fourteenth "		33 50
Eighth "	21 50	Fifteenth "		35 50

APPEALS from Federal Bureau to Federal Department........... 20 00
  "   " Federal Department to Federal Council............ 50 00
‡ AMENDMENT of specification and drawings, if required, from
$2.00 up.
ASSIGNMENTS... 10 00
WORKING, Nominal.. 25 00

* The above charge includes translation of the specification up to 2,000 words, 35 cents must be added for each 100 words in the specification in excess of 2,000.
† A definitive patent will be granted, and a provisional patent changed into a definitive patent, only when the existence of the machine itself, or of a model thereof, is proven to the satisfaction of the Federal Bureau. See remarks under heading of "Special."
‡ Amendment of the specification and drawings are sometimes required by the Federal Bureau. Our charge for such work will be based upon the actual amount of work involved in making the changes demanded by the Bureau.

LAW AND PRACTICE.

Who may be Patentee.—Only the true inventor or his lawful successors are entitled to claim a patent.

Patents, Kind and Term.—Provisional Patents are granted for a term of two years from the date of the filing of the application. They secure priority, but no protection against infringements, which can only be obtained by a Definitive Patent. It is not necessary to prove the existence of the object for which the patent is asked, or of a model of the same, to secure a Provisional Patent. Definitive Patents are only granted when it is proven that the object itself, for which the patent is demanded, or a model thereof, is in existence, and is granted for a term of fifteen years, subject to the payment of the prescribed taxes and the proper working of the invention. Patents are dated as of the day and hour upon which the complete papers are filed in the Federal Bureau, or posted in a post office in Switzerland. If the papers sent are incomplete or require amendment, the patent bears the date of the day upon which the corrected papers are filed. Patents of Addition are granted for the unexpired term of the original patent upon which they are based, and expire therewith. They are only granted when the existence of the object for which the patent is asked, or of a model of the same, is proven.

Unpatentable.—Patents are granted for such inventions only, as "may be realized in trade," and if they can be represented in models ; methods and processes cannot be patented. Only one invention can be claimed in a single application ; a machine and its product cannot be covered by the same patent.

Novelty, Effect of Prior Patent or Publication.—To obtain a valid patent the invention must be new as to Switzerland at the time the application therefor is filed. An invention is not considered as new, if at the time the application is filed, it is so well known in Switzerland that its employment is possible by any one skilled in the trade to which it relates. Switzerland is a member of the International Union for the protection of industrial property, and citizens or subjects of other countries which belong to the Union may file their applications in Switzerland at any time within seven months from the dates upon which they filed their applications in their own country, without the validity of their patents being endangered by the publication of the invention or the applications of third parties. Provision is also made for the protection of inventions exhibited in national or international exhibitions in Switzerland, the inventor being allowed to file his application at any time within six months from the day of admission of the articles to the exhibition.

Taxes.—All Patents (except Patents of Addition) are granted subject to the payment of annual taxes, payable in advance, counting from the date of the filing of the application. Three months' grace is allowed for making payment, and without fine. No further prolongation of time can be obtained. The tax amounts to 20 francs for the first year, 30 francs for the second, and so on increasing 10 francs, each year. No taxes are payable on Patents of Addition after their issue.

Assignments.—The documents should be in duplicate and must be legalized by a Swiss Consul.

We can obtain the legalization here, when desired, at a cost of $3.00 for each legalization.

Working.—Art. 9 of the law provides that a patent expires when the invention has not been carried into effect before the expiration of the third year from the date of the application. Inasmuch as there have been no decisions upon this point up to the present time, it is impossible to state what the exact requirements as to working will be. It is thought however that the practice will be the same as in Germany ; we would advise that an actual and thorough working be made in each case. We quote a price for nominal workings in anticipation of a demand for them, but it must be understood that we disclaim all responsibility as to their sufficiency.

Special.—*MODELS.*—The permanent deposit of models is obligatory :

    a. For inventions concerning the movements or the cases of watches;

    b. For inventions in the line of portable fire-arms;

    c. For inventions in which the object invented is composed in whole or in part of substances or combinations of substances which it is difficult to determine.

PROVING THE EXISTENCE OF MACHINE OR MODEL.—The law requires that an invention to be patentable, must be capable of being illustrated in a model, and a Definitive Patent will not be granted, nor will a Provisional Patent be changed into a Definitive Patent, until the existence of the article itself, or of a model representing the same be proven to the satisfaction of the Federal Bureau. If it is impracticable, or too expensive, to send the article itself, or to construct a model thereof, it will be sufficient to send photographs of the article, but it is necessary that such photographs shall show clearly, and give plain proof of the existence of each and every part of the invention described and claimed. Exterior views of casings, such as boiler-shells, retorts, filters, etc., which enclose parts which are the subject of claims, are not sufficient. Such parts must be photographed, separately if necessary. When photographs are relied upon to show the existence of a model, it is exceedingly important to see to it that they clearly prove the existence of every part of the invention, as if these proofs are submitted to the Federal Bureau at or near the expiration of the term of the Provisional Patent, and are rejected as insufficient, the patent may become forfeited by reason thereof. Photographs must either be sent unmounted, or mounted upon thin cardboard measuring 21 centimetres (8¼ inches) wide, and 33 centimetres (13 inches) in height, or they must be capable of being folded into this size. The working of an invention in Switzerland is considered equivalent to the production of a model.

MARKING PATENTED ARTICLES.—Every proprietor of a Definitive Patent must mark all articles made according to the same, which are to be exposed or sold in Switzerland, in a conspicuous place with the Federal Cross (✠) and the number of the patent. If this mark cannot be affixed upon the article itself, it must be represented upon the wrappers containing such articles.

DOCUMENTS REQUIRED.

1. **One Copy of the Specification.**—Written or printed on any paper of any size No signatures required.

2. **Drawings in duplicate.**—One copy to be on smooth, white, bristol board and the other on tracing cloth. The sheets must measure exactly 33 centimetres (13 inches) in height, by either 21, 42 or 63 centimetres (8¼, 16½ or 24¾ inches) wide, with a single marginal line all around, one-half an inch from the edge of the sheet. No signatures necessary. It should be noted that the Swiss office is exceedingly particular in the matter of drawings, and unless the following requirements are followed in every particular, it is almost certain that the drawings will be rejected. (1) All reference letters and numbers must be made plainly and not less than ⅛ inch in size. (2) There must be no writing upon the drawings except the reference letters and numbers. (3) The ink used must be deep black, and the lines clean and sharp. (4) The largest sized sheet must never be used except in cases where the whole of a view cannot be put upon a sheet of a smaller size. (5) A second sheet must not be used until the whole of the space upon the first sheet which can be used for drawing purposes is entirely used. (6) Where one sheet of the smallest size is sufficient, the drawing should be made upon the largest possible scale. (7) In other cases great care must be exercised in deciding upon the size of the sheet to be employed. The Patent Office demands that all the working space of one sheet be used before another sheet is taken, and that as few sheets be used as is practicable for the full illustration of the invention. Therefore the following rule should be followed: If the drawing space required is equal to that of two sheets of the smallest size, use one sheet of the middle size for the drawing. If the space required is equal to three small sheets, use one sheet of the middle size and one small sheet. If equal to four small sheets, use two sheets of the middle size. If equal to five small sheets, use two sheets of the middle size and one small sheet, and so on.

3. **Power of Attorney.**—Signed by the applicant, all names in full. No witnesses or legalization necessary. Either the usual French or the usual German form is sufficient.

If the applicant is the assignee, an assignment must be forwarded, which must be legalized by a Swiss Consul, and give the applicant the right to apply for the patent in his own name.

If the application is for a Definitive Patent, the application must be accompanied by a sample or model of the article to be patented, or by proof of the existence of such article or model.

Tahiti.

See France.

Tasmania.

CHARGES.

```
* PROVISIONAL PROTECTION, for six months................$30 00
* COMPLETING PATENT, all taxes paid for three years......... 70 00
                                                           _____
           Total cost.....................................$100 00
* Or, COMPLETE PATENT in first instance, taxes paid for three
      years                                                  90 00
† TAXES, on or before the expiration of the third year........... 85 00
      "           "              "        seventh "  ........... 110 00
‡ ASSIGNMENTS............................................... 15 00
```

* This charge does not cover the cost of possible opposition or referee's fees, but such extra expenses are almost never incurred; should they be, however, they will be made the basis of a special agreement as to amount.

+ The receipts for taxes must be endorsed upon the patent, which should always be forwarded when giving the order for payment. In case it is impracticable to do so, the Office will receive the tax without the production of the document, giving an interim receipt, and endorse the patent when presented.

‡ If the consideration expressed exceeds £100 ($500), there is an *ad valorem* duty of five shillings for every additional £50, or any fractional part thereof. Our charge includes the duty upon a consideration of £100 only, and when the amount is in excess of this sum, the additional duty must be added to our charge.

LAW AND PRACTICE.

Who may be Patentee.—The true and first inventor, which is interpreted to include the true and first importer, as in Great Britain. Patents are granted for communicated inventions as in England.

Patents, Kind and Term.—Provisional protection is granted for a term of six months. Patents of Invention are granted for a term of fourteen years counting from the date of the filing of the application. The term may be extended in exceptional cases for a further period not exceeding fourteen years. In case of prior foreign patents, the patent will expire with the first expiring foreign patent.

Unpatentable.—The law is silent upon this point.

Novelty, Effect of Prior Patent or Publication.—The application must be filed before the invention has been published or publicly used in Tasmania. Prior publication or prior patenting of the invention in another country will not prevent the obtaining of a perfectly valid patent provided the invention is new as to Tasmania at the time the application is filed.

Taxes.—A tax of £15 must be paid before the expiration of the third year of the life of the patent, counting from the date upon which the application was filed, and a further tax of £20 before the expiration of the seventh year. No prolongation of the time for making payment can be obtained. The payment of these taxes must be endorsed upon the patent, which should be forwarded when ordering the payment.

Assignments.—The documents should be in duplicate unless the assignee is content to allow the original document to remain in the Registrar's office. If the purchase money exceeds £100, there is an *ad valorem* duty of 5 shillings for every additional £50 or fractional part thereof.

Working.—There are no requirements.

DOCUMENTS REQUIRED.

1. **Power of Attorney.**—On any suitable paper. Signed by applicant.

2. **Petition.**—Signed by applicant. This may be written on any paper, and does not require to be witnessed.

3. **Declaration.**—Signed by applicant. This may be written on any paper, but *must* be made under some statute in force in the country or State where the declaration is made. It may be made before any person competent to take it. (See note under "Declarations" in article on Queensland.)

4. **Specification in duplicate.**—One copy must be on parchment and the other on paper. They must be written bookwise on both sides of the sheets, which must measure exactly 20 inches long and 15 inches wide, inclusive of a margin all around of

not less than one inch and a half. The parchment document must be signed and sealed by the applicant. The paper document must not be signed. No witnesses required.

5. Drawings in duplicate.—One copy must be on drawing paper (not tracing paper) and the other on parchment (not vegetable parchment). The sheets should measure 20 inches long by 15 inches wide, including a margin all round of not less than one and one-half inches.

FORMS.

POWER OF ATTORNEY.

Know all men by these presents :—

That I, (*Edward Henry Johns, mechanic, of Boston, in the State of Massachusetts, United States of America*) do hereby retain, constitute and appoint.........................of........................ Licensed Patent Agent, my true and lawful attorney, for me and in my name to sign, and as my act and deed to seal and deliver all necessary documents relating to obtaining Letters Patent in the Colony of Tasmania for an invention entitled (*Improvement in Plows*), and to alter and amend such documents, and at pleasure, to appoint a substitute or substitutes under him for any and all of the purposes aforesaid : I hereby ratifying and affirming, and engaging to ratify and confirm, all that my said attorney or his substitutes shall lawfully do by virtue hereof.

In witness whereof, I, the said (*Edward Henry Johns*), have hereunto set my hand and seal this..........day of.............................18....

Signed, sealed and delivered by the said)

(*Edward Henry Johns*) in presence of   )   (*Signature.*) [L. S]

    (*John Doe.*)
    (*Richard Roe.*)

PETITION.

To His Excellency the Governor of the Colony of Tasmania :

The humble Petition of (*Edward Henry Johns, mechanic, of Boston, in the State of Massachusetts, United States of America*), for, &c., Showeth :

That your Petitioner is in possession of an invention for (*Improvement in Plows*), which invention he believes will be of great public utility ; that he is the true and first inventor thereof ; and that the same has not been before made or used in the Colony of Tasmania by any other person or persons, to the best of his knowledge and belief.

Your Petitioner therefore humbly prays that Your Excellency will be pleased to grant unto him, his executors, administrators, and assigns, Letters Patent for the term of fourteen years, pursuant to the provisions of " *The Patent Law Act.*"

(*Signature.*)

And your Petitioner will ever pray, &c.

DECLARATION.

I, (*Edward Henry Johns, of Boston, in the State of Massachusetts, United States of America*), do hereby solemnly and sincerely declare, that I am in possession of an invention for (*Improvement in Plows*) which invention I believe will be of great public utility ; that I am the true and first inventor thereof ; and that the same has not been before made or used in the Colony of Tasmania by any other person or persons, to the best of my knowledge and belief ; and that the instrument in writing under my hand and seal, hereunto annexed, particularly describes and ascertains the nature of the said invention and the manner in which the same is to be performed. And I make this solemn declaration conscientiously believing the same to be true, and under and by virtue of the provisions of (*proceeding to recite the Statute under which the declaration is made*).

(*Signature.*)

Declared at..................................the............day of........................18......
before me (*signature and title of person taking declaration*).

SPECIFICATION.

To all to whom these presents come :

I, (*Edward Henry Johns, mechanic*), of (*Boston, in the State of Massachusetts, United States of America*), send greeting :

Whereas, I am desirous of obtaining Letters Patent for securing unto me Her Majesty's special License that I, my executors, administrators, and assigns, or such others as I or they should, at any time agree with, and no others, should and lawfully might, from time to time, and at all times during the term of fourteen years, to be computed from the day on which this instrument is left at the Office of the Registrar of Patents at Hobart, in the Colony of Tasmania, make, use, exercise and vend, within the said Colony of Tasmania, an invention for (*Improvement in Plows*); and, in order to obtain the said Letters Patent, I must, by an instrument in writing, under my hand and seal, particularly describe and ascertain the nature of the said invention, and in what manner the same is to be performed. Now, know ye that I, the said (*Edward Henry Johns*), do hereby declare the nature of the said invention, and the manner in which the same is to be performed, to be particularly described and ascertained in and by the following statement—that is to say:

(*Describe the Invention.*)

In witness whereof, I, the said (*Edward Henry Johns*), have hereunto set my hand and seal, this...........................day of.............................18....

(*Signature.*)   (L. S.)

Tobago (West India).

This island has been annexed to Trinidad, and by order in Council the Trinidad laws have been extended to apply to Tobago, and are now in force there.

Tonquin.

See France.

Trinidad.

CHARGES.

PATENT, cost of, all taxes paid...............................$125 00
ASSIGNMENTS, preparing and recording.................. ... 15 00

LAW AND PRACTICE.

Who may be Patentee.—The true and first inventor, or the true and first importer into Trinidad.

Patents, Kind and Term.—Patents of Invention (or Importation) granted for fourteen years, counting from the grant of the certificate by the Registrar-General.

Unpatentable.—The law is silent upon this point.

Novelty, Effect of Prior Patent or Publication.—To obtain a valid patent, the application therefor must be filed before any public use or exercise of the invention within the Colony of Trinidad. Prior patenting or publication of the invention in any other country will not prevent the obtaining of a perfectly valid patent, provided the invention is new in Trinidad at the time the application is filed.

Taxes.—There are none after the issue of the patent.

Assignments.—The documents should be in duplicate. Any usual form may be used.

Working.—There are no requirements.

DOCUMENTS REQUIRED.

1. **Petition.**—Signed by applicant.

2. **Declaration.**—Signed by applicant.

3. **Specification in duplicate.**—May be signed either by the applicant or the agent.

4. **Drawings in duplicate.**—On drawing board or tracing cloth, any suitable size. No signatures required.

5. **Power of Attorney.**—Signed by applicant.

FORMS.

The forms are the same as for Mauritius (which see), excepting the name of the Colony, which should read "Island of Trinidad," and the title of the Act, which for Trinidad is "Ordinance No. 25 of 1867."

The declaration should specify "that the same is not in use by any person or persons in the Island of Trinidad."

Tunis.

CHARGES.

```
* PATENT, cost of, all taxes paid for one year....................$50 00
* PATENTS OF ADDITION, all taxes paid...................... 50 00
  TAXES, payable yearly, counting from the date of application.
    Each year.......................................................... 20 00
  ASSIGNMENTS (Notarial). See "Assignments"................ 5 00
  WORKING, Nominal.................................. . 50 00
```

* The above charge includes translation of the specification up to 2,000 words; 35 cents must be added for every 100 words in the specification in excess of 2,000.

LAW AND PRACTICE.

Who may be Patentee.—Anyone; a person, firm or corporation.

Patents, Kind and Term.—Patents of Invention are granted for five, ten or fifteen years, as elected by the applicant, subject to the payment of the prescribed taxes and the proper working of the invention.

Unpatentable.—Plans and combinations of credit or finance; inventions, the use of which would be contrary to the laws and good manners, alimentary products and medicines, although processes relating to the manufacture of the latter may be made the subject of a patent.

Novelty, Effect of Prior Patent or Publication.—To obtain a valid patent, the application therefor must be filed before the invention has been published, or otherwise received sufficient publicity to allow of its being put into practice, either in the Regency of Tunis or in any other country.

Taxes.—A tax of 100 piastres is payable upon every patent (except Patents of Addition), before the expiration of each year of its life, counting from the date of the filing of the application. No prolongation of the time for making payment can be obtained.

Assignments.—Before an assignment can be recorded, all the taxes for the full term of the patent must be paid. As this is an expensive proceeding it is usual to prepare a Power of Attorney authorizing a Notary to effect the assignment. This is signed by both assignor and assignee and two witnesses, and should then be legalized by a French Consul. This document is retained by the assignee until he is ready to have the assignment made and recorded, which can be done at any time.

We can obtain the legalization here, when desired, at a cost of $3.00 for each legalization.

Working.—The patent must be worked within two years from the date of the issue of the patent, and the working must not be interrupted thereafter for any two whole years at a time. As there have been no decisions upon this point as yet, it is impossible to say just what construction will be put upon the law, but as the latter is, to all intents and purposes, a copy of the French law, it is believed that the practice will be the same as in France, and that an actual and effective working will be required. We will obtain estimates of the cost of actual workings upon receipt of particulars. We quote a price for nominal workings, but it must be understood that we do not recommend them and that we will not be responsible for their sufficiency.

Special.—*IMPORTATION OF PATENTED ARTICLES.* A patentee may be deprived of his rights if he shall have imported into the Regency, objects manufactured in foreign countries which are similar to those protected by his patent. A permit may, however, be obtained from the Prime Minister for the importation of : 1. Models of machines. 2. Objects manufactured abroad destined for public exhibitions or for trials made with the consent of the government. As Tunis is a member of the International Union, citizens and subjects of States belonging to the Union may, however, import patented articles without risk of forfeiting their patents.

DOCUMENTS REQUIRED.

1. **Specification.**—On any suitable paper. No signatures.

2. **Drawings in duplicate.**—On tracing cloth, any suitable size.

3. **Power of Attorney.**—Signed by the applicant. No witnesses or legalization necessary. The usual French form should be used, for which, see France.

Turkey.

CHARGES.

* PATENT, cost of, all taxes paid for one year	$100 00
* PATENT OF ADDITION, all taxes paid	60 00
TAXES, payable in advance, on or before March 13th, each year..	25 00
ASSIGNMENTS (see "Assignments" below) nominal	5 00
WORKING, exclusive of cost of manufacturing	50 00

* The above charge includes translation of the specification up to 2,000 words. Beyond that number $1.00 must be added for each 100 words.

LAW AND PRACTICE.

Who may be Patentee.—Practically, anyone, a person, firm, or corporation.

Patents, Kind and Term.—Patents of Invention granted for five, ten or fifteen years, as the applicant may elect, subject to the payment of the required taxes, and the proper working of the invention. Patents of Addition granted for the unexpired term of the original patent upon which it is based, and expiring therewith. In case of a prior foreign patent, the duration of the Turkish patent will not exceed that of the foreign patent. Extensions can only be secured by the enactment of a special law.

Unpatentable.—Pharmaceutical compounds and medicines of every kind; devices or combinations relating to banking or finance; inventions or discoveries contrary to public order or safety, to morals, or to the laws of the Empire; theoretical principles, methods, systems, discoveries and conceptions which are not capable of industrial application.

Novelty, Effect of Prior Patent or Publication.—To obtain a valid patent, the application therefor must be filed before the invention has received, either in Turkey or elsewhere, sufficient publicity to enable the same to be worked. Subject to the above provision, inventions already patented in any other countries may be patented in Turkey.

Taxes.—A tax of two Turkish pounds must be paid upon every patent (except a patent of addition) during each year of its life. All taxes are payable on the 1st of March of every Turkish fiscal year, or before the 13th of March, according to the Gregorian calendar, or new style. There are no taxes upon patents of addition after issue.

Assignments.—The assignment should be in duplicate and must be made by Notarial deed or by an Act passed before a civil tribunal of first instance in localities where there are no Notaries. Before an assignment can be recorded, all the taxes must be paid for the entire term of the patent. The practice is the same as for French assignments. Assignments must be legalized by a Turkish Consul.

We can obtain the legalization here, when desired, at a cost of $3.00 for each document.

Working.—The invention must be worked within two years of the date of the issue of the patent, and the working must not entirely cease thereafter for any two consecutive years. The law requires the actual manufacture of the invention in Turkey, the practice being the same as in France.

Special.—*IMPORTATION OF PATENTED ARTICLES.*—The importation of patented articles is strictly prohibited under the penalty of the forfeiture of the patent, with the exception that the Minister of Commerce and Agriculture may authorize the introduction into the Empire of models of machines and articles manufactured abroad, intended for public exhibitions or for experiments made with the consent of the government.

DOCUMENTS REQUIRED.

1. **Specification.**—Written or printed on any paper. No signatures necessary.

2. **Drawings in duplicate.**—On tracing cloth, of any convenient size, leaving ample margin. No signatures necessary.

3. **Power of Attorney.**—Signed by applicant and legalized by a Turkish Consul. The usual French power should be used. (See France.)

We can obtain the legalization here, when desired, at a cost of $3.00, which includes Consular and Agency fees.

Turks Island.

This island is now under the government of Jamaica.

Uruguay.

CHARGES.

PATENT, cost of, all taxes paid for one year.....................$300 00
PATENT OF ADDITION, all taxes paid for one year............ 250 00
TAXES, *payable yearly, counting from date of patent, with ten days' grace.*
    Each year, upon Original Patents........................... 40 00
    "   " Patents of Addition, when the holder is the original patentee......................... 25 00
    "   " Patents of Addition when the holder is a third party.................................. 35 00
ASSIGNMENTS, preparing and recording...................... 50 00
WORKING. The charges are variable, about.................... 100 00

*The above charge includes translation of the specification up to 2,000 words. Beyond this number, $1.00 must be added for each 100 words.

LAW AND PRACTICE.

Who may be Patentee.—The inventor, his agent, or assignee, and the owner of a prior foreign patent, who is allowed one year from the date of said patent to file his application in Uruguay.

Patents, Kind and Term.—Patents of Invention, granted for three, six, or nine years, as the applicant may elect, subject to the payment of the prescribed taxes and proper working. Patents of Addition, for improvements upon inventions for which a patent is already issued, granted for the unexpired term of the original patent, and expiring therewith. The term cannot be prolonged except by special Legislative Act.

Unpatentable.—Financial schemes; discoveries or inventions well known in the country and abroad by means of written works or printed periodicals; inventions that are purely theoretical, and do not admit of practical application; chemical compositions; and inventions that are contrary to the laws of morality and the Republic.

Novelty, Effect of Prior Patent or Publication.—To obtain a valid patent the application therefor must be filed before the invention has been published, or become well known in Uruguay and abroad. The owner of a foreign patent has, however, a priority of one year from the date of his foreign patent within which to file his application, and if the application be filed within this time, a valid patent may be obtained without regard to any publication or public use of the invention.

Taxes.—Patents of Invention are subject to a yearly tax of 25 pesos, which must be paid in advance, counting from the date of the patent. There is ten days' grace for making payment, and without fine. Patents of Addition are subject to a yearly tax of one-third of the amount of the yearly tax upon the original patent if the owner is the original patentee ; and to a yearly tax of two-thirds of the amount of the yearly tax upon the original patent if the owner of the Patent of Addition is not the original patentee. No prolongation of time for making a payment can be obtained.

Assignments.—The documents should be prepared in the Spanish language and be in duplicate. They should be legalized by a Uruguayan Consul.

We can obtain the legalization here, when desired, at a cost of $3.00 for each legalization.

Working.—The Executive power designates "a reasonable time" within which to commence working the industry to which the patent refers. If the working is stopped thereafter for one year the patent becomes void. It is sometimes possible to obtain an extension of the time for working, when the working has been interrupted by accident or *force majeure*, which event must be proved by the interested party within the term of one month, or the patent will be declared forfeited. In the absence of any judicial decisions upon this point it is not possible to determine just what will constitute a sufficient and legal working. There is little doubt, however, that the intent of the law is to require an actual and practically continuous working of the invention (manufacture) in Uruguay. We will obtain estimates of the cost of actual workings upon receipt of full particulars. We quote a price for nominal workings, as we frequently receive orders for them, but it must be clearly understood that we do not hold ourselves in any way responsible for their sufficiency.

DOCUMENTS REQUIRED.

1. **Specification**—On any paper and in any form. No signatures necessary.

2. **Drawings in duplicate.**—On drawing board or tracing cloth, any suitable size, made to metric scale. No signatures necessary.

3. **Power of Attorney.**—Signed by the applicant. This should be legalized by a Uruguayan Consul. The form is the same as for the Argentine Republic (which see).

4. **If a prior foreign patent exists,** a certified copy, legalized by a Uruguayan Consul should be furnished.

5. **If no prior foreign patent exists,** a declaration stating that the invention has not been patented in the country of its origin. This document must be signed by the applicant, and be legalized by a Uruguayan Consul. The form is the same as for the Argentine Republic, (which see).

When desired we can obtain the legalization here at a cost of $3.00 for each document, which amount includes Consular and Agency fees.

Venezuela.

CHARGES.

```
* PATENT, Cost of, for five years, all taxes paid.................$220 00
    "         "      ten     "        "     ...................  300 00
    "         "      fifteen "        "     ...................  375 00

ASSIGNMENT, preparing and recording.......................   40 00
WORKING, exclusive of freight or cost of manufacture.........   50 00
```
*The above charge includes translation of the specification up to 2,000 words. $1.00 must be added for each 100 words in the specification in excess of 2,000.

LAW AND PRACTICE.

Who may be Patentee.—An inventor, or any person who has had a patent granted to him in a foreign country.

Patents, Kind and Term.—The patent is granted for five, ten or fifteen years, as elected by the applicant, counting from the date of the issue of the patent, subject to the required working. In case of a prior foreign patent, the Venezuelan patent will be granted for a period equal to the unexpired term of the foreign patent.

Unpatentable.—Inventions prejudicial to health, public order, morals, or prior rights ; pharmaceutical preparations and medicines.

Novelty, Effect of Prior Patent or Publication.—The application must be made before the invention is known to or used by others in Venezuela, or has been patented to another or described in a public print published either in the Republic or abroad, or before the invention has been in public use or offered for sale for more than two years, but an invention already patented in a foreign country may be patented in Venezuela, provided that it has not already been patented by another person.

Taxes.—There are none after the issue of the patent.

Assignments.—The documents must be in duplicate and in the Spanish language and be legalized by a Venezuelan Consul.

We can obtain the legalization here, when desired, at a cost of $3.00 for each document.

Working.—Patents are granted for five, ten and fifteen years, and become void six months, one year, and two years, respectively, after the grant, unless the invention has been carried into operation. The working must not be discontinued for as much as a whole year at a time. In the absence of any judicial decisions regarding workings it cannot be determined with certainty just what will constitute a legal working. We are advised, however, that in case of machinery or apparatus, it is considered sufficient to import one or more into Venezuela and put them into operation there. In case of a process, it must be carried into practice in the country.

DOCUMENTS REQUIRED.

Specification.—Written or printed on any paper. No signatures necessary.

Drawings in duplicate.—On tracing cloth, any convenient size, leaving ample margins. No signatures required.

Power of Attorney.—Signed by applicant and legalized by a Venezuelan Consul. The form is the same as for the Argentine Republic (which see).

If a prior foreign patent exists, a certified copy of the same, legalized by a Venezuelan Consul, must be supplied.

The law requires an oath, but as this may be signed by the agent under Power of Attorney, it is not necessary to send one.

We can obtain the legalization here, when desired, at a cost of $3.00, which includes Consular and Agency fees.

Victoria.

CHARGES.

*PROVISIONAL PROTECTION, for 12 months	$25 00
COMPLETING PATENT, all taxes paid for three years	45 00
Total cost	$70 00
*Or COMPLETE PATENT, in first instance, taxes paid for three years	60 00
†TAXES, before the expiration of the third year	20 00
" " " " seventh "	20 00
ASSIGNMENTS, preparing and recording (including 10s. stamp)	12 50

* In case the application is opposed, or rejected by the Examiner there will be extra charges in addition to the above amounts. These will be seldom incurred however, and will be made the subject of special agreement in each case.

† In case a tax is not paid within the required time an extension of time for paying same may be obtained, not however to exceed six months at most, upon payment of a fine of 15 shillings ($3.75), for each month of such extension. To the amount of the fine must be added our agency charge of $7.50 for obtaining such extension and paying the fine. An application for extension of time must be made according to a prescribed form and must be accompanied by a statutory declaration; we will furnish forms when desired.

LAW AND PRACTICE.

Who may be Patentee.—(1) The actual inventor or his assigns. (2) The actual inventor jointly with the assigns of a part interest in the invention. (3) The legal representatives of a deceased actual inventor or of his assigns, provided they file their application within twelve months of the decease of such inventor. (4) Any person to whom the invention has been communicated by the actual inventor, his legal representatives or assigns, if the actual inventor, his legal representatives or assigns is or are not resident in Victoria. (5) A corporation, either as the assignee of, or as a communication from the inventor. (6) Joint inventors.

Patents, Kind and Term.—Provisional Protection is granted for a term of twelve months, counting from the day the application is filed. In such case the complete specification should be filed within nine months from the date of application. An extension of one month's time may be had for filing the complete specification upon payment of a fine. Patents of Invention, granted for fourteen years, counting from the date of the filing of the application, subject to the payment of the prescribed taxes. The patent may sometimes be extended for an additional term of fourteen years.

Unpatentable.—Inventions, the use of which would be, in the opinion of the Supreme Court law officer or Commissioner, contrary to law or morality, or dangerous, or injurious or prejudicial to the public interest.

Novelty, Effect of Prior Patent or Publication.—The application should be filed before the invention has been published or publicly used in Victoria, but where a patent has been obtained in a foreign country for any invention first invented in any country outside of Victoria, a patent may be obtained for such invention at any time within one year from the date of the granting of any such patent, notwithstanding that such invention has been used or published in Victoria, within such period of one year, provided that such use or publication has not been made with the consent of the inventor. The exhibition, publication, or public use of an invention at an industrial or international exhibition will not prevent the obtaining of a valid patent, provided the inventor gives the Commissioner one month's notice of his intention to make such exhibition, and files his application within twelve months from the opening of the exhibition.

Taxes.—A tax of £2.10.0 is payable before the expiration of the third year of the life of the patent, counting from the date of the filing of the application, and a further tax of £2.10.0, before the expiration of the seventh year. In case a payment is not made within the required time, an extension of such time, not to exceed six months, at most, may be had upon filing an application made in the prescribed form, accompanied by a statutory declaration setting forth the grounds upon which such extension is asked, and upon payment of a fine of 15 shillings ($3.75) for each month of such extension. See "Charges" for our terms for obtaining extensions.

Assignments.—These should be in duplicate, and may be in any suitable form. When forwarding the same for registration, a request to enter name upon the register must also be supplied.

Working.—There are no requirements.

DOCUMENTS REQUIRED.

These should be prepared upon strong (not thin), white paper, of a size exactly 8 inches wide by 13 inches high, leaving a margin of 2 inches on the left hand side thereof.

Black ink only should be used, as we are advised that the Commissioner will in future refuse documents prepared in analine or other colored inks.—Carbon copies will not be accepted.

1. **Authorization.**—Signed by applicant.

2. Application for Patent and Copy Thereof, must be signed by the applicant except in the case of a corporation applying, when it must be signed by the Agent. The copy must be marked "true copy," and this certificate must also be signed. The application can be made before a British Consul, Notary Public, or any person competent to take declarations by the law of the country where the same is to be taken.

3. Specification in duplicate.—May be signed by either the applicant or by the Agent. One of the copies must be marked "true copy," and this certificate must be signed by the person signing the specification.

4. Drawings in duplicate.—On sheets of pure, white drawing paper or bristol board, 8 inches wide by 13 inches high, or 16 inches wide by 13 inches high. A single margin line must be drawn all around, one-half inch from the edge of the sheet. No signatures necessary.

5. A Fac-simile of the Original Drawings.—This may be made upon tracing cloth. No signatures necessary.

When the applicant is the assignee, an assignment (with an examined copy thereof), must be supplied.

FORMS.

AUTHORIZATION.

Victoria.

I hereby appoint..
to act as my agent in respect of my application for a Patent for (*insert title of invention*) and I request that all notices, requisitions, and communications relating thereto may be sent to such agent at the above address.

Dated the..................day of................one thousand eight hundred and ninety.........

(*Signature.*)

APPLICATION FOR PATENT BY A SINGLE INVENTOR.

Victoria.

Application for Patent.

(*By a single Inventor.*)

I, (*insert name, address, and occupation of inventor*), do solemnly and sincerely declare that I am in possession of an invention for (*insert title of invention ;*) that I am the actual inventor thereof : and that the said invention is not in use in Victoria by any other person or persons to the best of my knowledge and belief. And I desire that a Patent may be granted to me for the said invention.

And I make this solemn declaration conscientiously believing the same to be true, and under and by virtue of (*here recite the Statute in force in the country in which the declaration is made*).

(*Signature.*)

Declared this......................day of............ .....one thousand eight hundred and ninety ......
......at.................................in the..........................of..........................
Before me (*Signature of official before whom the declaration was made*).

APPLICATION FOR PATENT BY JOINT INVENTORS.

Victoria.

Application for Patent.

(*By Joint Inventors.*)

We (*insert names, addresses, and occupations*), do severally, solemnly and sincerely declare that we are in possession of an invention for (*insert title of invention*) ; that we are the actual inventors, thereof ; and that the said invention is not in use in Victoria by any other person or persons to the best of our knowledge and belief ; and we desire that a Patent may be granted to us for the said invention.

And I, (*insert name of first declarant*), make this solemn declaration conscientiously believing the same to be true and under and by virtue of (*here recite the Statute in force in the country in which the declaration is made.*)

(*Signature of first Declarant.*)

And I, *(insert name of second declarant)*, make this solemn declaration, conscientiously believing the same to be true and under and by virtue of *(here recite the Statute in force in the country in which the declaration is made)*.

(Signature of second Declarant.)

Declared this..day of...
one thousand eight hundred and ninety......................at......................................
in the.....................of....................by the above-named...............................

Before me...

(Person taking declaration of first Applicant to sign here.)

Declared this..day of...
one thousand eight hundred and ninety......................at......................................
in the.....................of....................by the above-named...............................

Before me...

(Person taking declaration of second Applicant to sign here.)

APPLICATION FOR PATENT BY INVENTOR AND ASSIGNEE JOINTLY.

Victoria.

Application for Patent,

(By an Inventor and an Assignee jointly.)

We, *(insert names, addresses and occupations)*, do severally, solemnly, and sincerely declare that we are in possession of an invention for *(insert title of invention)*; that I the said *(insert name of actual inventor)*, am the actual inventor thereof, and that I the said *(insert name of assignee)*, am the assignee of the said *(insert name of inventor)*, of a part or share of and in the said invention; and that the said invention is not in use in Victoria by any other person or persons to the best of our knowledge and belief; and we desire that a Patent may be granted to us jointly for the said invention.

And I, *(insert name of one of the parties)*, make this solemn declaration conscientiously believing the same to be true, and under and by virtue of *(here recite the Statute in force in the country in which the declaration is made.)*

(Signature of first Declarant.)

And I, *(insert name of other party)*, make this solemn declaration conscientiously believing the same to be true, and under and by virtue of *(here recite the Statute in force in the country in which the declaration is made)*.

(Signature of second Declarant.)

Declared this....................day of..................one thousand eight hundred and ninety....
at........................in the........................by the above-named........................

Before me..

(Person taking declaration of first Declarant to sign here.)

Declared this....................day of..... ....one thousand eight hundred and ninety....
at........................in the................by the above-named........................

Before me..

(Person taking declaration of second Declarant to sign here.)

APPLICATION FOR PATENT BY ASSIGNEE ALONE.

Victoria.

Application for Patent,

(By the Assignee of the Inventor alone.)

I, *(insert name, address and occupation)*, do solemnly and sincerely declare that I am in possession of an invention for *(insert title of invention)*, that I am the assignee of *(insert name of actual inventor)*, who is I verily believe the actual inventor thereof; and that the said invention is not in use in Victoria by any other person or persons to the best of my knowledge and belief. And I desire that a Patent may be granted to me for the said invention.

And I make this solemn declaration conscientiously believing the same to be true and under and by virtue of *(here recite the Statute in force in the country in which the declaration is made.)*

(Signature.)

Declared this..............day of.................one thousand eight hundred and ninety..........
at............in...

Before me..

(Person taking declaration to sign here.)

PROVISIONAL SPECIFICATION.

Provisional Specification.

(Title of Invention.)

I, *(insert name, address and occupation)*, do hereby declare the nature of my invention for *(insert title of invention)*, to be as follows:

(Here follows description.)

(Signature.)

Dated this...........................day of.................189 ....

COMPLETE SPECIFICATION.

Complete Specification.

(Title of Invention.)

I, *(insert name, address and occupation)*, do hereby declare the nature of my invention for *(insert title of invention)*, and in what manner the same is to be performed to be particularly described and ascertained in and by the following statement:

(Here insert full description of Invention.)

Having now particularly described and ascertained the nature of my said Invention and in what manner the same is to be performed, I declare that what I claim is:

(Signature.)

Dated this.....................day of.....................................189

ASSIGNMENT FROM INVENTOR, WHEN APPLICANT APPLIES AS ASSIGNEE.

Assignment.

THIS DEED, made the....................day of...............................one thousand eight hundred and........................ between *(insert name, address and occupation of inventor)*, (hereinafter called the assignor), of the one part, and *(insert name, address and occupation of assignee)* (hereinafter called the assignee) of the other part. Whereas, the said assignor is the inventor of an invention entitled *(insert title of invention)*.

Now, this Deed Witnesseth that, in consideration of the premises and of the sum of *(insert consideration)*, sterling, in hand well and truly received by the said assignor from the said assignee at or before the signing and sealing of these presents, the receipt whereof the said assignor does hereby acknowledge, the said assignor does hereby sell and assign, transfer and set over, unto the said assignee, his executors, administrators and assigns, all his right, title and interest of and in the said invention, so far as the Colony of Victoria is concerned, with full power to the said assignee to apply for and obtain Letters Patent therefor in his own name, in Victoria aforesaid.

In Witness whereof, the said assignor has hereto set his hand and seal the day and year first above written.

(Signature.)   [L. S.]

Signed and Delivered by the said }
.... }
in the presence of.............. }

Name. Address. Occupation.

APPOINTMENT OF AGENT.

(To be used for communications.)

Whereas I, *(insert name, address and occupation)*, am the actual inventor *(or the assignee of the actual inventor)*, of an invention for *(insert title of invention)*, for which I am desirous of obtaining Letters Patent in the colony of Victoria, do hereby nominate and appoint...........................
Patent Agent, my agent to represent me in all matters relating to the said application for Letters Patent. And I hereby give him full power to apply for the said Patent in his name as upon a communication from me.

Dated this.......................day of...one thousand eight hundred and..

(Signature.),....................................

Witness............................
Name. Address. Occupation.

Western Australia.

CHARGES.

LETTERS OF REGISTRATION, cost of, all taxes paid $110 00
* PATENT, cost of, all taxes paid, for 4 years.................... 90 00
† TAXES, On Letters of Registration........................... none.
    On Patents before the expiration of the 4th year......... 35 00
       "   "   "   " 7th year......... 35 00
ASSIGNMENTS... 25 00

  * The above charge does not cover the cost of possible opposition, or of amendment, if the application is rejected by the Examiner. Extra expenses are seldom incurred, and will be made the subject of special agreement in each case.

  † The time for paying a tax may be extended, not to exceed six months, upon payment of a fine of £10. Our charge for procuring the extension and paying the fine is, including fine, $65.00.

LAW AND PRACTICE.

Who may be Patentee.—The *bona fide* holder of a foreign patent may obtain Letters of Registration, which have the same force as Letters Patent. The originator or discoverer of any new invention, for which no patent, or instrument in the nature of a patent has been issued in any other country, may apply for and obtain Letters Patent. Joint inventors may obtain a joint patent. An inventor and an assignee may join in making an application for Letters Patent. The legal representatives of a deceased inventor may file an application for a patent within six months from the date of his decease.

Patents, Kind and Term.—Letters of Registration are granted for the unexpired term of the foreign patent upon which they are based, and expire therewith. Letters Patent are issued for a term of fourteen years, counting from the date of the filing of the application, subject to the payment of the prescribed taxes. The Patent may, in exceptional cases, be extended for a further term of seven, or even fourteen years.

Unpatentable.—Letters Patent will not be granted for any invention known to be already patented in Great Britain or in any other country. Letters of Registration may, however, be obtained in such cases.

Novelty, Effect of Prior Patent or Publication.—Letters of Registration may be obtained at any time during the life of a foreign patent, for the unexpired term of such foreign patent. To obtain valid Letters Patent, the application therefor should be filed before any publication or public use of the invention within Western Australia. The exhibition, publication or public use of an invention at an international or industrial exhibition, will not prevent the obtaining of valid Letters Patent, provided notice of the intention to exhibit is given the Registrar, and the application is filed within six months from the date of the opening of the exhibition.

Assignments.—These should be in duplicate and may be in any suitable form.

Working.—There are no requirements.

DOCUMENTS REQUIRED (LETTERS PATENT).

1. **Application.**—Signed by applicant.

2. **Specification in duplicate.**—No signature required.

3. **Drawings in duplicate.**—No signatures necessary.

4. **Statement of Address.**—Signed by applicant.

  No forms of applications for Letters Patent have ever been issued by the Government; but from the Registrar's remarks, there is little doubt but that documents prepared in accordance with the British rules will be accepted.

DOCUMENTS REQUIRED. (LETTERS OF REGISTRATION.)

1. **Petition.**—Signed by applicant.

2. **Certified Copy of Letters Patent** held by applicant. May be either printed or written on any material.

3. **Certified Copy of Specification** on which such Patent has been granted, unless printed, must be written on brief or foolscap paper, on one side only. If printed, the certification will be held to include the correctness of the drawings also, if the whole is bound up together.

4. **Certified Copy of Drawing** on which such Patent has been granted. Whether printed or not, can be on paper or cloth.

5. **Declaration by Applicant.**—Signed by applicant.

6. **Declaration by Professional Man.**—Signed by a Patent Solicitor or Agent, preferably.

7. **Power of Attorney.**—Signed by applicant.

If the applicant be the assignee of the patentee, a certified copy of the assignment must also be supplied.

Declarations may be made before a Notary Public or other competent official.

FORMS.

PETITION.

Petition.

To His Excellency the Governor of the Colony of Western Australia.

The humble Petition of (*here insert name and address of Petitioner*)
Sheweth:

That your Petitioner is the *bona fide* holder of (*insert name of country*) Letters Patent, dated the
............................day of.., granted to him for an invention entitled (*here insert title of invention*).

That your Petitioner is desirous of obtaining Letters of Registration for the said invention, and has accordingly deposited the sum of £15 with the Colonial Treasurer, in accordance with the provisions of the "*Patents Act* 1888."

Your Petitioner therefore humbly prays that your Excellency will be pleased to grant unto him, his executors, administrators, and assigns, Letters of Registration for the said invention, in accordance with the provisions of the "*Patents Act* 1888."

And your Petitioner will ever pray, &c.

(Signature.)

DECLARATION OF PROFESSIONAL MAN.

Declaration.

I, (*insert name, address and occupation*), do solemnly and sincerely declare:

That I have searched the Register of Proprietors of Patents, which is kept at the Patents Office, (*insert name of place*), and that so far as is disclosed by this record (*insert name of owner of patent*), is the Sole Proprietor of Letters Patent, granted to (*insert name of original patentee*), for an invention entitled (*insert title of invention*).

That the said Letters Patent are dated the.........................day of.........................
and are now in full force.

And I make this solemn declaration, conscientiously believing the same to be true, and under and by virtue of (*here recite the Statute under which the declaration is made*).

(Signature.)

Declared at..
Before me (*Signature of official before whom declaration is taken*).

DECLARATION OF APPLICANT.

Declaration.

I, (insert name, address and occupation), do solemnly and sincerely declare :

That I am the person named in, and the bona fide holder of (insert name of country), Letters Patent granted to me for an invention entitled (title of invention), which said Letters Patent are dated the..................day of ....

And I make this solemn declaration conscientiously believing the same to be true, and under and by virtue of (here recite Statute.)

(Signature.)

Declared at..................before me (signature of official before whom declaration is made).

—

If the applicant be the assignee, he must furnish, in lieu of this declaration, a copy of the deed of assignment and the following statutory declaration :

FORM OF DECLARATION OF APPLICANT WHEN HE IS NOT THE GRANTEE OF LETTERS PATENT.

I, (insert name, address and occupation of applicant), do solemnly and sincerely declare:

That I am the assignee of the person named in, and the bona fide holder of (insert name of country) Letters Patent granted to one (insert name of patentee), of (insert address), for an invention entitled (insert title of invention), which said Letters Patent are dated the........day of.........18

That I am the person named in the copy deed hereto annexed and marked "A," and that such copy deed is a true and correct copy of the original deed of assignment of which it purports to be a copy.

And I make this solemn declaration, conscientiously believing the same to be true, and under and by virtue of (here recite Statute.)

(Signature.)

Declared at..

Before me...............................(Signature of official before whom declaration is made.)

Zanzibar.

There is as yet no patent law in force. It is probable that the government would give protection to inventions by way of special grant, provided the invention was likely to be of use in the country.

As yet we have had no demand for such grants, and have made no arrangements as to prices, etc. We have a reliable agent there, however, and will undertake the transaction of any business in that country upon terms to be agreed upon in each individual case.

The International Union

FOR

THE PROTECTION OF INDUSTRIAL PROPERTY.

On January 1st, 1891, the following countries were members of the International Union :

Belgium,
Brazil,
France (and her Colonies Martinique, Guadaloupe, St. Mary de Madagascar, La Re-union, Cochin-China, St. Pierre and Micquelon, French Guiana, Senegal, Congo, Gaboon, Mazotte, Nassi-Bé, French India, New Caledonia and Tahiti),
Great Britain,
Guatemala,
Italy,

Netherlands (and her East and West Indian Colonies),
Norway,
Portugal,
San Domingo,
Servia,
Spain,
Sweden,
Switzerland,
Tunis,
United States of America.

These countries have associated themselves together, forming an international union, for the protection of inventions, trade and other commercial marks, and similar industrial property. The principal provisions of the regulations of the Union are as follows:

1. Aliens have the same rights as Natives.—The subjects or citizens of each of the contracting States, shall in all the other States of the Union, in matters concerning patents, industrial designs or models, trade and commercial marks, and trade-names, enjoy the advantages that their respective laws now grant, or shall hereafter grant to natives.

2. Right of Priority for Filing Applications.—Any person who has duly lodged an application for a patent, an industrial design or model, or trade or commercial mark in one of the contracting States, shall enjoy, for lodging the application in the other States, and reserving the rights of third parties, a right of priority during the terms hereinafter named.

Consequently, a subsequent application in any of the other States of the Union before the expiration of these periods shall not be invalidated through any acts accomplished in the interval, either, for instance, by another application, by publication of the invention or by the working of it by a third party, by the sale of copies of the design or model, or by the use of the mark.

The above-mentioned terms of priority shall be six months for patents, and three months for industrial designs and models, and for trade and commercial marks. The terms are increased by a month for countries beyond the sea (North and South America, etc.).

3. Protection for Inventions Exhibited in Exhibitions.—Temporary protection will be granted for any patentable invention, industrial design or model, or trade or commercial mark, for articles exhibited at official or officially recognized international exhibitions.

This temporary protection is granted for the term of six months from the day of the admission of the article at the exhibition, and is independent of the "term of priority" mentioned in the preceding article. During this term, the exhibition, publication, or working not authorized by the owner of the invention, design, model or mark thus protected, shall not hinder the party who has obtained the said temporary protection from making good in the course of said term his application for patent, or the registration necessary to secure definite protection in the entire territory of the Union. This temporary protection shall not be operative unless, while it still continues, an application for patent is made, or some specimen deposited for the purpose of securing to the respective article definite protection in one of the States belonging to the Union.

4. The Right to Import Patented Articles.—The importation of patented articles by the patentee into any country where a patent has been issued, does not entail forfeiture of the patent. Nevertheless, the patentee remains subject to the obligation to work his patent in conformity with the laws of the country into which he introduces the patented articles.

5. Protection of Trade-Names.—A trade-name is protected in all of the countries of the Union without the necessity of registration.

6. Confiscation of Infringing Articles.—All products illegally bearing a trade or commercial mark or trade-name, or a spurious or misleading mark with regard to the place of production, may be confiscated either in the country where the false mark was affixed, or in the country where the product has been introduced.

7. Rights of Aliens Domiciliated in States of Union.—Subjects or citizens of States not forming part of the Union, who are domiciled in the territory of any of the States of the Union, shall enjoy equal rights with the subjects or citizens of States belonging to the Union. Those possessing industrial or commercial establishments in any of the States of the Union, but not residing there, shall possess equal rights if they are the exclusive owners of the said establishments, and are represented there by a general agent. In case of contestation, such persons are bound to prove that they actually and continuously exercise their industry or business there.

CHARGES, TAXES AND WORKINGS.

(Copyrighted, 1891, by Richards & Co.)

Table showing the Countries in which Yearly Taxes are payable upon Patents; the amount of same, and when payable; together with our charge for a complete application for patent; our charge for extra translations for each 100 words in the specification in excess of 2,000; the kind of working required, times when due, and our charge for nominal workings.

Country	Charge for Patents	Translation per 100 words in excess of 2,000	Payable from	Grace	2nd year	3rd year	4th year	5th year	6th year	7th year	8th year	9th year	10th year	11th year	12th year	13th year	14th year	15th year	*Workings Kind	*Workings Due	Charge for nominal workings
Austria-Hungary	$35.00	$.35	issue	none	$20.00	$20.00	$20.00	$20.00	$25.00	$30.00	$33.00	$36.00	$39.00	$45.00	$52.00	$58.00	$64.00	$70.00	actual	1 + 2	$20.00
Belgium (Note 1)	15.00	.35	application	1 month without fine, 1 month with fine	6.50	6.50	10.50	12.50	14.50	16.50	18.50	20.50	22.50	24.50	26.50	28.50	30.50	32.50	actual	(Note 2)	20.00
Brazil	130.00	2.00	issue	none	22.00	26.25	34.00	40.00	46.00	52.00	57.50	63.50	69.00	75.50	82.00	87.50	93.50	99.50	actual	3 + 1	50 to 100
France	35.00	.35	application	none	22.50	22.50	22.50	22.50	22.50	22.50	22.50	22.50	22.50	22.50	22.50	22.50	22.50	22.50	actual	3	30.00
Germany	30.01	.35	application	3 months	15.00	27.50	40.00	52.50	65.00	77.50	90.00	102.50	115.00	127.50	140.00	152.50	165.00	177.00	actual	1 + 2	15.00
Guatemala	175.00	1.00	issue	none	The tax is fixed by the Government, and may be from $5.00 to $50.00 per year.														nominal	1 + 1	40.00
Great Britain	27.50	.....	application	3 months with fine	.....	.....	52.50	52.50	52.50	52.50	77.50	77.50	77.50	105.00	105.00	105.00	105.00	105.00	none	none	none
India	50.00	.....	application	3 months with fine	.....	.....	27.50	27.50	27.50	32.50	32.50	32.50	42.50	42.50	42.50	55.00	55.00	55.00	none	none	none
Italy	35.00	.35	application	3 months	12.50	12.50	17.50	17.50	17.50	22.50	22.50	22.50	27.50	27.50	27.50	32.50	32.50	32.50	nominal	1 + 1 or 2 + 2	20.00
Luxembourg	25.00	.35	application	3 months	7.50	9.50	11.60	13.50	16.50	17.50	19.50	21.50	23.50	23.50	27.50	29.50	31.50	33.50	nominal	3	15.00
Norway	35.00	.50	application	with fine	6.25	7.50	8.75	10.00	11.25	12.50	13.75	15.00	16.25	17.50	18.75	20.00	21.25	22.50	nominal	3	20.00
Peru	300.00	1.25	application	none	115.00	115.00	116.00	115.00	115.00	115.00	116.00	115.00	115.00	115.00	115.00	115.00	115.00	115.00	actual	2	75.00
Queensland	60.00	.....	application	3 months with fine	.....	.....	.....	.....	.....	.....	.....	.....	.....	.....	.....	.....	.....	.....	none	none	none
Spain (Note 3)	36.00	.35	application	none	8.50	10.50	12.50	14.50	16.50	18.50	20.50	22.50	24.50	26.50	28.50	30.50	32.50	34.50	actual	2 + 1	30.00
Sweden	45.00	.50	application	3 months with fine	10.00	10.00	10.00	10.00	18.00	18.00	18.00	18.00	18.00	25.00	25.00	25.00	25.00	21.00	nominal	3	30.00
Switzerland	35.00	.35	application	3 months	9.50	11.50	13.50	15.50	17.50	19.50	21.50	23.50	25.50	27.50	29.50	31.50	33.50	35.50	actual	3	25.00
Tunis	50.00	.35	application	none	20.00	20.00	20.00	20.00	20.00	20.00	20.00	20.00	20.00	20.00	20.00	20.00	20.00	20.00	actual	2 + 2	50.00
Turkey	100.00	1.00	March 13 yearly	none	25.00	25.00	25.00	25.00	25.00	25.00	25.00	25.00	25.00	25.00	25.00	25.00	25.00	25.00	actual	2 + 2	50.00
Uruguay	300.00	1.00	yearly issue	10 days	40.00	40.00	40.00	40.00	40.00	40.00	40.00	40.00	40.00	40.00	40.00	40.00	40.00	40.00	actual	yearly	100.00

NOTE 1.—The tax in Belgium for the 16th year is $34.50; 17th, $36.50; 18th, $38.50; 19th, $40.50; and 20th year, $42.50.

NOTE 2.—The Belgian patent must be worked within one year from the first commercial working in any other country, and must not be interrupted thereafter for any twelve consecutive months.

NOTE 3.—The tax in Spain for the 16th year is $36.50; 17th, $38.50; 18th, $40.50; 19th, $42.50; and 20th, $44.50.

*In the second column under "Due," the figures indicate the term of years within which the patent is to be worked, thus: 1 + 2 indicates that the patent is to be worked during the first year of its life, and the working is not to be interrupted for any two consecutive years thereafter, etc., etc. Where one figure only is given, the law contains no provision calling for subsequent or continuous workings.

CHARGES, TAXES AND WORKINGS.

(Copyrighted, 1891, by Richards & Co.)

Condensed Table of Charges for Applications for Patents in Countries in which taxes are payable on patents after their issue, but not yearly; our charge for paying such taxes; the requirements as to workings, and our charge for nominal workings.

COUNTRY.	Charge for Patent.	Translations each 100 words beyond 2,000.	Payable from.	Grace.	Taxes. When Due and Amount.		Workings. Kind.	Due.	Cost Nominal.
Bahama Islands	$75.00	......	application	none	7th year, $66.00	14th year, $115.00	none	none	none
Barbadoes	75.00	......	"	"	7th " 100.00	14th " 150.00	nominal	3	$30.00
British Guiana	290.00	......	"	"	7th " 115.00		none	none	none
British Honduras	175.00	......	"	"	3rd " 60.00	7th " 110.00	"	"	"
Canada	27.50	......	"	"	5th " 22.50	10th " 22.50	nominal	2	$20.00
Cape Colony	110.00	......	"	"	3rd " 60.00	7th " 110.00	none	none	none
Leeward Islands	250.00	......	"	"	3rd " 60.00	7th " 110.00	"	"	"
Malta	75.00	......	"	"	About $15.00 every second year, and five per cent. of profits of the exclusive manufacture.		nominal	1-|-1	$40.00
Natal	90.00	......	"	"	3rd year, $35.00	7th year, $60.00	none	none	none
* New Zealand	50.00	......	"	3 months with fine	4th " 35.00	7th " 60.00	* See Note.		
Orange Free State	325.00	$1.00	"	3 months with fine	3rd " 35.00	7th " 65.00	none	none	none
South African Republic	300.00	1.00	"	3 months with fine	3rd " 26.00	7th " 65.00	"	"	"
† South Australia	60.00	......	"	none	3rd " 22.50	7th " 22.50	†	3	......
Tasmania	90.00	......	"	"	3rd " 85.00	7th " 110.00	none	none	none
Victoria	60.00	......	"	"	3rd " 20.00	7th " 20.00	"	"	"

* There are no requirements for the working of patents granted on and after January 1, 1890. Patents granted before that date should be worked within two years of their date.

† The South Australian law provides for the working of patents within three years of their date, but this provision has never been enforced in a single instance.

CHARGES AND WORKINGS.

Condensed Table of Charges for Applications for Patents, in Countries in which no taxes are due or payable upon patents after their issue; together with requirements as to workings in such countries, and our charge for nominal workings.

COUNTRY.	Charge for Patent.	Translations each 100 words beyond 2,000.	WORKING. Kind.	WORKING. Due.	WORKING. Cost. Nominal.
Argentine Republic, 5 year	$150.00				
10 "	275.00	$1.00	actual	2 + 2	$50 to $100
15 "	430.00				
Bolivia	400.00	1.25	"	1	$100.00
Ceylon, if no English patent	150.00	....			
if an " "	110.00	....	none	none	none
Chili	250.00	1.00	actual	1 to 3	75.00
Colombia, 5 year	150.00				
10 "	200.00				
15 "	250.00	1.00	actual	1 + 1	100.00
20 "	300.00				
Congo Free State	110.00	.35	none	none	none
Danish West Indies	75.00	.50	nominal	1 + 1	50.00
Denmark	85.00	.50	nominal	1 + 1	30.00
Ecuador	200.00	1.00	nominal	1	75.00
Faroe Islands	75.00	.50	nominal	1 + 1	50.00
Fiji Islands	175.00	....	none	none	none
Finland	200.00	1.00	nominal	2 + 1	$50 to $100
Hawaii	90.00	....	none	none	none
Hong Kong	115.00	....	none	none	none
Iceland	75.00	.50	nominal	1 + 1	50.00
Jamaica	185.00	....	nominal	2	50.00
Liberia	200.00	....	nominal	8	75.00
Mauritius	180.00	....	none	none	none
Mexico	150.00	.75	nominal	5	50.00
Newfoundland	150.00	....	nominal	2	50.00
New South Wales	60.00	....	none	none	none
Portugal, 1 year	90.00				
5 "	125.00				
10 "	175.00	.50	nominal	2 + 2	$50 to $75
15 "	225.00				
Russia, 3 year	90.00			within first quarter of term	
5 "	120.00	.85	nominal		$40 to $50
10 "	300.00				
St. Helena	100.00		none	none	none
Straits Settlements	125.00		none	none	none
Trinidad	125.00		none	none	none
Venezuela, 5 year	220.00			6 months, 1 year, 2 years; and yearly	
10 "	330 00	1.00	nominal		50.00
15 "	375.00				

CHARGES, TAXES AND WORKINGS.
Special Grants—See page 160.

EXTRA TRANSLATIONS.

(Copyrighted, 1891, by Richards & Co.)

A table showing the exact cost of extra translations for any number of words up to 10,000, at the different rates charged. In counting the number of words in a specification, every word, reference letter, figure and number must be counted as a word; for fractions of 100 words, over 50 is charged for as 100 words; for a fraction less than 50, no charge is made.

NUMBER OF WORDS.	At 35 Cts. per 100.	At 50 Cts. per 100.	At 75 Cts. per 100.	At 85 Cts. per 100.	At $1.00 per 100.	At $1.25 per 100.	At $2.00 per 100.
100	$ 35	$ 50	$ 75	$ 85	$1 00	$1 25	$2 00
200	70	1 00	1 50	1 70	2 00	2 50	4 00
300	1 05	1 50	2 25	2 55	3 00	3 75	6 00
400	1 40	2 00	3 00	3 40	4 00	5 00	8 00
500	1 75	2 50	3 75	4 25	5 00	6 25	10 00
600	2 10	3 00	4 50	5 10	6 00	7 50	12 00
700	2 45	3 50	5 25	5 95	7 00	8 75	14 00
800	2 80	4 00	6 00	6 80	8 00	10 00	16 00
900	3 15	4 50	6 75	7 65	9 00	11 25	18 00
1000	3 50	5 00	7 50	8 50	10 00	12 50	20 00
1100	3 85	5 50	8 25	9 35	11 00	13 75	22 00
1200	4 20	6 00	9 00	10 20	12 00	15 00	24 00
1300	4 55	6 50	9 75	11 05	13 00	16 25	26 00
1400	4 90	7 00	10 50	11 90	14 00	17 50	28 00
1500	5 25	7 50	11 25	12 75	15 00	18 75	30 00
1600	5 60	8 00	12 00	13 60	16 00	20 00	32 00
1700	5 95	8 50	12 75	14 45	17 00	21 25	34 00
1800	6 30	9 00	13 50	15 30	18 00	22 50	36 00
1900	6 65	9 50	14 25	16 15	19 00	23 75	38 00
2000	7 00	10 00	15 00	17 00	20 00	25 00	40 00
2100	7 35	10 50	15 75	17 85	21 00	26 25	42 00
2200	7 70	11 00	16 50	18 70	22 00	27 50	44 00
2300	8 05	11 50	17 25	19 55	23 00	28 75	46 00
2400	8 40	12 00	18 00	20 40	24 00	30 00	48 00
2500	8 75	12 50	18 75	21 25	25 00	31 25	50 00
2600	9 10	13 00	19 50	22 10	26 00	32 50	52 00
2700	9 45	13 50	20 25	22 95	27 00	33 75	54 00
2800	9 80	14 00	21 00	23 80	28 00	35 00	56 00
2900	10 15	14 50	21 75	24 65	29 00	36 25	58 00
3000	10 50	15 00	22 50	25 50	30 00	37 50	60 00
3100	10 85	15 50	23 25	26 35	31 00	38 75	62 00
3200	11 20	16 00	24 00	27 20	32 00	40 00	64 00
3300	11 55	16 50	24 75	28 05	33 00	41 25	66 00
3400	11 90	17 00	25 50	28 90	34 00	42 50	68 00
3500	12 25	17 50	26 25	29 75	35 00	43 75	70 00
3600	12 60	18 00	27 00	30 60	36 00	45 00	72 00
3700	12 95	18 50	27 75	31 45	37 00	46 25	74 00
3800	13 30	19 00	28 50	32 30	38 00	47 50	76 00
3900	13 65	19 50	29 25	33 15	39 00	48 75	78 00
4000	14 00	20 00	30 00	34 00	40 00	50 00	80 00
4100	14 35	20 50	30 75	34 85	41 00	51 25	82 00
4200	14 70	21 00	31 50	35 70	42 00	52 50	84 00
4300	15 05	21 50	32 25	36 55	43 00	53 75	86 00
4400	15 40	22 00	33 00	37 40	44 00	55 00	88 00
4500	15 75	22 50	33 75	38 25	45 00	56 25	90 00
4600	16 10	23 00	34 50	39 10	46 00	57 50	92 00
4700	16 45	23 50	35 25	39 95	47 00	58 75	94 00
4800	16 80	24 00	36 00	40 80	48 00	60 00	96 00
4900	17 15	24 50	36 75	41 65	49 00	61 25	98 00
5000	17 50	25 00	37 50	42 50	50 00	62 50	100 00

EXTRA TRANSLATIONS—(Continued).

NUMBER OF WORDS.	At 35 Cts. per 100.	At 50 Cts. per 100.	At 75 Cts. per 100.	At 85 Cts. per 100.	At $1.00 per 100.	At $1.25 per 100.	At $2.00 per 100.
5100	$17 85	$25 50	$38 25	$43 35	$51 00	$63 75	$102 00
5200	18 20	26 00	39 00	44 20	52 00	65 00	104 00
5300	18 55	26 50	39 75	45 05	53 00	66 25	106 00
5400	18 90	27 00	40 50	45 90	54 00	67 50	108 00
5500	19 25	27 50	41 25	46 75	55 00	68 75	110 00
5600	19 60	28 00	42 00	47 60	56 00	70 00	112 00
5700	19 95	28 50	42 75	48 45	57 00	71 25	114 00
5800	20 30	29 00	43 50	49 30	58 00	72 50	116 00
5900	20 65	29 50	44 25	50 15	59 00	73 75	118 00
6000	21 00	30 00	45 00	51 00	60 00	75 00	120 00
6100	21 35	30 50	45 75	51 85	61 00	76 25	122 00
6200	21 70	31 00	46 50	52 70	62 00	77 50	124 00
6300	22 05	31 50	47 25	53 55	63 00	78 75	126 00
6400	22 40	32 60	48 00	54 40	64 00	80 00	128 00
6500	22 75	32 50	48 75	55 25	65 00	81 25	130 00
6600	23 10	33 00	49 50	56 10	66 00	82 50	132 00
6700	23 45	33 50	50 25	56 95	67 00	83 75	134 00
6800	23 80	34 00	51 00	57 80	68 00	85 00	136 00
6900	24 15	34 50	51 75	58 65	69 00	86 25	138 00
7000	24 50	35 00	52 50	59 50	70 00	87 50	140 00
7100	24 85	35 50	53 25	60 35	71 00	88 75	142 00
7200	25 20	36 00	54 00	61 20	72 00	90 00	144 00
7300	25 55	36 50	54 75	62 05	73 00	91 25	146 00
7400	25 90	37 00	55 50	62 90	74 00	92 50	148 00
7500	26 25	37 50	56 25	63 75	75 00	93 75	150 00
7600	26 60	38 00	57 00	64 60	76 00	95 00	152 00
7700	26 95	38 50	57 75	65 45	77 00	96 25	154 00
7800	27 30	39 00	58 50	66 30	78 00	97 50	156 00
7900	27 65	39 50	59 25	67 15	79 00	98 75	158 00
8000	28 00	40 00	60 00	68 00	80 00	100 00	160 00
8100	28 35	40 50	60 75	68 85	81 00	101 25	162 00
8200	28 70	41 00	61 50	69 70	82 00	102 50	164 00
8300	29 05	41 50	62 25	70 55	83 00	103 75	166 00
8400	29 40	42 00	63 00	71 40	84 00	105 00	168 00
8500	29 75	42 50	63 75	72 25	85 00	106 25	170 00
8600	30 10	43 00	64 50	73 10	86 00	107 50	172 00
8700	30 45	43 50	65 25	73 95	87 00	108 75	174 00
8800	30 80	44 00	66 00	74 80	88 00	110 00	176 00
8900	31 15	44 50	66 75	75 65	89 00	111 25	178 00
9000	31 50	45 00	67 50	76 50	90 00	112 50	180 00
9100	31 85	45 50	68 25	77 35	91 00	113 75	182 00
9200	32 20	46 00	69 00	78 20	92 00	115 00	184 00
9300	32 55	46 50	69 75	79 05	93 00	116 25	186 00
9400	32 90	47 00	70 50	79 90	94 00	117 50	188 00
9500	33 25	47 50	71 25	80 75	95 00	118 75	190 00
9600	33 60	48 00	72 00	81 60	96 00	120 00	192 00
9700	33 95	48 50	72 75	82 45	97 00	121 25	194 00
9800	34 30	49 00	73 50	83 30	98 00	122 50	196 00
9900	34 65	49 50	74 25	84 15	99 00	123 75	198 00
10000	35 00	50 00	75 00	85 00	100 00	125 00	200 00

DRAWINGS.

(Copyrighted, 1891, by Richards & Co.)

Table showing the requirements as to drawings in foreign countries.

COUNTRY.	No. of Drawings.		SIZE OF SHEETS.	Margin. In. from edge.
	Bristol.	*Tracings*		
Argentine Republic..	....	2	Any size...........................	none
Austria	....	2	" "	"
Bahama Islands	....	4	" "	"
Barbadoes	....	2	" "	"
Belgium	....	2	$13\frac{3}{8}$ inches high by $8\frac{3}{8}$ inches wide or any multiple of this size.......	$1\frac{3}{4}$
Bermuda	....	2	Any size...........................	none
Bolivia	....	2	" "	"
*Brazil	3	....	13 inches high by $8\frac{1}{4}$, $16\frac{1}{2}$ or $24\frac{3}{4}$ inches wide....................	$\frac{13}{16}$
British Guiana	....	2	Any size...........................	none
British Honduras....	....	2	" "	"
Canada	1	2	8 inches wide by 13 inches high......	"
Cape Colony........	....	2	Any size...........................	"
Ceylon	....	2	" "	"
Channel Islands, each	....	2	" "	"
Chili	....	2	" "	"
China Empire	....	2	" "	"
Colombia	....	2	" "	"
Congo Free State....	....	2	" "	"
Costa Rica..........	....	2	" "	"
Danish West Indies ..	....	2	" "	"
Denmark	....	2	" "	"
Ecuador............	....	2	" "	"
Falkland Islands	....	2	" "	"
Faroe Islands	....	2	" "	"
Fiji Islands	....	2	" "	"
Finland	....	2	" "	"
France	....	2	" "	"
Gambia (British)	....	2	" "	"
Germany	1	1	13 inches high by $8\frac{1}{4}$, $16\frac{1}{2}$ or $24\frac{3}{4}$ inches wide....................	$\frac{13}{16}$
Gibraltar	....	2	Any size...........................	none
Gold Coast Colony..	....	2	" "	"
Great Britain	2	....	13 inches high by 8, or 16 inches wide	$\frac{1}{2}$
Greece	....	2	Any size...........................	none
Grenada............	....	2	" "	"
Guatemala	....	2	" "	"
Hawaii	2	....	10 inches wide by 15 inches high....	1
Hayti	....	2	Any size...........................	none
Honduras	....	2	" "	"
Hong Kong	....	2	" "	
Iceland	....	2	" "	"
India	....	5	" "	"
Italy	....	3	$5\frac{5}{8}$ inches wide by $7\frac{7}{8}$ inches high $7\frac{7}{8}$ wide by $11\frac{13}{16}$ high; or $11\frac{13}{16}$ inches wide by $15\frac{3}{4}$ inches high. The smallest size possible should be used....	"

* All the drawings must be signed by the inventor in the lower right-hand corner above the margin line. No witnesses nor legalization required.

DRAWINGS—CONTINUED.

(*Copyrighted, 1891, by Richards & Co.*)

COUNTRY.	*No. of Drawings.* *Bristol.*	*Tracings*	SIZE OF SHEETS.	*Margin. In. from edge.*
Jamaica	....	2	Any size	none
Lagos	....	2	" "	"
Leeward Islands	....	2	" "	"
Liberia	2	....	" "	"
Luxembourg	....	3	" "	"
Malta	....	2	" "	"
Mauritius	....	2	" "	"
Mexico	....	2	" "	"
Natal	....	2	" "	"
Newfoundland	....	2	" "	"
New South Wales	1	1	13 inches high by 8 or 16 inches wide	½
New Zealand	2	....	Any size	none
Nicaragua	....	2	" "	"
Norway	....	2	13 inches high by 8¼, 16½ or 24¾ inches wide	13/16
Orange Free State	....	2	Any size	none
Paraguay	....	2	" "	"
Peru	....	2	" "	"
Portugal	....	2	" "	"
Queensland	2	....	13 inches high by 20 or 28 wide	½
Russia	....	2	Any size	none
St. Helena	none	none		
St. Lucia	....	2	" "	"
St. Vincent	....	2	" "	"
San Domingo	....	2	" "	"
San Salvador	....	2	" "	"
Sierra Leone	....	2	" "	"
S. African Republic	....	2	" "	"
South Australia	....	2	" "	"
Spain	....	2	" "	"
Straits Settlements	....	2	" "	"
Sweden	1	1	13 inches high by 8¼, 16½ or 24¾ inches wide	13/16
*Switzerland	1	1	13 inches high by 8¼, 16½ or 24¾ inches wide	"
†Tasmania	†	1	15 inches high by 20 inches wide	1½
Trinidad	....	2	Any size	none
Tunis	....	2	" "	"
Turkey	...	2	" "	"
Uruguay	....	2	" "	"
Venezuela	...	2	" "	"
Victoria	1	1	13 inches high by 8 or 16 inches wide	½
‡Western Australia	2	....	" " " " " "	"

* See remarks in body of book.

† Tasmania requires one copy on parchment and one on tracing cloth, and is now the only country requiring a drawing upon parchment.

‡ Drawings are required for Western Australia only when Letters Patent are to be applied for. When Letters of Registration are taken, no drawings except the certified copies need be furnished.

METRICAL WEIGHTS AND MEASURES.

The French Metrical System is based upon the (assumed) length of the fourth part of a terrestrial meridian. The ten-millionth part of this arc was chosen as the unit of measures of length, and called a *Metre*. The cube of the tenth part of the mètre was adopted as the unit of capacity, and denominated a *Litre*. The weight of a litre of distilled water at its greatest density was called a *Kilogramme*, of which the thousandth part, or *Gramme*, was adopted as the unit of weight. The multiples of these, proceeding in decimal progression, are distinguished by the employment of the prefixes *deca*, *hecto*, *kilo* and *myria*, from the Greek, and the subdivisions by *deci*, *centi* and *milli*, from the Latin:

Measures of Length (unit Metre).

Equal to	Inches.	Feet.	Yards.	Fathms.	Miles.
Millimètre	0·03937	0·003	0·001	0·000	0·000
Centimètre	0·39371	0·032	0·010	0·005	0·000
Décimètre	3·93708	0·328	0·109	0·054	0·000
Metre	39·37079	3·280	1·093	0·546	0·000
Décamètre	393·70790	32·808	10·936	5·468	0·006
Hectomètre	3937·07900	328·089	109·363	54·681	0·062
Kilomètre	39370·79000	3280·899	1093·633	546·816	0·621
Myriamètre	393707·90000	32808·991	10936·330	5468·165	6·213

Cubic, or Measures of Capacity (unit Litre).

Equal to	Cub. In.	Cub. Feet.	Pints.	Gallons.	Bushls.
Millilitre, or cubic centim.	0·06103	0·000	0·001	0·000	0·000
Centilitre, 10 cubic do.	0·61027	0·000	0·017	0·002	0·000
Décilitre, 100 cubic do.	6·10271	0·003	0·176	0·022	0·002
Litre, or cubic Décimètre	61·02705	0·035	1·760	0·220	0·027
Décalitre, or Centistère	610·27052	3·353	17·607	2·200	0·275
Hectolitre, or Décistère	6102·70515	3·531	176·077	22·009	2·751
Kilolitre, or Stère	61027·05152	35·316	1760·773	220·096	27·512
Myrialitre, or Décastère	610270·51519	353·165	17607·734	2200·966	275·120

Measures of Weight (unit Gramme).

Equal to	Grains.	Troy oz.	Avoir. lb.	Cwt. = 112 lb.	Tons = 20 cwt.
Milligramme	0·01543	0·000	0·000	0·000	0·000
Centigramme	0·15432	0·000	0·000	0·000	0·000
Décigramme	1·54323	0·003	0·000	0·000	0·000
Gramme	15·43235	0·032	0·002	0·000	0·000
Décagramme	154·32349	0·321	0·022	0·000	0·000
Hectogramme	1543·23488	3·215	0·220	0·001	0·000
Kilogramme	15432·34880	32·150	2·204	0·019	0·000
Myriagramme	154323·48800	321·507	22·046	0·196	0·009

Square, or Measures of Surface (unit Are).

Equal to	Sq. Feet.	Yards.	Perchs.	Roods.	Acres.
Centiare, or sq. mètre	10·764299	1·196	0·039	0·000	0·000
Are, or 100 sq. mètres	1076·429934	119·603	3·953	0·098	0·024
Hectare, or 10,000 sq. miles	107642·993419	11960·332	395·382	9·884	2·471

TABLE FOR CONVERTING METRIC WEIGHTS AND MEASURES.

Metres into yards.		Kilometres into miles and yards			Litres into gallons and quarts.			Hectolitres into quarters & bushls.			Kilogrammes into cwt. qr. lb. oz.					Hectares into acres r. p.			
1=	1·094	1=	0	1094	1=	0	0·880	1=	0	2·751	1=	0	0	2	3¼	1=	2	1	35
2=	2·187	2=	1	427	2=	0	1·761	2=	0	5·502	2=	0	0	4	6½	2=	4	3	31
3=	3·281	3=	1	1521	3=	0	2·641	3=	1	0·254	3=	0	0	6	9¾	3=	7	1	26
4=	4·374	4=	2	855	4=	0	3·521	4=	1	3·005	4=	0	0	8	13	4=	9	3	22
5=	5·468	5=	3	188	5=	1	0·402	5=	1	5·756	5=	0	0	11	0¼	5=	12	1	17
6=	6·562	6=	3	1282	6=	1	1·282	6=	2	0·507	6=	0	0	13	3½	6=	14	3	12
7=	7·655	7=	4	615	7=	1	2·163	7=	2	3·258	7=	0	0	15	7	7=	17	1	8
8=	8·749	8=	4	1709	8=	1	3·043	8=	2	6·010	8=	0	0	17	10¼	8=	19	3	3
9=	9·843	9=	5	1043	9=	1	3·923	9=	3	0·761	9=	0	0	19	13½	9=	22	0	38
10=	10·936	10=	6	376	10=	2	0·804	10=	3	3·512	10=	0	0	22	0¾	10=	24	2	34
20=	21·873	20=	12	753	20=	4	1·608	20=	6	7·024	20=	0	1	16	1½	20=	49	1	28
30=	32·809	30=	18	1129	30=	6	2·412	30=	10	2·536	30=	0	2	10	2¼	30=	74	0	21
40=	43·745	40=	24	1505	40=	8	3·215	40=	13	6·048	40=	0	3	4	3	40=	98	3	15
50=	54·682	50=	31	122	50=	11	0·019	50=	17	1·560	50=	0	3	26	3¾	50=	123	2	9
60=	65·618	60=	37	498	60=	13	0·823	60=	20	5·072	60=	1	0	20	4½	60=	148	1	3
70=	76·554	70=	43	874	70=	15	1·627	70=	24	0·585	70=	1	1	14	5¼	70=	172	3	37
80=	87·491	80=	49	1251	80=	17	2·431	80=	27	4·097	80=	1	2	8	6	80=	197	2	38
90=	98·427	90=	55	1627	90=	19	3·325	90=	30	7·609	90=	1	3	2	6½	90=	222	1	24
100=	109·363	100=	62	243	100=	22	0·039	100=	34	3·121	100=	1	3	24	7	100=	247	0	18
200=	218·727	200=	124	487	200=	44	0·077	200=	68	6·242	200=	3	3	20	15	200=	494	0	37
300=	328·090	300=	186	730	300=	66	0·116	300=	103	1·362	300=	5	3	17	6	300=	741	1	15
400=	437·453	400=	248	973	400=	88	0·155	400=	137	4·483	400=	7	3	13	14	400=	988	1	33
500=	546·816	500=	310	1217	500=	110	0·193	500=	171	7·604	500=	9	3	10	5	500=	1235	2	11

From Whitaker's Almanack, 1891.

ISSUE DAYS IN THE UNITED STATES PATENT OFFICE.

(Copyrighted, 1891, by Richards & Co.)

All United States patents are issued upon the third Tuesday after the first Thursday following the receipt of the final fee of $20.00 at the Patent Office. The intervening time is employed in photolithographing the drawings and printing the specification of the patent. The following tables show the issue days for 1891 and 1892 and the dates upon which the final fees must be paid to insure the issue of the patent upon any desired day.

1891.

	JANUARY	FEBRUARY	MARCH	APRIL	MAY	JUNE	JULY	AUGUST	SEPTEMBER	OCTOBER	NOVEMBER	DECEMBER
Final fees paid from	Dec. 12 to Dec. 18	Jan. 9 to Jan. 15	Feb. 6 to Feb. 12	Mar. 13 to Mar. 19	April 10 to April 16	May 8 to May 14	June 12 to June 18	July 10 to July 16	Aug. 7 to Aug. 13	Sept. 11 to Sept. 17	Oct. 9 to Oct. 15	Nov. 6 to Nov. 12
Patent will issue	Jan. 6	Feb. 3	Mar. 3	April 7	May 5	June 2	July 7	Aug. 4	Sept. 1	Oct. 6	Nov. 3	Dec. 1
Final fees paid from	Dec. 19 to Dec. 25	Jan. 16 to Jan. 22	Feb. 13 to Feb. 19	Mar. 20 to Mar. 26	April 17 to April 23	May 15 to May 21	June 19 to June 25	July 17 to July 23	Aug. 14 to Aug. 20	Sept. 18 to Sept. 24	Oct. 16 to Oct. 22	Nov. 13 to Nov. 19
Patent will issue	Jan. 13	Feb. 10	Mar. 10	April 14	May 12	June 9	July 14	Aug. 11	Sept. 8	Oct. 13	Nov. 10	Dec. 8
Final fees paid from	Dec. 26 to Jan. 1	Jan. 23 to Jan. 29	Feb. 20 to Feb. 26	Mar. 27 to April 2	April 24 to April 30	May 22 to May 28	June 26 to July 2	July 24 to July 30	Aug. 21 to Aug. 27	Sept. 25 to Oct. 1	Oct. 23 to Oct. 29	Nov. 20 to Nov. 26
Patent will issue	Jan. 20	Feb. 17	Mar. 17	April 21	May 19	June 16	July 21	Aug. 18	Sept. 15	Oct. 20	Nov. 17	Dec. 15
Final fees paid from	Jan. 2 to Jan. 8	Jan. 30 to Feb. 5	Feb. 27 to Mar. 5	April 3 to April 9	May 1 to May 7	May 29 to June 4	July 3 to July 9	July 31 to Aug. 6	Aug. 28 to Sept. 3	Oct. 2 to Oct. 8	Oct. 30 to Nov. 5	Nov. 27 to Dec. 3
Patent will issue	Jan. 27	Feb. 24	Mar. 24	April 28	May 26	June 23	July 28	Aug. 25	Sept. 22	Oct. 27	Nov. 24	Dec. 22
Final fees paid from			Mar. 6 to Mar. 12			June 5 to June 11			Sept. 4 to Sept. 10			Dec. 4 to Dec. 10
Patent will issue			Mar. 31			June 30			Sept. 29			Dec. 29

1892.

	JANUARY	FEBRUARY	MARCH	APRIL	MAY	JUNE	JULY	AUGUST	SEPTEMBER	OCTOBER	NOVEMBER	DECEMBER
Final fees paid from	Dec. 11 to Dec. 17	Jan. 8 to Jan. 14	Feb. 5 to Feb. 11	Mar. 11 to Mar. 17	April 8 to April 14	May 13 to May 19	June 10 to June 16	July 8 to July 14	Aug. 12 to Aug. 18	Sept. 9 to Sept. 15	Oct. 7 to Oct. 13	Nov. 11 to Nov. 17
Patent will issue	Jan. 5	Feb. 2	Mar. 1	April 5	May 3	June 7	July 5	Aug. 2	Sept. 6	Oct. 4	Nov. 1	Dec. 6
Final fees paid from	Dec. 18 to Dec. 24	Jan. 15 to Jan. 21	Feb. 12 to Feb. 18	Mar. 18 to Mar. 24	April 15 to April 21	May 20 to May 26	June 17 to June 23	July 15 to July 21	Aug. 19 to Aug. 25	Sept. 16 to Sept. 22	Oct. 14 to Oct. 20	Nov. 18 to Nov. 24
Patent will issue	Jan. 12	Feb. 9	Mar. 8	April 12	May 10	June 14	July 12	Aug. 9	Sept. 13	Oct. 11	Nov. 8	Dec. 13
Final fees paid from	Dec. 25 to Dec. 31	Jan. 22 to Jan. 28	Feb. 19 to Feb. 25	Mar. 25 to Mar. 31	April 22 to April 28	May 27 to June 2	June 24 to June 30	July 22 to July 28	Aug. 26 to Sept. 1	Sept. 23 to Sept. 29	Oct. 21 to Oct. 27	Nov. 25 to Dec. 1
Patent will issue	Jan. 19	Feb. 16	Mar. 15	April 19	May 17	June 21	July 19	Aug. 16	Sept. 20	Oct. 18	Nov. 15	Dec. 20
Final fees paid from	Jan. 1 to Jan. 7	Jan. 29 to Feb. 4	Feb. 26 to Mar. 3	April 1 to April 7	April 29 to May 5	June 3 to June 9	July 1 to July 7	July 29 to Aug. 4	Sept. 2 to Sept. 8	Sept. 30 to Oct. 6	Oct. 28 to Nov. 3	Dec. 2 to Dec. 8
Patent will issue	Jan. 26	Feb. 23	Mar. 22	April 26	May 24	June 28	July 26	Aug. 23	Sept. 27	Oct. 25	Nov. 22	Dec. 27
Final fees paid from			Mar. 4 to Mar. 10		May 6 to May 12			Aug. 5 to Aug. 11			Nov. 4 to Nov. 10	
Patent will issue			Mar. 29		May 31			Aug. 30			Nov. 29	

200-YEAR CALENDAR.

For ascertaining Any Day of the Week for any given time within Two Hundred Years from the introduction of the New Style, 1752 ¶ to 1952 inclusive.

Years 1753 to 1952.	Jan	Feb	Mar	Apr	May	Jun	July	Aug	Sept	Oct	Nov	Dec
1761 1767 1778 1789 1795 / 1801 1807 1818 1829 1835 1846 1857 1863 1874 1885 1891 * / 1903 1914 1925 1931 1942	4	7	7	3	5*	1	3	6	2	4	7	2
1762 1773 1779 1790 / 1802 1813 1819 1830 1841 1847 1858 1869 1875 1886 1897 / 1909 1915 1926 1937 1943	5	1	1	4	6	2	4	7	3	5	1	3
1757 1768 1774 1755 1751 / 1803 1814 1825 1831 1842 1853 1859 1870 1881 1887 1898 / 1910 1921 1927 1938 1949	6	2	2	5	7	3	5	1	4	6	2	4
1754 1765 1771 1782 1793 1799 / 1805 1811 1822 1833 1839 1850 1861 1867 1878 1889 1895 / 1901 1907 1918 1929 1935 1946	2	5	5	1	3	6	1	4	7	2	5	7
1755 1766 1777 1788 1794 1800 / 1806 1817 1823 1834 1845 1851 1862 1873 1879 1890 / 1902 1913 1919 1930 1941 1947	3	6	6	2	4	7	2	5	1	3	6	1
1758 1769 1775 1786 1797 / 1809 1815 1826 1837 1843 1854 1865 1871 1882 1893 1899 / 1905 1911 1922 1933 1939 1950	7	3	3	6	1	4	6	2	5	7	3	5
1753 1759 1770 1781 1767 1798 / 1810 1821 1827 1838 1849 1855 1866 1877 1883 1894 1900 / 1906 1917 1923 1934 1945 1951	1	4	4	7	2	5	7	3	6	1	4	6

LEAP YEARS.

								Jan	Feb	Mar	Apr	May	Jun	July	Aug	Sept	Oct	Nov	Dec
								..	29	..	..	..	..	..	..	..	..	..	..
1764	1792	1804	1832	1860	1888	..	1928	7	3	4	7	2	5	7	3	6	1	4	6
1768	1796	1808	1836	1864	1892	1904	1932	5	1	2	5	7	3	5	1	4	6	2	4
1772	..	1812	1840	1868	1896	1908	1936	3	6	7	3	5	1	3	6	2	4	7	2
1776	..	1816	1844	1872	..	1912	1940	1	4	5	1	3	6	1	4	7	2	5	7
1780	..	1820	1848	1876	..	1916	1944	6	2	3	6	1	4	6	2	5	7	3	5
1756	1784	1824	1852	1880	..	1920	1948	4	7	1	4	6	2	4	7	3	5	1	3
1760	1788	1828	1856	1884	..	1924	1952	2	5	6	2	4	7	2	5	1	3	6	1

NOTE.—To ascertain any day of the week, first look in the table for the year required, and under the months are figures which refer to the corresponding figures at the head of the columns of days below. *For Example:*—To know on what day of the week May 4 fell in the year 1891, in the table of years look for 1891, and in a parallel line, under May, is fig. 5, which directs to col. 5, in which it will be seen that May 4 fell on Monday.

¶ 1752 same as 1772 from Jan. 1 to Sept. 2. From Sept. 14 to Dec. 31 same as 1780 (Sept. 3—13 were omitted).

	1	2	3	4	5*	6	7
	Monday 1	Tuesday 1	Wednesd. 1	Thursday 1	Friday 1	Saturday 1	Sunday 1
	Tuesday 2	Wednesd. 2	Thursday 2	Friday 2	Saturday 2	Sunday 2	Monday 2
	Wednes. 3	Thursday 3	Friday 3	Saturday 3	Sunday 3	Monday 3	Tuesday 3
	Thursday 4	Friday 4	Saturday 4	Sunday 4	Monday* 4	Tuesday 4	Wednesd. 4
	Friday 5	Saturday 5	Sunday 5	Monday 5	Tuesday 5	Wednes. 5	Thursday 5
	Saturday 6	Sunday 6	Monday 6	Tuesday 6	Wednesd. 6	Thursday 6	Friday 6
	Sunday 7	Monday 7	Tuesday 7	Wednesd. 7	Thursday 7	Friday 7	Saturday 7
	Monday 8	Tuesday 8	Wednesd. 8	Thursday 8	Friday 8	Saturday 8	Sunday 8
	Tuesday 9	Wednesd. 9	Thursday 9	Friday 9	Saturday 9	Sunday 9	Monday 9
	Wednes. 10	Thursda. 10	Friday 10	Saturday 10	Sunday 10	Monday 10	Tuesday 10
	Thursda. 11	Friday 11	Saturday 11	Sunday 11	Monday 11	Tuesday 11	Wednes. 11
	Friday 12	Saturday 12	Sunday 12	Monday 12	Tuesday 12	Wednes. 12	Thursda. 12
	Saturday 13	Sunday 13	Monday 13	Tuesday 13	Wednes. 13	Thursda. 13	Friday 13
	Sunday 14	Monday 14	Tuesday 14	Wednes. 14	Thursda. 14	Friday 14	Saturday 14
	Monday 15	Tuesday 15	Wednes. 15	Thursda. 15	Friday 15	Saturday 15	Sunday 15
	Tuesday 16	Wednes. 16	Thursda. 16	Friday 16	Saturday 16	Sunday 16	Monday 16
	Wednes. 17	Thursda. 17	Friday 17	Saturday 17	Sunday 17	Monday 17	Tuesday 17
	Thursda. 18	Friday 18	Saturday 18	Sunday 18	Monday 18	Tuesday 18	Wednes. 18
	Friday 19	Saturday 19	Sunday 19	Monday 19	Tuesday 19	Wednes. 19	Thursda. 19
	Saturday 20	Sunday 20	Monday 20	Tuesday 20	Wednes. 20	Thursda. 20	Friday 20
	Sunday 21	Monday 21	Tuesday 21	Wednes. 21	Thursda. 21	Friday 21	Saturday 21
	Monday 22	Tuesday 22	Wednes. 22	Thursda. 22	Friday 22	Saturday 22	Sunday 22
	Tuesday 23	Wednes. 23	Thursda. 23	Friday 23	Saturday 23	Sunday 23	Monday 23
	Wednes. 24	Thursda. 24	Friday 24	Saturday 24	Sunday 24	Monday 24	Tuesday 24
	Thursda. 25	Friday 25	Saturday 25	Sunday 25	Monday 25	Tuesday 25	Wednes. 25
	Friday 26	Saturday 26	Sunday 26	Monday 26	Tuesday 26	Wednes. 26	Thursda. 26
	Saturday 27	Sunday 27	Monday 27	Tuesday 27	Wednes. 27	Thursda. 27	Friday 27
	Sunday 28	Monday 28	Tuesday 28	Wednes. 28	Thursda. 28	Friday 28	Saturday 28
	Monday 29	Tuesday 29	Wednes. 29	Thursda. 29	Friday 29	Saturday 29	Sunday 29
	Tuesday 30	Wednes. 30	Thursda. 30	Friday 30	Saturday 30	Sunday 30	Monday 30
	Wednes. 31	Thursda. 31	Friday 31	Saturday 31	Sunday 31	Monday 31	Tuesday 31

From Whitaker's Almanack, 1891.

GREEK AND RUSSIAN CALENDAR.

A.D. 1891, A.M. 7399–8000.

OLD STYLE.	CERTAIN HOLY DAYS.	NEW STYLE.
Jan. 1	Circumcision	Jan. 13
" 6	Theophany (Epiphany)	" 18
" 20	First Sunday of the Triodion	Feb. 1
" 27	Sunday of the Carnival	" 8
" 30	First Day of Lent	" 11
Feb. 2	Hypapante	" 14
" 10	Orthodox Sunday	" 22
Mar. 2	Accession of Emperor*	Mar. 14
" 10	Palm Sunday	" 22
" 15	Great Friday (Good Friday)	" 27
" 17	Holy Pasch (Easter Day)	" 29
" 25	Annunciation of Theotokos	Apr. 6
Apr. 23	St. George	May 5
" 25	Ascension	" 7
May 5	Pentecost (Whit Sunday)	" 17
" 6	All Saints	" 18
" 12	First Day of Fast of Apostles	" 24
" 15	Coronation of Emperor*	" 27
June 29	Peter and Paul, Chief Apostles	July 1
Aug. 1	First Day of Fast of Theotokos	Aug. 13
" 6	Transfiguration	" 18
" 15	Repose of Theotokos	" 27
" 30	St. Alexander Nevsky*	Sept. 11
Sept. 8	Nativity of Theotokos	" 20
" 14	Exaltation of the Cross	" 26
Oct. 1	Patronage of Theotokos	Oct. 13
Nov. 15	1st day of Fast of Nat. of Christ	Nov. 27
' 21	Entrance of Theotokos	Dec. 3
Dec. 9	Conception of Theotokos	" 21
" 25	Nativity (Christmas)	1892 Jan. 6

* Peculiar to Russia.

MOHAMMEDAN CALENDAR.

(1308–1309.)

Year.	Name of Month.	Month Begins.
1308	Jomada II	January 12
"	Rajab	February 10
"	Shaaban	March 12
"	Ramadân	April 10
"	Shawall	May 10
"	Dulkaada	June 8
"	Dulheggia	July 8
1309	Muharram .1809	August 7
"	Saphar	September 6
"	Rabia I	October 5
"	Rabia II	November 4
"	Jomada I	December 3

THERMOMETER.

Comparison between Scales of Fahrenheit, Réaumur and the Centigrade.

To convert degrees. Boiling point = 212° F = 100° C = 50° R; Freezing point = 32° F = 0° C = 0° R. Centigrade or Réaumur into degrees Fahrenheit, or vice versa, use one of the following formulas: Let F = Number of degrees Fahrenheit, C = Number of degrees Centigrade, and R = Number of degrees Réaumur, then:

$$F = C + R + 32 \qquad R = \frac{4(F-32)}{9}$$
$$F = \frac{9R}{4} + 32$$
$$F = \frac{9C}{5} + 32 \qquad C = \frac{5(F-32)}{9}$$

CENT.	FAH'T	RMR.	CENT.	FAH'T	RMR.
100B.	212B.	80B.	25	77	20
99	210·2	79·2	24	75·2	19·2
98	208·4	78·4	23	73·4	18·4
97	206·6	77·6	22	71·6	17·6
96	204·8	76·8	21	69·8	16·8
95	203	76	20	68	16
94	201·2	75·2	19	66·2	15·2
93	199·4	74·4	18	64·4	14·4
92	197·6	73·6	17	62·6	13·6
91	195·6	72·6	16	60·8	12·8
90	194	72	15	59	12
89	192·2	71·2	14	57·2	11·2
88	190·4	70·4	13	55·4	10·4
87	188·6	69·6	12	53·6	9·6
86	186·8	68·8	11	51·8	8·8
65	185	68	10	50	8
84	183·2	67·2	9	48·2	7·2
83	181·4	66·4	8	46·4	6·4
82	179·6	65·6	7	44·6	5·6
81	177·8	64·8	6	42·8	4·8
80	176	64	5	41	4
79	174·2	63·2	4	39·2	3·2
78	172·4	62·4	3	37·4	2·4
77	170·6	61·6	2	35·6	1·6
76	168·8	60·8	1	33·8	0·8
75	167	60	Zero	32	Zero
74	165·2	59·2	1	30·2	0·9
73	163·4	58·4	2	29·4	1·6
72	161·6	57·6	3	26·6	2·4
71	159·8	56·8	4	24·x	3·2
70	158	56	5	23	4
69	156·2	55·2	6	21·2	4·8
68	154·4	54·4	7	19·4	5·6
67	152·6	53·6	8	17·6	6·4
66	150·8	52·8	9	15·8	7·2
65	149	52	10	14	8
64	147·2	51·2	11	12·2	8·6
63	145·4	50·4	12	10 4	9·6
62	143·6	49·6	13	8·6	10·4
61	141·8	48·8	14	6·8	11·2
60	140	48	15	5	12
59	138·2	47·2	16	3 2	12·8
58	136·4	46·4	17	1·4	13·6
57	134·6	45·6	18	—	14·4
56	132·8	44·8	19	2·2	15·2
55	131	44	20	4	16
54	129·2	43·2	21	5·9	16·8
53	127·4	42·4	22	7·6	17·6
52	125·6	41·6	23	9·4	18·4
51	123·8	40·8	24	11·2	19·2
50	122	40	25	13	20
49	120·2	39·2	26	14·8	20·8
48	118·4	38·4	27	16·6	21·6
47	116·6	37·6	28	16·4	22·4
46	114·6	36·8	29	20·2	23·2
45	113	36	30	22	24
44	111·2	35·2	31	23·8	24·8
43	109·4	34·4	32	25·6	25·6
42	107·6	33·6	33	27·4	26·4
41	105 8	32·6	34	29·2	27·2
40	104	32	35	31	28
39	102·2	31·2	36	32·8	28·8
38	100·4	30·4	37	34·6	29·6
37	98·6	29·6	38	36·4	30·4
36	96·8	29·3	39	38·2	31·2
35	95	28	40	40	32
34	93·2	27·2	41	41·8	32·8
33	91·4	26·4	42	43·6	33·6
32	89·6	25·6	43	45·4	34·4
31	87·8	24·8	44	47·2	35·2
30	86	24	45	49	36
29	84·2	23·2	46	50·8	36·8
28	82·4	22·4	47	52·6	37·6
27	80·6	21·6	48	54·4	38·4
26	78·8	20·8	49	56·2	39·2

UNIFORMITY.—One of the laws promulgated by King Edgar decreed that there should be but one Standard Measure, that kept at Winchester, and by the 27th section of Magna Charta there was to be one Weight for all England. But no effort appears to have been made to render this compulsory; consequently numerous customary weights and measures continued in use. Laws were from time to time promulgated, but custom was stronger than law, especially with regard to land, corn, and wool. In 1824, however, an Act was passed rendering uniformity compulsory. This came into force on 1st of January, 1826, since which time the Imperial Statute System of Weights and Measures has been in general use.

Avoirdupois Weight.

Drachm.... dr. = 27½ grains (27·34375).
Ounce .... oz. = 16 drachms, 437·5 grains.
Pound .... lb. = 16 oz., 256 dr., 7,000 grains.
Stone....... st.,= Butcher's Meat, &c. = 8 lbs.
Stone ...... st. = Horseman's weight = 14 lbs.
Quarter .... qr. = 28 lbs.
Cental or Quintal, cent. = 100 lbs.
Hundredweight, cwt. = 4 qrs., 112 lbs.
Ton .... T. = 20 cwt., 2,240 lbs.

Avoirdupois weight is used in almost all commercial transactions and common dealings, but in addition to the above there are special weights for various articles, the chief of which are:—

A Quartern Loaf....................... =	4	lbs.
A Peck of Flour, 2 Gallons.......... =	14	"
A Firkin of Butter................... =	56	"
A Firkin of Soft Soap............... =	64	"
A Box of Fish, about................ =	90	"
A Barrel of Gunpowder.............. =	100	"
A Barrel of Raisins.................. =	112	"
A Seam of Glass, 24 stones of 5 lbs.. =	120	"
A Barrel of Butter—4 firkins........ =	224	"
A Barrel (or pack) of Soft Soap..... =	256	"
A Faggot of Steel.................... =	120	"
A Pig of Ballast..................... =	56	"
A Fodder of Lead, London and Hull =	19½	cwt.
A do. Derby=22½ cwt.; Newcastle =	21¼	"
A Cask of Blacklead................. =	11½	"

A Sack—Potatoes, 168 lbs.; Flour, 280 lbs.; Coals, 224 lbs.; a ton of Coals, 10 sacks, 2,240 lbs.

The Metrical system of weights is used in Belgium, France, Germany, Italy, Portugal, Spain, Sweden and Norway, and some other countries, the unit of which is the Gramme= 15·432 grains; the chief multiple of the Gramme is the Kilogramme=2·2046 lbs; in practical use this is found inconvenient for small purchases, and nearly all commodities are sold by the demi or half kilo. The Centner of ·50 kilos=110¼ lbs., very nearly represents the English cwt.; but heavy goods are sold by the Tonneau of 2204·621 lbs., about 19 cwt. 7 lbs., the Myriagramme being ignored.

In the United States and in Canada the cwt. is generally reckoned as 100 lbs., and the ton of 20 cwt.=2,000 lbs.

In Russia the Pood of 36 lbs. is the commercial weight; 63 Poods=1 English ton.

Indian Weights (Bengal).

Tola, unit of postage=180 grains.
Chittak=5 Tolas; Seer (16 Chittaks)=2 $\frac{3}{8}$ lbs.
Imperial or Indian Maund=82$\frac{2}{7}$ lbs.

Madras.

Viss=3·09 lbs., Maund=25 lbs., Candy=500 lbs.

Troy Weight.

Carat .... = 3.17 grains.
Pennyweight ...dwt. = 24 grains.
Ounce...............oz. = 20 dwts., 480 grs.
Pound............lb. = 12 oz., 240 dwts., 5,760 grs.
Hundredweight.cwt. = 100 lbs.

TROY is the weight used by goldsmiths and jewelers. The grains Troy, Apothecaries and Avoirdupois are equal, and the same in England, France, the United States, Holland, and in most other countries; but the carat varies; in France it is 3·18 grains; in Holland, 3·0 grains, and in the U. S., 3·2 grains. The jewelry ounce is divided into 151½ carats or 600 pearl grains.

The oz. Troy and Apothecaries = 1·09714 oz. Avoirdupois; but the lb. Troy and lb. Apothecaries = only 0·82286 lb. Avoirdupois; while 175 lb. Troy and Apothecaries = 144 lb. Avoirdupois.

STANDARD gold consists of 22 parts pure gold alloyed with 2 parts of copper or other metal, and according to the quantity of alloy is called 9, 12, 15 or 18 carat, i. e., that number of parts of pure gold out of the twenty-four. Standard silver is of fineness 11 oz. 2 dwt. fine to 18 dwt. alloy ; there is also another obsolete legal standard, the Britannia, of 11 oz. 10 dwt. fine. One lb. of silver is coined into 66 shillings.

Apothecaries' Weight.

Scruple ℈ = 20 Grains.............=	20	grs.
Drachm ʒ = 3 Scruples ....=	60	"
Ounce ℥ = 8 Drachms..........=	480	"
Pound ℔ = 12 Ounces...........=	5760	"

The avoirdupois oz. of 437½ grains, and the lb. of 7,000 grains, are the weights named in the British Pharmacopœia; drugs are purchased by Avoirdupois, but compounded by Apothecaries' weight. The Apothecary's oz. and lb. may now be considered obsolete.

Hay and Straw.

Truss of Straw, 36 lbs.
Truss of Old Hay, 56 lbs.
Truss of New Hay (up to September 1st), 60 lbs.
Load, 36 Trusses—Straw, 11 cwt. 2 qrs. 8 lbs.; Old Hay, 18 cwt.; New Hay, 19 cwt. 1 qr. 4 lbs.

Wool.

Clove, cl. = 7 lbs.
Stone, st. = 2 cloves, 14 lbs.
Tod, td. = 2 Stones 1 qr.
Wey, wy. = 6½ Tod 1 cwt. 2 qrs. 14 lbs.
Pack, pk. = 240 lbs.
Sack, sk. = 2 Weys 13 qrs.
Last, la. = 12 Sacks 39 cwt.

Since the advent of SHODDY, some of the above weights have become nearly obsolete, although the terms are still in use with different values: thus 16 lbs. = 1 st.; 28 lbs. = 1 Tod; 20 lbs. = 1 Score ; 12 Score or 240 lbs. = 1 Pack.

Cotton Wool.

Cotton Wool, bale variable; U. S. A. and Egyptian, about 450 lbs.; East Indian, 380 lbs.; Brazil, 180 lbs.

Cotton Yarn.

Skein, skn. = 120 Yards,
Hank, hk. = 7 Skeins.
Spindle, spdl. = 18 Hanks.
Bundle Hanks to the weight of 10 lbs.

Reels of Cotton vary from 30 to 1,760 yards, but by the new act must be marked correctly. Balls of Cotton are chiefly made up for export, and are of all weights.

Liquid Measure.

The Gill contains 8·665 cubic inches.
The Pint contains 4 gills or 34·660 inches.
Quart=2 pints=8 gills.

Gallon=4 quarts=32 gills.	Gals.	Qts.	Pts.
Firkin or Quarter Barrel	9	36	72
Anker (10 gallons)	10	40	80
Kilderkin, Rundlet, or ½ Barrel	18	72	144
Barrel	36	144	288
Tierce (42 gallons)	42	168	336
Hogshead of Ale (1½ barrel)	54	216	432
Puncheon	72	288	576
Butt of Ale (3 barrels)	108	432	864

Practically, the only measures in use are gallons, quarts, pints and gills, the others are merely nominal; *e. g.*, the hogshead of 54 gallons, *old measure*, contains but 52 gallons, 1 quart, 1 pint, and 3·55 gills imperial measure, and of wine six nominal quart bottles go to the gallon. Of wines imported in casks the following are the usual measurements:—

Pipe of Port or Masdeu	= 415	gallons
" Teneriffe	= 100	"
" Marsala	= 93	"
" Madeira and Cape	= 92	"
Butt of Lisbon and Bucellas	= 117	"
" Sherry and Tent	= 108	"
Aum of Hock and Rhenish	= 30	"
Hogshead of Claret	= 46	"

In the United States the old British or "Winchester" wine gallon of 231 cubic inches is in use; the names of measures are the same, but the capacity of the gill is only 7·21875 cubic inches.

Apothecaries' Fluid Measure. Marked

60 Minims ♏ (drops) = 1 Fluid Drachm.....f ʒ
8 Drachms......... = 1 Ounce.... ....f ℥
20 Ounces.......... = 1 Pint................ O
8 Pints............ = 1 Gallon......C., or Cong.

1 Drachm =1 Tea-spoonful.
2 Drachms=1 Dessert-spnful
4 Drachms=1 Table-spnful.
2 Ounces =1 Wine glassful.
3 Ounces =1 Teacupful.

Prescribing medicine by the spoon, glass, or cupful, is unsafe, as all those vessels vary in size. Graduated glass measures may be purchased for a few pence, and one should be found in every house.

Dry or Corn Measure.

Quart.. = 2 Pints.	Strike... = 2 Bushels.
Pottle.. = 2 Quarts.	Coomb.. = 4 Bushels.
Gallon.. = 4 Quarts.	Quarter. = 8 Bushels.
Peck.... = 2 Gallons.	Load.... = 5 Quarters.
Bushel.. = 4 Pecks.	Last.... =10 Quarters.

Boll of Meal = 140 lb.; 2 Bolls = 1 Sack.

Wheat and other cereals are commonly sold by weight, the bushel being thus reckoned:—
Wheat, English, 63 lbs. Foreign, 62 lbs.
Barley, English, 52 and 56 lbs. French, 52½ lbs. Mediterranean, 50 lbs.
Oats, English, 40 and 42 lbs. Foreign, 38 and 40 lbs.
Rye and maize, 60 lbs.
Buckwheat, 52 lbs. to the bushel.
Grain of all kinds is frequently sold by the stone of 14 lbs.

Coals were formerly sold by measure: 3 heaped bushels = 1 sack, 12 sacks = 1 chaldron. Coke, apples, potatoes, and some other goods are still sold by heaped measures and the sack of three bushels; of coke, four bushels are commonly given.

Fruit.—The Covent Garden bushel basket is 17½ inches in diameter at top, 10 inches at the bottom, and is 10 inches deep. The smaller market baskets are said to vary in size according to the season and the supply.

Cubic or Solid Measure.

Cubic foot .... = 1,728 Cubic Inches.
Cubic Yard.... = 27 Cubic Feet, 21·033 Bushels.
Stack of Wood = 108 Cubic Feet.
Shipping Ton.. = 40 Cubic Feet merchandise.
Shipping Ton.. = 42 Cubic Feet of Timber
Ton of displacement of a Ship=35 Cubic Feet.

Measures of Length.

Inch, *in*............ = 72 Points, or 12 Lines.
Nail, 1/16............ = 2¼ Inches.
Palm .... = 3 Inches.
Hand .... = 4 Inches.
Link .... = 7·92 Inches.
Quarter (or a Span) = 9 Inches.
Foot .... = 12 Inches.
Cubit .... = 18 Inches.
Yard .... = 36 Inches.
Pace, Military...... = 2 Feet 6 Inches.
Pace, Geometrical. = 5 Feet.
Fathom .... = 6 Feet.
Rod, Pole, or Perch. = 5½ Yards.
Chain (100 Links)... = 22 Yards (4 Poles).
Cable's Length ..... = 120 Fathoms, 720 Feet.
Furlong............ = 40 Rods, 220 Yards.
Mile............... = 8 Furlongs, 80 Chains, 320 Rods, 1,760 Yards, 5,280 Feet, 63,360 Inches.

Mile Geographical, or Nautical Knot = 6,082·66 Feet.
Admiralty Knot or Nautical Mile, 6,080 Feet = 1·151 Mile Statute Degree.
League = 3 Miles.
Degree = 60 Geographical, or 69·121 Statute Miles.

Although no longer sold by that measure Calicos, &c., are sometimes said to be "Ell wide"—the English Ell being 1¼ yards, the Flemish Ell ¾ yard, and the French Ell 1½ yard.
The old *Scottish Mile* was 5,920 feet; ten Scots Miles being about equal to 11¼ Statute Miles. Eleven *Irish Miles* were equal to 14 Statute Miles.

Square, Surface, or Land Measure.

The Square Foot contains 144 Square Inches.
Yard = 9 feet = 1,296 inches.
Rod, Pole, or Perch = 30¼ yards = 272¼ feet.
Chain = 16 rods = 484 yards = 4,356 feet.
Rood = 40 rods = 1,210 yards = 10,890 feet.
Acre = 4 roods = 160 rods = 4,840 yards.
Yard of Land = 30 acres = 120 roods.
Hide = 100 acres = 400 roods.
Mile = 640 acres = 2,560 roods = 6,400 chains = 102,400 rods, poles or perches, or 3,097,600 square yards.

A Square Acre *roughly* stated has four equal sides of 69⅓ yards: *accurate* measurement gives each side 208·71 feet.
The sides of a square half-acre would be 147·581 feet, and of a square quarter-acre, 104·355 feet.
The above Imperial Measure is now employed in the United Kingdom, in Canada, Australia, and the Colonies generally, also in the United States; but occasionally some older measurements are referred to, of these—
The Lancashire Acre of 160 perches, each containing 49 square yards = 7,840 square yards.
The Cheshire Acre of 160 perches, each containing 64 square yards = 10,240 square yards.
The Irish Acre, equal to 1·619835 Statute; or 1 Statute equal to 0·617347 Irish.
The Cunningham Acre, equal to 1·291322 Statute; or 1 Statute Acre is equal to 0·7744 Cunningham.
The Scottish Acre = 1·261183 statute (nearly 6,104 square yards.)

Measures of Time.

60 Seconds................ = 1 Minute.
60 Minutes................ = 1 Hour.
24 Hours (*23h. 56m. 4s.*).. = 1 Day.

From Whitaker's Almanack, 1891.

7 Days	= 1 Week.
28 Days	= 1 Lunar Month.
28, 29, 30, or 31 Days	= 1 Calendar Month.
12 Calendar Months	= 1 Year.
365¼ Days	= 1 Common Year.
366 Days	= 1 Leap Year.

The Astronomical Day commences at noon, and is computed from 1 to 24 hours.

In 400 years 97 are Leap-years and 303 common.

Angular Measure.

60 Seconds"	= 1 Minute.
60 Minutes'	= 1 Degree.
30 Degrees°	= 1 Sign.
90 Degrees	= 1 Quadrant.
4 Quadrants, or 360°	= 1 Circumference, or Great Circle.

The Earth moves at a velocity of 15 degrees an hour, about 17·366 miles a minute; 1° is therefore equal to 4 minutes.

Circular Measure.

The Diameter is a straight line passing through the centre from opposite parts of the Circumference, or perimeter.

The Radius is half the Diameter, or a Straight line from the centre to the Circumference.

The Diameter is to the Circumference about as 7 is to 22, or more nearly as 1 is to 3·1416.

The Diameter × 3·1416 gives the Circumference.

The Radius squared × 3·1416 gives the Area.

The Diameter squared × 3·1416 gives the Area of a Sphere or Globe.

One sixth of the Cube of the Diameter × 3·1416 gives the Solidity of a Sphere.

A Circular Acre is 235·504 feet, a Circular Rood 117·752 feet in diameter. The Circumference of the Globe is about 24,855 miles, and the Diameter about 7,900 miles.

Timber and Wood.

40 cubic feet rough, 50 cubic feet squared = 1 load.

50 cubic feet of planks = 1 load.

100 superficial feet = 1 square of flooring.

100 Deals = 100.

Width of Battens, 7 inches; Deals, 9 inches; Planks are 2 to 4 inches thick, and 10 or 11 inches wide.

Carpenters', Bricklayers' and Builders' Measurements.

Stock or kiln bricks	8¾ inches	× 4½	× 2¾
Welsh fire-bricks	9 "	× 4½	× 2¾
Paving bricks	9 "	× 4½	× 1¾
Square tiles	9¾ "	× 9¾	× 1
"	6 "	× 6	× 1
Dutch clinker bricks	9¼ "	× 3	× 1½

A rod of Brickwork 16½ feet × 16½ feet × 1½ brick thick = 306 cubic feet, or 11⅓ cubic yards, and contains about 4,500 bricks with about 75 cubic feet of mortar.

A Square of Flooring is 100 square feet.

Ordinary bricks weigh about 7 lbs. each; a load of 500 weigh over 1½ tons.

Sizes of Slates.

	in. in.		in. in.
Empress	26 × 16	Ladies	16 × 10
" Small	26 × 14	" Small	16 × 8
Princesses	24 × 14	" Large	14 × 12
Duchesses	24 × 12	" "	14 × 8
Marchionesses	22 × 12	Plantations	13 × 11
" Small	22 × 11	Doubles	13 × 10
Countesses	20 × 10	"	13 × 7
" Wide	20 × 12	Smalls	12 × 8
Viscountesses	18 × 10	"	12 × 6
" Small	18 × 9	"	11 × 5¼

Water.

Cubic inch	= .0361 lbs.
Gallon	= 10.0000 "

Cubic foot = 62·3210 lb. or 6·2321 gallons.

35·943 cubic feet (210 gallons) = 1 ton.

The gallon is = 277¼ cubic inches = 0·16 cubic feet, = 10 lb. distilled water.

Water for Ships: Ton 210 gals., Butt 110, Puncheon 72, Barrel 36, Kilderkin 18.

Cisterns, 1 cubic foot, is equal to about 6¼ gallons, or 62·321 lb. A Cistern 4 feet by 2½ and 3 deep will hold about 187 gallons, and weigh nearly 16 cwt. in addition to its own weight.

The No. 3 Navy Tank is 49 in. long, 49 in. broad and 49 in. deep: it holds 400 gals. of Water, weighing 1 ton 9½ cwt., in addition to the tank itself (6 cwt. 3 qrs. 25 lbs.).

A TON WEIGHT OF THE FOLLOWING WILL AVERAGE IN CUBIC FEET.

Earth	21	Coal, Newcastle	43
Clay	18	Pit Sand	22
Chalk	14	River ditto	19
Thames ballast	20	Marl	18
Coarse gravel	19	Shingle	23
Coal, Welsh	40	Night Soil	18

A cubic foot of pure gold weighs 1,210 lb., pure silver 655 lb., cast iron 450 lb., copper 550 lb., lead 710 lb., pure platinum 1,220 lb., tin 456 lb.

Old Scotch Measures.

Liquids.

4 Gills... = 1 Mutchkin.
2 Mutchkins = 1 Choppin.
2 Choppins = 1 Pint.
2 Pints....... = 1 Quart.
4 Quarts.... = 1 Gallon.
8 Gallons.... = 1 Barrel.

Corn Measure.

4 Lippies = 1 Peck.
4 Pecks.. = 1 Firlot.
4 Firlots = 1 Boll.
16 Bolls = 1 Chalder.

Old Scotch Weights.

16 Drops 1 Ounce, 16 Ounces 1 Pound, 16 Pounds 1 Stone.

From Whitaker's Almanack, 1891.

CHARGES, TAXES, AND WORKINGS.

(Copyrighted, 1891, by Richards & Co.)

Condensed Table of Charges for Applications for Special Grants in countries which have no patent law, but which grant protection by way of special Legislative Act.

Country.		Cost of Grant.
Bermuda		$400 00
Channel Islands	Guernsey	75 00
	Jersey	75 00
China, Empire		225 00
Costa Rica		300 00
Falkland Islands		150 00
Gambia (British)		200 00
Gibraltar		175 00
Gold Coast Colony		200 00
Greece		250 to 2,500 00
Grenada		150 00
Hayti		400 00
Honduras		400 00
Lagos		200 00
Nicaragua		300 00
Paraguay		400 00
St. Lucia		175 00
St. Vincent		150 00
San Domingo		400 00
San Salvador		300 00
Sierra Leone		200 00